A Planet Through a Field of Stars

To Paul
from
Andrew
March '93

C000212352

For May and Elizabeth

A
PLANET THROUGH A
FIELD OF STARS

BEING A SPANISH PILGRIMAGE

ANDREW PATTERSON

THE SACRED LAND
• PROJECT •

Copyright © Andrew Patterson 1997

ISBN 1 872350 37 2

Printed and bound in Great Britain by
Hartnolls Limited, Bodmin, Cornwall

GC Book Publishers Ltd.
Wigtown
SCOTLAND DG8 9HL
Tel/Fax: 01988 402499
email: sales@gcbooks.demon.co.uk
website: http://www.gcbooks.demon.co.uk

Foreword

It is commonplace amongst writers of travel books to claim that it is not the arrival that counts but the journey that leads to the arrival. For most books on travel and pilgrimage this is true. But not this one. For when ever Andrew Patterson stops along his way, you feel he has arrived! Whichever community, individual or place he stays at or meets en route, becomes an event, a coming home in some sense. It is perhaps this above all which marks out this extraordinary book.

I am delighted to have been asked to write this foreword. This book will be, I hope, the first amongst a growing number in a Sacred Land Project series. The Sacred Land Project is the UK's largest and most ambitious religious conservation project and Andrew has been centrally involved in it, for it picks up on themes in his own journey. So what is the Sacred Land Project about?

Within every religious tradition that has flourished in Britain, there is a shared belief in the sacred significance of nature and in the emotional and spiritual power of the landscape which surrounds us. This belief has been expressed throughout our history: through the ancient sites of the Celts; through the pilgrimage routes and monasteries of the medieval Christians; and today through the parish churches, the chapels, the mosques, the temples - wherever people of faith gather.

However, today the importance of valuing land from a religious perspective seems to have been ignored or forgotten by many. Too often, we view the land as a purely instrumental resource that is "ripe for development" or has "good business potential". There needs to be a re-discovery, a change in our modern attitude towards the land in order to prevent and redress environmental damage and neglect. It is an issue which has a direct impact on everyone and everything that lives in Britain today.

The Sacred Land Project stems from this belief that the land and our surroundings have an emotional and spiritual significance. Throughout Britain there are thousands of shrines, wells. Pilgrimage routes and other features of the landscape which for centuries have been regarded as special or sacred. Some of theses are still a focus of pilgrimage or festival and attract many visitors, but the history or significance of many has been lost or forgotten. The Sacred Land Project aims to re-establish the spiritual and environmental significance of these sites. It also seeks to keep alive the tradition of sacred space in today's society, by creating new spaces for peace, quiet and reflection within our towns and cities.

The Sacred Land Project is a five year scheme (April 1997 - March 2002) run by WWF UK, ARC and ICOREC, assisted by MOAS International. The project involves groups and activities across the United Kingdom, ranging from national and government bodies to small local groups, both secular and religious. The project is working in partnership with members of all the major faiths in the UK. It also aims to act as an umbrella organisation for existing initiatives which would benefit from partnership with other groups. WWF UK and ICOREC will provide a network for exchange of information between individual projects as well as bringing together possible partners in larger projects.

It seems only too appropriate that the first book in the Sacred Land Pilgrim's Series should be by such an inveterate pilgrim as Andrew. His outstanding work on reopening the Ninian's Way in Galloway and his involvement with the recovery of the sacred within the lived landscape is the outward manifestation of an inner journey which Andrew has been making. A journey which in many ways echoes the journey of so many people in contemporary society who wish for a deeper spirituality and relationship with this world, than much of formal religion can easily provide.

It is perhaps this journey, the journey of souls in search of meaning which is the key note of the last half of the 20th century and seems set to dominate the religious scene of the 21st century. For many of us, the old secure landmarks of faith have crumbled or been obscured by fogs of doubt and rainstorms of criticism. We can no longer hold to certain images or patterns of faith which sustained our ancestors. Yet the longing to belong and the spiritual yearning for truth and community is as strong today as it has ever been. Perhaps stronger for you never notice your need for something until is has gone.

It is this search that takes many of us back into our past to look for myths and adventures, places and communities which can give us a hint that the Christian faith can be different from that which we were told. That the Christian is not confined to Western European capitalism or the linguistic and liturgical forms of the post-Reformation mind.

But while recovery of different traditions of faith strengthen our own sense of the purpose of our search, ultimately we need to find a language for today. It is this which emerges from the account of Andrew's journey. There are hints here of how Christianity in aboriginal lands of Europe can be different and can breath life into our bodies and souls.

Such a journey is not a comfortable one. It is not a journey of unanimity - I certainly do not agree with everything Andrew says, often far from it - but he would be horrified if I did! Perhaps what Andrew most clearly shows is that the future of faith is diversity - difference. That the old days of a monolithic faith with hierarchies and power structures is largely a thing of the past. Instead it is the encounters with communities, people and places which seems to be forming the new way in which faith will be found and lived.

So enjoy this book, a journey into the past though the present opening vistas of the future, where your guide is one of nature's great idiosyncratic individuals who yet manages to make you feel part of a wider community and more exciting world.

Martin Palmer

Photo: Galloway Gazette

Andrew Patterson was born in 1949 and educated at St. Andrew's and Edinburgh universities. He has worked as a forester, organic gardener, teacher and minister. Now living in Wigtown with his wife and family, he was involved in the setting up of the Whithorn Pilgrimage Trust. He is currently serving as a councillor for the Dumfries & Galloway Council.

PROLOGUE

The word, pilgrim, shares the same linguistic origin with the word for planet in the language of ancient Greece. Planets travel through the seeming stillness of the night stars and human pilgrims traveled through landscapes in a similar footloose way.

Compostela in Spain was a hugely popular pilgrim destination during the Middle Ages. Many people thought the name Compostela derived from the Latin for a "field of stars".

"A Planet through a Field of Stars" is the account of an idiosyncratic journey through the by ways of Scotland, Ireland, Brittany and France, through Spain to Compostela, and the eventual journey home to Galloway through Cornwall, Wales, England and the Isle of Man. The miles of the physical journey on an old motorbike help reveal the rich tapestry of European history and the spiritual expression of the human soul throughout the centuries. Two wheels follow in the footsteps of saints and sinners, of ploughmen and kings.

"Foot holy pilgrims who walked in wishes" as Padraic Fallon phrased it.

A Spanish Pilgrimage

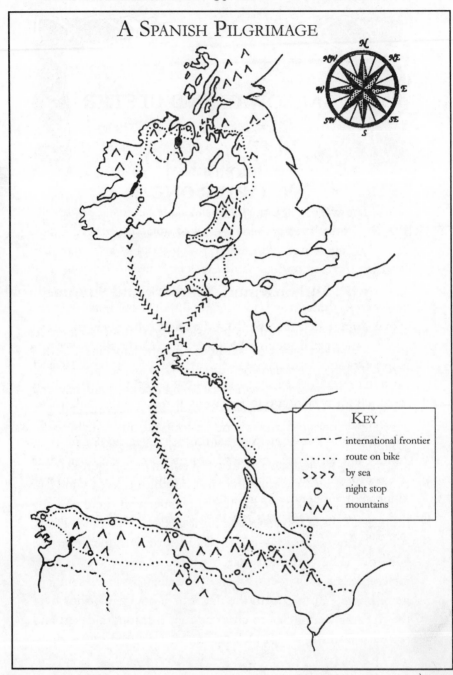

GALLOWAY AND ULSTER

CHAPTER ONE

*"The road goes ever on and on
down from the door where it began"*
J.R.R. Tolkien

Wigtown, Torhousemuir, Mindork and Stranraer.

After a short and restless sleep wakefulness emerged through the last wisps of slumber. Bright sunshine flooded through chinks between the curtains. It was the last week in May and for a month the wind had been brisk and cold, blowing off the Atlantic from the ice of Greenland. The wind had only slowed to allow sharp frosts at night to nip the buds and blossom of apple trees. There had been little growth in field or garden and the fresh lime greens of new leaves had only begun to cover the naked lattice of winter branches, but the weeks of wind had blown away the damp dankness of winter and there was the promise of the short weeks and the long days of summer ahead.

Spring comes late at 55 degrees of latitude from the equator. The continual march of the ocean waves is only interrupted by a few rocks, roosts of the albatross in the southern hemisphere. In the north the dawn of a new day begins over the freezing Bering Sea to cross permafrost, tundra-desert and trackless forests of spruce and marsh until there is a slight warming where the rivers of Russia flow to the Baltic. At this latitude dawn over America matches Eurasia for the harshness of landscape and climate from Labrador to Alaska, but from the Baltic coast of Lithuania the daily journey of the morning light travels through the fertile farms of Denmark before rising over the greenery of Northumbria, Galloway and Ulster in the offshore islands of Europe.

Only in this small segment so far from the equator are rich harvests of arable and pasture to be found. It is the gift of the Atlantic whose Gulf Stream brings tropical waters and milder air to soften northern winters. Even so, a midwinter day is just six hours of pale illumination from an orb low in the sky and often obscured by grey cloud. The sun barely dips below the horizon for a brief two hours of night at midsummer, but warmth is slow to return after the long darkness of winter.

A month before midsummer and the sun was high in the sky at 6 o'clock in the morning as I rose to draw the curtains. Home is a small terraced house on a hill in Wigtown, the old county town of the most south-westerly shire in Scotland. If visibility is clear the drawn curtains reveal an enormous vista over the Solway Firth to the Lake District mountains of England. Wakefulness on this particular morning brought with it the realisation that this was the beginning of an unusual day. A long journey was to begin after a hasty breakfast. Bags were packed downstairs and they were to accompany me far away to the south beyond Biscay and over the Pyrenees.

After final preparations and the farewells of parting from my family I would step onto the tarmac outside the front door and follow it for 4,500 miles until it brought me home again.

A frisson of anxiety and anticipation ran down my spine. There had been no morning like this for many years. Once before I had left Scotland for a six month journey in the U.S.A. and Canada, but that had been before two decades of married life, of growing children and the mundane tribulations of paid employment. There had been family holidays when we had travelled by car to Holland, Germany and France, but this time I was to journey alone to the most westerly projection of continental Europe in Galicia. It was my intention to avoid motorways with their roaring lorries, and cities with their congestion and foul air. Instead I would follow quiet roads westwards from Wigtown through the familiar landscape of the old shire to the port of Stranraer. There I would take ship for Northern Ireland and journey to Donegal in the Republic before travelling through the middle of Ireland to Cork. An overnight journey by sea would bring a continental landing at Roscoff in Brittany. Beyond the Loire and the Gironde the pine forests of Gascony would shade the road until the high wall of the Pyrenees marked the end of France and the beginning of the Iberian peninsula. The road would turn to the west beyond the mountains to lead through Navarre, Castile and Leon until the granite of Galicia begins to climb above the heat of the Spanish lowlands. The journey home promised the Asturian and Cantabrian coastlines with a ship from Santander to Plymouth and wanderings in the western extremities of Cornwall and Wales. Last on the itinerary before an already longed for safe return was to be the Isle of Man.

Scotland, both parts of Ireland, Brittany, Galicia, Cornwall, Wales and Man constitute those areas of Europe where populations are largely descended from that distinctive people known to history as the Celts. In the centuries before the legions of ancient Rome had marched north of the Alps Celtic tribes had dominated the continent from the Danube to the Rhine. They were eclipsed over most of Europe by the rise of the Roman Empire and the subsequent invasions of German tribes. However, the Celts were to survive with varying degrees of success and independence in small nations on the edge of the

Atlantic. Their neighbours thereafter down the centuries were the expanding power centres of England, France and Spain which periodically embroiled the continent in their mutual antipathies and rivalries.

These small Celtic nations share the same historical experience of over powerful neighbours and they all face similar problems in the modern world. The immutable facts of geography place them far from the levers of power in Madrid, Paris, London and Brussels. Compared with averages throughout the rest of the European Union, the Celtic west suffers from very high levels of unemployment and relatively low incomes.

The journey was not intended as a sentimental exploration of a mythical Celtic twilight.. Ethnocentric nationalism had little part in the agenda for we are all mongrels and travel down that road soon leads to Mussolini and Hitler. My destination was the ancient city of Compostela. It had been the most important centre of Christian pilgrimage after Jerusalem and Rome during the mediaeval centuries. Travellers from many nationalities went to marvel at the supposed burial site of the apostle James. In the gospel story he was the brother of John and Jesus called them Sons of Thunder. Over the centuries this Galilean friend of the Nazarene carpenter had been adopted as the particular patron of the church in Spanish speaking lands. The impulse to make this journey had been slowly germinating since the seed had been sown on a cold December day in Edinburgh. Along with 30,000 others under a forest of blue and white saltire banners I was in the old capital of Scotland to add my voice to the demand for direct democratic representation in the European Union through a Scottish Parliament. A European summit was taking place in Holyrood Palace where heads of government and their delegations deliberated over weighty matters.

Only the Republic of Ireland from among the ancient Celtic nations had direct representation at the top table. The interests of Galicia were in the hands of the Spanish, those of Brittany were encompassed by France, and Scotland, Wales, Cornwall and Northern Ireland had no direct representation apart from that afforded them by the London government in which the English enjoyed a perpetual majority. The demand for Scottish constitutional reform and home rule was voiced by the biggest political demonstration seen in the streets of Edinburgh since the Second World War.

On the way home to Galloway I had arranged to see a man about an old motorbike which had been advertised for sale. I found a 1952 James Comet rusting gently in a shed beneath a generous coating of chicken droppings. Months of work would be needed to restore this neglected survivor from the days before Japanese manufacturers came to dominate the market, but the idea was sown. I would travel to Compostela on the old James and visit the traditional burial place of the apostle of that name. On the way there would be much to learn in the other Celtic nations about their relationships with their larger, powerful neighbours. Was there a future for the ancient cultural identities of the Scots, Irish, Bretons and Welsh in the new European Union?

I hoped to find answers to this question because the Sacred landscape of Europe would be my companion throughout the long miles of each day, but there was sadness in the excitement of departure. I was leaving those who made my life delightful, but the open road beckoned. In a haze of two stroke oil I waved farewell.

Travel on a small motorbike is quite different from journeying by car. Few belongings can be taken on a bike. Everything I was to need for several weeks had to be packed into a small rucksack. Sleeping bag, torch, knife, cup, bowl, spoon, a change of clothes and of shoes, maps and waterproofs all had to be stowed alongside tools and a selection of spare parts for the James.

The little motorbike shared its simple 98cc Villiers engine with a distinguished stable of lawnmowers, autoscythes and rotovators. The single cylinder engine generated less than 3 horsepower and its top speed was thought with optimism and a following wind to be close to 40m.p.h. There was no speedometer on the basic machine. The engine was mounted in a low, rigid frame and the only suspension to take the bruising out of the road were the springs in the saddle and a spring above the front forks. These small Villiers engines had been made by the 100,000 and they had a reputation for reliability even if their performance was modest by modern standards. A bright red tank, alloy mudguards, a stainless exhaust and a leather saddle-cover completed the machine. Bold and interlaced Celtic lettering proclaimed the name "James" on the side of the tank.

Wigtown sits on its round green hill in a landscape of similar drumlin mounds through which the River Bladnoch winds towards the sea. The old town was founded over a millennium ago when Vikings used the Celtic Sea between Britain and Ireland as a highway between Scandinavia and the rich southern lands they plundered. Doubtless it was once an unsavoury nest of pirates, but Kings of Scots were eventually to tame the town and make it a centre for the administration of royal authority. It never made the transition into industrialised modernity and in recent years even the local creamery and distillery have been closed down. It is a quiet place to live.

In previous centuries it was a thriving place with a large fishing fleet and several trading schooners. Pollution and overfishing have destroyed the fish stocks of the Solway, and the age of coastal shipping has long since passed. The harbour is empty, but two weeks of favourable wind would have brought a Galloway schooner or a Viking longboat to Galicia in previous centuries. It was going to take longer on the James.

Wigtown is 30 miles from the ferryport of Stranraer. The road out of town to the west is lined with cherry trees. Their blossom fell like snow to carpet the road as the old bike clattered and whirred its way out of town. The route followed the course of the Bladnoch with the hills and beech copses of Torhousemuir to the north. In Viking days their god of thunder, Thor, was remembered here. To the south, the long peninsula of the Machars stretches down to Whithorn, a town more ancient than Wigtown. The quiet finger of land between Wigtown Bay and Luce Bay has claim to be the cradle of the faith given by the Hebrews to the Celts of the north. Ancient legends insist that in 397A.D. a bishop called Ninian began the building of a church which was called Candida Casa, the Shining Place of Whithorn.

The new religion spread throughout the Celtic world in the century that followed Ninian's work. Their church was a unique exultancy in the divine. It nurtured the arts of peace: of literacy, music, medicine, architecture, horticulture, pharmacy, distilling, farming, smelting, boat building, metal work and much else besides. Celtic churchmen were great travellers and sailors. Dialogue between the Celtic nations was continual through their itinerant clergy. The two wheels of the James would travel where they had walked and sailed.

Whithorn became a great focus for pilgrimage in mediaeval times. The antiquity of its foundation and reverence for the pioneering spirit of Ninian held a fascination for travellers, but in 1581 the Scots Parliament outlawed pilgrimage. The 16th century was a time of turmoil and schism. Reformers like Martin Luther, John Calvin and John Knox had broken with the papacy and in so doing they had denounced the age old practice of pilgrimage as an antique superstition. They taught that the true pilgrim journey was only to be found in the interior voyage of an individual in search of the still small voice of God. All over northern Europe, and wherever the Reformation held sway, ancient pilgrim shrines were swept away. Pilgrim roads went unfrequented and venerable buildings declined into dereliction and decay.

Compostela far in the south was never subjected to this Protestant scorn The old city and its cathedral survive to reveal a mediaeval pilgrim centre. Compostela would help to show what had been lost for better and for worse at Whithorn.

As well as removing many of the accretions of tradition, the Reformation also brought much that was new to the life of Scotland. Foremost was the astonishing attempt to create a literate nation with a school in every parish, an academy in every burgh and four universities when England had only two, but there was also the renunciation of the alliance with Roman Catholic France and the development of a new community of interest with the embattled Protestant regime in England and Wales. After the death of Elizabeth Tudor in 1603 this led to James VI of Scotland becoming James I of England and the United Kingdom was born.

Pilgrim journeys remained outlawed in Scotland as the influence of John Calvin gripped the lives of the people ever tighter.

However, in 1987 the Council of Europe decided to redevelop the historic pilgrim trails to Compostela as a gesture to underline the new internationalism that was sweeping through the continent. I hoped to see how the resurrected Pilgrim Way to Compostela was developing. An enthusiasm in recent years had been a project to waymark for walkers and cyclists a similar route through Galloway to Whithorn as a symbol that the narrow days of 1581 are long since ended and that in the modern world a courteous dialogue is possible between communities of differing religious persuasions. The signposting of the first section between Glenluce Abbey and Whithorn had been completed, and a guide book for the Whithorn Pilgrim Way had been published. This little book had gained a bursary from the Scottish Arts Council. It was that bursary which was providing the funds for the journey to Compostela.

The James had been designed during the time of rationing and shortage in the thin years that followed Hitler's war. As a result it was utilitarian and frugal in its use of fuel giving 160 miles for a gallon of petrol. Thirty gallons would suffice, or so I thought, for the adventure. The first mile of the road to Compostela was in a flurry of cherry blossom. It was a glorious departure.

The road passes an ancient stone circle some three miles from Wigtown. It stands as a mute witness to the lives of Galloway farming families more than 4000 years ago. The great pyramids of Egypt and the journeys of Abraham lay in the future when these stones were already covered in lichen and had stood for centuries. Similar monuments were to decorate the landscape all the way to Compostela. The people of the Neolithic and the Bronze Age who had raised these monuments lived in no less of an international culture than that nurtured thousands of years later by the Celtic Church. The circle at Torhouse has met many dawns whirling in from the Barents Sea.

A traveller is shut away from the wind and the elements in a car. It is different perched on a motorbike. The wind off the Atlantic was in my teeth. There was shelter when I dipped down to cross the river before a single track ribbon of tarmac leaves the main road to lead through Mindork Forest. The interior of the peninsula gradually turns from arable and pasture to bleak moorlands. Much of this heathland has been planted with conifers. The larch stood clothed in new green needles in contrast to the dun and brown of the heather and bracken that had not yet come into bud.

Beyond Mindork it was necessary to rejoin the main road. From the vantage point of the hill above Glenluce the waters of

Loch Ryan began to glint in the distance. Loch Ryan was gouged out by a glacier which carved south through Luce Bay to flow around and over the Isle of Man during the last Ice Age. The thawing of this immense glacier was only complete little over 100 centuries ago. When the waters drained away a sandy spit of land was left to separate high tide in Luce Bay and Loch Ryan. The main bulk of Galloway is connected by this narrow isthmus to the last and most south westerly length of land in Scotland, the Rhins of Wigtownshire.

Stranraer shelters in the lee of the low hills of the Rhins at the head of Loch Ryan. It is the main ferry port for Northern Ireland. In the old Celtic tongue Loch Ryan means the King's loch and Stranraer was the King's beach. They have provided safe anchorage and wide landing places for seafarers throughout the centuries. In the modern world trains and buses from London and Glasgow deliver their passengers to the town and a huge volume of lorries and cars also use the port facilities. The rise and fall of fierce Atlantic tides have made necessary the construction of long jetties out into the shallow waters of the loch.

The railway station is at the end of the long pier, marooned from the town by a wasteland of tarmac and parked vehicles waiting to board the ferries. The main ferry terminal for foot passengers is beside the station. Across the loch at Cairnryan, the hill of the King, a rival shipping company has docking facilities, and a new competitor has recently introduced a service to Belfast by fast catamaran. The imprint of the royal title in the names of Loch Ryan, Stranraer and Cairnryan reflect the strategic importance of this tip of Galloway to the defence of Scotland when enemies came over the seas from England, Ireland and Scandinavia.

Stranraer is a small place compared to Dover or the continental ferry ports, but a large proportion of the imports and exports of Ireland pass through its harbour. The town contains nearly a third of the 30,000 souls who live in the old shire. During the last war there were twice as many servicemen as civilian residents in Wigtownshire. Loch Ryan offered one of the safest landfalls in the whole island of Britain for Atlantic convoys, the lifeline from America, when the menace of the U-Boats was at its worst. Enormous flying boats whose range could take bombs and depth charges into the mid Atlantic used to thunder down Loch Ryan in a flurry of foam, no less spectacular than the new catamarans, before clawing their weight into the air.

That was 50 years ago. The last 25 years have involved Loch Ryan in another war, the euphemistically called Troubles in Northern Ireland. Security is very tight in the harbour area. It is a reminder that I am leaving the quiet of rural Scotland for other lands.

The Galloway Princess is due to sail shortly before noon. I arrive with time to spare. It has taken little over an hour from Wigtown at the leisurely gait of the James. Other motorcyclists arrive. Their machines dwarf the old bike. These modern motorbikes have been designed to cope for hour after hour of motorway speeds. Using a large modern machine on motorways the journey to Galicia could be achieved in three or four days of rush and hurry, but I hoped to meander through the ruralities and enjoy those places that still survived remote from the influence of giant cities. The James was a fine machine for such a journey, and the cost of its frugal fuel consumption would be a fraction of that needed by more powerful and thirsty machines.

Motorcyclists are often a gregarious bunch full of the exhilaration of fresh air. We were first on the ferry to secure the bikes to bulkheads with ropes in case of heavy weather. The cavernous vehicle deck reverberated with the pulse of the ship's engines, and the racket of lorries, cars, vans and caravans arriving in this steel cave soon drove us to the upper decks.

Many differing accents mixed in the cafeteria. One accent above all others rang through the conversation of Newcastle, Manchester and Glasgow. Northern Irish voices pronounce their vocables in a unique way. So often this Ulster twang has been associated with hard faced spokesmen from terrorist groups justifying on television the latest atrocity...... a parent killed in front of his children, a farmer shot in his fields, a teenager killed at a security barrier.

The change in the beat of the ship's great engines signalled that the Galloway Princess was casting off her moorings. From the upper deck the low painted and whitewashed buildings of Stranraer receded into the distance as propellers churned up the yellow sediment beneath the hull, and momentum came to thousands of tons of steel in shallow waters.

The Rhins looked impossibly green in the new growth of summer as the length of Loch Ryan was reached and the ship took course in the open sea for Larne. The great rock of Ailsa Craig, called by generations of voyagers "Paddy's Milestone", and the peaks of Arran in the Firth of Clyde rose to the north.

A thin, keening wind drove grey waves against the hull and the sun was pale behind high clouds. My disreputable old leather jacket lost the struggle with the wind and I went to seek warmth and shelter. It was a reminder that life on a motorbike is open to the elements, and on the journey there would be days when the weather would be endured rather than enjoyed. It was a consoling thought that soon the route would veer for the south, for vineyards, olive groves, figs and warm winds: but before me as I gazed from the deck of the ship lay the wide lands of Northern Ireland drawing nearer with every minute.

Larne at first sight does not seem so very different from Stranraer. The roads and road signs are the same as they are in Scotland, Wales and England; and very good roads they are too because the London Government has invested hugely in road building, house building and public works in an attempt to keep life in the local economy. The same names above shop fronts and petrol stations sell the same products for the same currency as in Galloway, but there are profound differences.

The older parts of Scottish towns are built in stone. In Northern Ireland the prevalent method of construction in Victorian and Edwardian times was in brick, which was then cement rendered and painted. These flat areas provide a good surface for the graffiti artists whose varying messages are displayed in every town. Larne is predominantly a Loyalist place whose Protestant inhabitants refuse to consider becoming citizens of a United Ireland ruled from Dublin. Union Jacks and portraits of the Queen proclaim their defiance of the I.R.A. and their loathing of Irish Nationalism. Sinister acronyms insist that this is home turf to the Ulster Defence Association, the Ulster Freedom Fighters and the Red Hand Commando; organisations which have murdered more people in recent years than Republican terrorists.

Wigtownshire is a foreign land compared with all this. Ireland and Scotland face each other over narrow waters, but in Galloway murder is a rare and terrible event. In Northern Ireland it had become almost routine, each successive life lost or maimed only giving rise to a passing moment of disgust.

The route from Larne headed north along the coast of County Antrim. This is the Loyalist heartland. Union Jacks fluttered everywhere. The destination for the day was Corrymeela near Ballycastle. There were 40 miles to cover as the high afternoon sun slanted into the west. The coast of Galloway was still visible, a low grey smudge in the east. Closer were the hills and islands of Argyle. Beyond Glenarm and Carnlough Bay it was time for a rest.

I parked the James and climbed over the parapet of a low

bridge to find a warm and windless spot, making a note as I did so that loch is spelt lough in the island of Ireland. Others had been there before me to dump a litter of unwanted rubbish in the small valley with its limpid stream in bluebells. I was to see the waste and selfish thoughtlessness of modern European lifestyles on every day of the journey and in the loveliest of places. On the other side of the road the sea lapped a shingle beach with its tideline of plastic cast-offs. The road continued past headlands to Cushendall and Cushendun, where the James would have to face its first real climb on the long hill up to Loughaveema. Antrim provides fair, high country with wide sweeping moors. Basalt uplands overly hugh chalk and limestone beds from the Jurassic. These rock beds from the time of the dinosaurs are a fossil hunters' paradise. I had been to this same coast on a geology field trip from St. Andrews as a young student 25 years earlier, when murder had begun to stalk and blight the towns and villages of this lovely land.

It has been said that "the past is another country". At the beginning of the Troubles young idealists used the language of Martin Luther King in emulation of the struggle by black people in the United States for Civil Rights. The Roman Catholic population of Northern Ireland had become an underclass. They had the worst housing, the lowest incomes, the highest unemployment and the least access to public services.

Civil Rights marches demanding an end to discrimination were attacked by Protestant mobs, and the predominantly Protestant police behaved with great brutality. Emboldened by the collapse of civil order there followed a widespread campaign of arson to destroy Roman Catholic neighbourhoods. The British Army was initially deployed in Northern Ireland to protect the poverty stricken ghettos that were under attack.

Of course this was not the beginning of the Troubles. There has been war in Ireland and simmering resentments between differing communities in every century, but the horror of the violence in Northern Ireland has been made more stark because the factions of enmity proclaim their identity and the justification of their actions according to their religious affiliations. Such loyalties seem arcane in the liberal ethos of western Europe after Hitler's war. Only the Basques in the Pyrenees in their feud with the Spanish state compare with the ferocity of the violence of the two communities in Ireland; until Croatia and Bosnia reminded us of what is possible.

I hoped that the miles to Compostela would bring some understanding of the causes of conflict in Ireland, not least when I was to be among the Basques, but the Pyrenees were two weeks away and Corrymeela was far enough for this day.

Corrymeela is a community that is dedicated to bridging the divides of enmity so that the work of reconciliation is made possible. It was founded by people who had noted the work of the Iona Community in Scotland. If Whithorn had been the cradle of Christianity in Lowland Scotland, then it was Iona, a small island off the coast of Mull in the Hebrides, which was the beacon of the Celtic Church in the Highlands and Islands. It had been also the burial place of the Kings of Scots for centuries. An Ulsterman called Columba had been the founder of the original Christian community on Iona in the 6th century. The cathedral and abbey on the island fell into ruin after the Reformation, but, during the dark days of the economic depression before Hitler's war, unemployed ship yard workers from Glasgow used their skills to begin the process of rebuilding the abbey. For over 50 years the new Iona Community has hosted gatherings throughout the summer months which brought people together from every background, but especially the urban poor, for a few days of peace and reflection. In particular Iona became a focus for dialogue between the Protestant traditions of Scotland and the Roman Catholic community in the country.

In the 19th century there had been a huge immigration of Irish people into Scotland. They were predominantly Roman Catholic farming families who were driven out of their homeland by the evil years of the Potato Famine. They settled in the industrial heartland of central Scotland. Their arrival by the hundred thousand over a few short years profoundly affected the well-being of the host communities in Ayrshire, Clydeside, Lanarkshire and Lothian where they chiefly settled. The newcomers were competitors in the labour market and depressed wages. Many native breadwinners lost their livelihoods as a result. Resentment and antipathy between the two communities of industrial Scotland widened into mutual bigotry and mistrust, but not to the desperate extent of Northern Ireland. In this context the Iona Community has worked from its inception to develop understanding and friendship. The Iona community has brought new life to ecclesiastical waters that were becoming stagnant. Both my wife and myself had been accepted as members of the community

The Corrymeela Community was set up to achieve the same aims. Throughout the Troubles groups of people have found peace there and barriers have melted. Many relatives of victims from both sides have found healing for the trauma and anger of savage bereavement. Many fearful people fleeing their homes under threat have found refuge there and the foundations of a new life. Corrymeela is not housed within the grand stone walls of a rebuilt mediaeval abbey. It is centred on a rambling timber house around which has grown a small complex of new buildings. Its situation on a cliff top high above the sea is astonishingly beautiful. Long blue hills tumble into the waves in huge cliffs which climb up to Fair Head. The northern horizon is studded with the mountains of the Hebridean islands.

As the James pulled up the last rise before Corrymeela the clouds and mountains of Barra and the Outer Hebrides were just visible above water that was the deep blue of the Atlantic. Large lazy waves rolled in from Greenland to crash on the foreshore in flurries of spume. The reception area of the community is beside a landscaped bowl of garden through which a stream tumbles in troughs and channels. The sounds of flowing water, and the rumble of the ocean were a relief after the busy clattering of the old Villiers motor; and a helmet can be a burden on the neck after long hours in the saddle. It was good to arrive.

Cheerful young volunteers staff Corrymeela and provide the domestic framework which caters for many dozens of people each week. When I arrived a party of deaf children and their mothers were up for a few days from Belfast. An enthusiastic and noisy game of football was in progress as I was shown to a room overlooking the sea. On this night at least I would sleep in a bed. Weary, middle-aged bones demanded repose. I dozed off even though it was only late afternoon.

I was woken a short while later by a concerned member of staff. My arrival had caused some trepidation among the mothers of the deaf children. There had been an unfortunate incident during their previous visit the year before. Two young men had been at Corrymeela recovering from a punishment beating by the I.R.A. who frequently use such tactics to enforce their authority in districts under their control. Their arms had been broken by baseball bats and hurling sticks, but that hadn't stopped these two likely lads from visiting Ballycastle and getting uproariously drunk. On their return they had propositioned some of the mothers and been a fearful nuisance. A sinister man arriving on a motor bike had disquieted them. The young volunteer explained the awkward predicament and offered another room in one of the newer buildings. Half asleep I gathered my bags and followed her to the new room.

Shortly afterwards it was time for the evening gathering in the building called the Cruive or the Heart of the community.

This is an underground spiral dug into the hill with turf surrounded windows which look out over the ocean to the offshore lights of Rathlin Island. These had begun to twinkle through the growing twilight and the gleam of a lighthouse intermittently pierced the long gloaming of May.

Rathlin Island is reputed to have been the refuge of King Robert the Bruce. The 13th century had seen the growing might of England under its Plantagenet Kings overwhelm the power of the native princes in Wales and in Ireland, but Robert the Bruce destroyed English power for a generation at Bannockburn in 1314. He ensured the survival of Scottish independence into the future. It had not been easy. Shortly after his coronation a succession of swift defeats had driven the Bruce from Scotland to Rathlin. Legend has it that sheltering in a cave on the island the hunted fugitive watched the antics of a persistent spider trying to spin its web. Initial failure did not daunt the insect which eventually swung to extend its gossamer successfully. Encouraged by this example of persistence King Robert returned to Scotland and ultimate victory.

The Bruce was to return to Ireland with his brother Edward after Bannockburn, in an attempt to destroy the English garrisons there. It was too great a task for the slender resources of the northern kingdom.

Shortly before the old king died he made a request that his heart be embalmed and placed in a casket. He then asked his great friend Sir James Douglas to take this casket on a pilgrimage. For all of his reign the old warrior had fought to contain the growing might of England. On his deathbed he wished that he had been free to fight as a Crusader against Islam. Moorish armies out of Africa had threatened the Christian north of Spain. It is said that loyal Sir James fulfilled the request and left with a strong escort of Bannockburn veterans for Compostela. I would be following in the footsteps of loyal Sir James

Every morning and evening there is a gathering for a time of quiet at Corrymeela. Sometimes the more formal litanies of traditional worship are followed. Sometimes, out of unstructured silence, scripture or music rise to fill the space, and echoes of eternity and even Eden can be heard in the Cruive.

All over Europe the art of worship is neglected. The inherited institutions of ecclesiastical continuity, both Protestant and Roman Catholic, have appeared to wither into irrelevance in the modern world. Rigorous intellects have dissected the contradictions in the philosophy and the integrity of the history of the Church, but that night in the Heart of Corrymeela I felt that I was given something which has survived unsullied by the casual brutality of the centuries. Having sat in silence with closed eyes for several minutes I was unaware of who was behind until singing began. Incredible and subtle nuances in harmony and rhythm washed over everyone. Three South African ministers brought this unexpected delight and vibrance. They were visiting Northern Ireland to study the effects of long term violence on war-torn communities. Afterwards in conversation they explained that much of South Africa is traumatised by the same cruelties that Corrymeela knows, but on a scale that dwarfs the local Troubles. They pointed out that Johannesburg is the most violent city on the planet, and that the murder rate in Northern Ireland is less than it is in New York.

Despite their well informed appraisal of circumstances in their homeland they are joyful at recent events. They are full of hope for a better future after the ending of apartheid and the victory that spring of Nelson Mandela in the elections. Their optimism is infectious and an ending of the recent dire epoch in the history of Northern Ireland seems possible. Saying farewell to my chance met friends I watch rabbits wander fearlessly on Corrymeela's lawns as the last fire of the setting sun brimmed the horizon.

All serenity fled with the realisation that I had forgotten the location of my new room. It was eventually found, but the African ministers had left me thinking.

The Protestant people of Northern Ireland have been likened by Republican propagandists to the Boers of southern Africa, descendants of Dutch traders who set up a supply base at the Cape of Good Hope early in the 17th century. Stout European hulls with their newly-developed and efficient sails and rigging combined with gun powder and cannons to begin the process during which Europeans subjugated Africa, Asia and the Americas in the following centuries. The merchants of the United Provinces of the Low Countries in the delta lands of the River Rhine wished to challenge the monopoly of trade in the Indian Ocean that had been gained by the Portuguese when they had crushed the lightly built dhows of Arabia. The power of Portugal was replaced by the Dutch whose replenishing base at the Cape was slowly to develop an agricultural hinterland and a settled European population. The first indigenous people they met were the Khoi and San, kin of the Bushmen of the interior. These sparse populations of hunter-gatherers who used no metal tools or weapons were very different from the populous, iron wielding tribes of Bantu agriculturists who had migrated from the north to settle the coastlands east of the Cape, driving the Khoi and the San before them. Agriculture and iron gave the Bantu advantage over their Stone Age enemies, but Bantu spears were no match for European guns.

These first Dutch settlers were Protestants. As people who had read in their bibles the ancient historical tales of the Hebrews they related their new life and wanderings in a distant and very different land from Holland to the journeys made by the Israelites on their way to the land of milk and honey in Palestine. Africa for them was their Promised Land, gifted to them by God. In this they were little different from another group of northern European settlers in New England who were to become known to posterity as the Pilgrim Fathers and who thought they had a divine right to settle in the New World of the Americas.

Musket and gunpowder carved the Dutch a niche at the Cape, but another power coveted the strategic harbour commanding the South Atlantic and Indian Oceans. The British Empire began a new wave of colonisation at the Cape in the early 19th century. Resentful at usurpation by incomers many of the Boers left the lands of the old colony and trekked into the interior over huge grasslands in long caravans of ox-drawn wagons. They were moving into an empty land. While Cape Colony had been preoccupied with the European wars of Napoleon, the Bantu tribes of south eastern Africa had undergone the "Mfecane" or the Killing Times. The Zulu peoples under Chaka, an African Napoleon, had cut a swathe of conquest and massacre through the tribal lands of their neighbours. Only scattered remnants of the defeated observed the Boer advance, until it was halted by Zulu regiments which had known nothing but victory. Gunpowder prevailed over spears and hide shields. The Boers went on to become the masters of two independent republics in the Orange Free State and the Transvaal.

The British Empire wanted to extend its authority over the Boers because gold and diamonds were found in the Transvaal near to where the great city of Johannesburg has grown. The dawn of this century saw the vicious fighting of the Boer War. One technical advance in the history of warfare achieved in this conflict was the use of barbed wire by the British. Developed for agricultural purposes, it was to extend in a dense mesh from the Alps to the Channel and cause the deadly stalemate of the First World War, but in South Africa the British used it to enclose concentration camps in which tens of thousands of civilians were incarcerated. Typhoid and cholera killed many thousands.

Perhaps the trauma of this suffering affected the Boer psyche to enable the hard-faced intransigence which maintained apartheid for so long despite international calumny.

The new wave of young Irish Nationalists at the beginning of the Troubles adopted the rhetoric of Martin Luther King in their demand for Civil Rights, but they also likened their plight to that of the native people of South Africa against colonial repression and prejudice. The Protestants of Northern Ireland were painted as bigots in the same colours as the Klu Klux Klan and the Boer supporters of apartheid. To this heady verbal picture was added the sadness and past glories of Irish history, in which for over a millennium they had been the victims of repeated invasions from the island of Britain and from the continent. Vikings, Normans and mediaeval English settlers established themselves in the coastlands and estuaries. These incomers soon became assimilated into the predominantly Celtic language and culture of the island but this did not happen with the last great wave of settlement which occurred at the same time as the Dutch began to build their Cape Colony in 17th century Africa. The new incursion was mostly in the north of Ireland, in those areas which had rebelled against rule by Elizabeth Tudor of England. The O'Neil Earl of Ulster who came of the same line as the old High Kings of Ireland had been the leader of the insurgents. His lands and those of his supporters were forfeited, and Protestant farmers from southern Scotland and northern England came to the nine counties of the old administrative province of Ulster. They were lured to Ireland by the promise of grants of land at a time when hunger was rife in Britain. If it was greed to usurp the lands of the defeated then that is not unique to Ireland, but for the most part these incomers were poor folk driven by the need to feed their hunger. The London Government wanted them as a garrison in case of rebellion by the native Irish.

It was said that *"England's danger was Ireland's opportunity".* The great powers of France and Spain had largely remained loyal to the Roman Catholic understanding of Christianity whilst England, Wales, the Netherlands, Scotland, Scandinavia and northern Germany supported the Reformation. In the 17th century the Protestant powers were on the defensive against the resurgent powers of the south. Spanish or French successes in Ireland would have endangered an invasion of Britain. It was this strategic necessity in a bitter, continental war of religion that was the context for the Protestant colony in the lands of the defeated Earls of Ulster. The Protestant churches attracted few converts from the native Irish who made affiliation to what had become the traditional form of the Church a talisman of their unquenched thirst for independence from London.

If the Boers were embittered by the slaughter of the Boer War, then similar results were caused to the collective psyche of the Ulster Protestants in the hardship they suffered in their first generations. Two massive uprisings by the native Irish turned their wrath against the settlers in the 17th century. During the first years of the Civil War between Parliament and Crown in Scotland, Wales and England the colonists in Ireland were hard pressed, and where defeat followed massacre was merciless. Help first came with an army of Scottish Lowlanders who defended the survivors. When Oliver Cromwell landed to destroy the last centres of resistance in the south of Ireland his troops exacted a terrible retribution.

The same occurred in 1689, before Dutch King William gained his victory at the Battle of the Boyne, an event which Ulster Protestants still celebrate every July as their liberation from enemies who had shown little pity.

So deep were the wounds of these experiences that this last wave of settlers did not assimilate into Irish culture and society. The religious divide separated them as it had not earlier settlements. The new incomers did not adopt Gaelic speech, and the accents of north country England and lowland Scotland blended to produce the sonorous and distinctive vocables I began to hear that morning on the ferry in Stranraer.

I rested, ready for another day of travel in the morning, glad of the soft warmth of a bed within walls and under a roof.

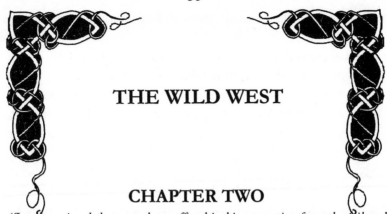

THE WILD WEST

CHAPTER TWO

"I am convinced that man has suffered in his separation from the soil and from the other living creatures of the world; the evolution of his intellect has outrun his needs as an animal, and yet he must still, for security, look long at some portion of the earth as it was before he tampered with it"
Gavin Maxwell "Ring of Bright Water"

Corrymeela, Coleraine, Larne, Wigtown; and Wigtown, Antrim, Stroke City, and Gartan Lough

Friday dawned bright and clear but the wind was still brisk and less than warm. I left Corrymeela before many people were up and about. The James was reluctant to start and I notice an ominous patch of oil on the tarmac beneath it. Perseverance and spannerwork eventually produced a spark. Spluttering movement followed.

I intended to travel westwards through County Londonderry and into Donegal. The prefix London was added to the old Irish Derry, meaning oak woods, in the 17th century when that great English city was involved with the settlement of Protestant colonists in the county. My planned resting place for that night was at Gartan Lough on the edge of the empty Derryveagh Mountains. Tent and sleeping bag would have to suffice against the elements. It was at Gartan that Columba of Iona knew his childhood years.

From Corrymeela it is a short mile to the town of Ballycastle. A magnificent electric tramway like the one which still operates on the Isle of Man used to run along the north Antrim coast and connect with the railway from Belfast. Ballycastle still has the faded glamour of a seaside resort from the days when excursions of factory workers would throng the streets.

Coleraine was the next town on the route, some fifteen miles from Ballycastle. It is built at the highest point salt water reaches up the estuary of the River Bann. Many departments of the University of Ulster are based there and it has a large population of students. Roman Catholic and Protestant youngsters go to separate schools in Northern Ireland. University and college are often the first situations in which they meet individuals from the other community and discover a mutual humanity. Students also come to Coleraine from Scotland, England and Wales. The busy town has a cosmopolitan feel to it. It seems little touched by the Troubles, and little different from Ayr or Dumfries over the water. There was no visible political graffiti on its buildings and no soldiers on the streets. I knew it would be different at the city on the next great estuary to the west beside the River Foyle.

I had been advised at Corrymeela, half in jest, that if I needed directions I should ask the way for Stroke City. It is called Londonderry by Protestants and it was there that their ancestors, had endured months of siege before being liberated by William of Orange. For Irish Nationalists the prefix "London", as in Londonderry, is anathema. The city is called Derry. To avoid offending prickly sensitivities Londonderry/ Derry is often called Stroke City.

The coast between Ballycastle and Coleraine is as lovely

as any. It leads past headlands and tall basalt cliffs to the columns of the Giant's Causeway. Along this coast is the famous Bushmills Distillery. It claims to be the oldest in the world, but I had avoided the busy traffic on the coast road, heading inland before following the River Bann to the bridges at Coleraine. The way had meandered between tall hedges through a pastoral countryside very similar to Wigtownshire, but the fields were smaller. Antrim farms are not large and they tend to be owner occupied, whereas large tracts of Galloway are estate lands with tenanted farms.

The high moorlands of East Antrim gently tilt westwards to the wide valley of the Bann. Frost is a rarity in these lowlands. The grass grows for ten months in the year and provides rich pasture for dairy cattle. Dun and speckled hides shone in the sun and placid eyes gazed through the hedges at my passing.

Bann is the Gaelic word for woman. The river flows wide and deep for 30 miles to the sea from Lough Neagh, the largest body of freshwater in all the British Isles. The southern headwaters of the Bann rise in the hills of County Armagh before widening into the great lough. To the east of the waters of the Bann and Lough Neagh is the heartland of the Ulster Protestants. Nine out of ten of the inhabitants of County Antrim and seven out of ten in County Down are Protestant. Much of east Belfast is staunchly Republican, however, and they insist on rule from Dublin. To the west of the River Bann the proportion of Protestants diminishes.

I stopped at Coleraine not only to watch the swirling waters of the river and to get the feel of a Northern Irish town going about its business, but also to check on the James. It had been running very rough and seemed to be losing power from its already modest performance. The Villiers engine had been functioning perfectly for months, but shortly before departure I had replaced the clutch plates. This task involved splitting the engine casings. I was to discover later that a tiny gudgeon pin

had been incorrectly placed during the rebuild. This had worked
its way loose and was beginning the process of wrecking the
piston and rings in the cylinder. The increasing vibrations of
the distressed engine were virtually to disassemble the bike in
the 5 miles after Coleraine on the Limavady road. Realisation
dawned that the James was not going to get to Compostela. It
wasn't even going to get to Stroke City. Only the trees on the
Fermoyle hills heard the Villiers engine clunk to a standstill and
the imprecations that followed.

I needed to find a phone. While I sat morosely by the side
of the road exchanging baleful glances with the immobile bike
and wondering what to do to extricate myself from the
predicament, a cheerful biker on a powerful race-replica machine
with garishly painted fairings stopped to offer assistance. There
was nothing he could do that I had not already tried, but he gave
directions to the nearest telephone down the hill at a small garage
run by the MacIntyre brothers. The James free wheeled down
the slope.

MacIntyre is the family name of the lady I married. It was
a reminder that movements of people between Ireland and
Scotland have always been a two way process. Much of western
and highland Scotland was settled by tribes out of Ireland in the
5th and 6th centuries. A story associated with the MacIntyres
claims that their ancestor on the voyage from Ireland to Scotland
plugged a leak in the boat by hacking off a finger as a makeshift
bung to halt the inrush of water. MacIntyre means "son of the
carpenter", and anciently they lived in the Sperrin Mountains of
County Tyrone.

The brothers at the garage could not have been more
friendly and helpful. They refused payment for the phone. I
went outside to await the arrival of the yellow A.A. van which
would return the bike to Larne. A gudgeon pin had wrecked
months of planning, and I thought of the three South Africans

from the previous evening. Telling them of my journey I had shown them a little Celtic cross I was taking to Compostela as a gift from the Iona Community. In my haste to show it to them and unwrap the packaging I had snapped the stem from its mount with clumsy fingers. Clumsy fingers had done for the engine also. I was not pleased with myself.

The minutes became an hour as I sat chewing stems of grass and pondering the situation. I had made contingency plans in case the James misbehaved. Another motorbike lay in my garden shed in Wigtown. If the James was proving difficult it had been my intention to take a ferry for Wales from south eastern Ireland, and meet up with a friend to exchange machines before the continental part of the journey. As it was, the A.A. would take me back to Wigtown and I would return to Larne the next day on the other machine. It was a light-weight, two-stroke twin with a 125c.c. race developed engine which gave 18 horsepower. The little Yamaha was very fast and only 14 years old. I had every confidence that it would cover the miles to Spain and back again, but it would use much more fuel than the James.

Despite its mechanical treachery I was grateful to the little machine that had been found rusting under its coat of chicken droppings on the day of the great demand for a Scottish Parliament. It had given the idea and the inspiration for the journey. I vowed that on my return from Compostela the James would be repaired by fingers more clever than my own.

The A.A. van eventually arrived. The driver was a talkative chap from the Waterside district of Stroke City. The neighbourhood is on the eastern bank of the River Foyle, opposite the main part of the city on the western shore. The Waterside is a Protestant stronghold and the two communities live in as tight an apartheid as had existed in South Africa. In Northern Ireland it is self imposed. Loyalist Waterside glares across the river at the Nationalist and Republican slogans which bedaub Derry. I asked him what he thought would be the chances of a lasting peace in Northern Ireland. In answer to my question the loquacious A.A. man shrugged his shoulders and was silent. After 25 years the Troubles had developed into a crazy normality. False hopes of peace had been dashed too often. His stoic lack of hope in any lasting resolution to the ever repeating circle of violence spoke volumes in that one mute gesture. It was so sad.

I pushed the bike onto the ferry at Larne. The A.A. had arranged for another van to meet me in Stranraer. The next A.A. man was the son of a friend from Whithorn. We talked about travelling, when he eventually stopped laughing at my little misfortune. He said he was off to climb Annapurna in the Himalayas. He was also a part-time soldier in the Territorials and he had been chosen to be part of a British Army mountaineering expedition that summer. Compostela did not seem so impossibly far away in comparison. I was encouraged.

Back in Wigtown the cherry blossom was still falling and my family were more amused than sympathetic to see me home so soon. The third morning of the adventure dawned with the same view as on the first. On with the pack, helmet, goggles, gloves, and my great companion throughout the weeks ahead, an ancient jacket of battered, black leather. I would need it this day, for the wind from the west was redoubled in force beneath a cold, grey sky.

Merriment and comments about how far the next motorbike would manage filled the moments of our farewells. I told them I was going to spend a quiet few weeks in Blackpool. Farewell, again.

Less than 30 years of technical development stood between the James and the Yamaha, but they were like animals of a different species. The James performed its function in an unspectacular fashion, puttering along at low, economical revolutions as a good lawnmower should. It only had two gears:

slow and even slower, but it was an immensely pleasurable way to travel on quiet roads.

The Yamaha had a 5 speed gearbox that transferred power onto the tarmac from an engine capable of over 10,000 revolutions per minute. Between 7,000 and 9,000 r.p.m. there was a spectacular power band providing bursts of acceleration that could outperform most cars. Disc brakes provided stopping power, and telescopic forks and sprung shock absorbers gave a comfortable ride on a padded saddle. It was luxury in comparison with the bone jarring from the rigid frame of the James, but the Yamaha was still a lightweight when compared to modern touring bikes with engines bigger than many cars and over 100 horse power under the tank.

I could expect to cover twice as far in a day as on the James. The tyres ran on a carpet of cherry blossom as I headed once again for Stranraer and Larne. I was determined to reach Stroke City and Gartan Lough in Donegal by nightfall.

I took the main road out of Larne and headed for Antrim town beside its freshwater bay on Lough Neagh. The longer legs of the newer machine enabled me to more than keep up with the flow of traffic as we sped westwards into the lush lowlands that fringe the great lough. Soon the road merged with the motorway from Belfast heading northwards until the quieter Randalstown road beckoned along the northern shore of this inland sea. Tideless, sweet waters teem with eels and fish. Wildfowl nest among the reeds, but the well-being of the lough is imperilled by the growth of algae which turn the waters green. Sunlight and oxygen are destroyed in the depths, and other forms of life die. The algae thrive on the effluent coming off the surrounding land which is intensively farmed and heavily stocked. An accumulations of chemical fertilisers has contributed to the spread of the algic plague. At a straggle of buildings called Toome the road crosses the bridge over the wide outflow where the too green River Bann departs from the lough.

The ancient Celtic peoples who named the rivers and mountains of the landscape in pre-Christian centuries believed that divine beings had their dwelling in rivers and woodlands. The quiet waters of the lough and the river still murmur the song of the goddess they once thought had lived there.

The first people to live in the British Isles after the Ice Age were Mesolithic hunters and gatherers. The river, lough, marsh, forest, hillsides and coastlands of this countryside provided a multitude of game. A heavy population of these Mesolithic aboriginals thrived around Lough Neagh. When Neolithic people were later to arrive with a knowledge of gardening, rudimentary farming and animal husbandry, the hunters around the lough seem to have quickly adapted to a farming lifestyle. In time, bronze and sharp iron came into use, and incoming warrior families rose to local prominence. The rich basin of Lough Neagh is separated from the rest of Ireland to south and west by mountains, marsh and barriers of drumlin hills.

There is a legend concerning this land apart with an inland sea as its centre. It concerns a Hebrew princess from Jerusalem. After the glory days of David and Solomon, ancient Israel fell on harder times. Eventually only the hill country of Judah around Jerusalem were still unconquered. Assyria had been repulsed, but a new army threatened out of Babylon. Fearful that the city would fall, one of the daughters of the dynasty descended from David and Solomon was instructed to flee the city to the ends of the earth to keep a rivulet of the royal blood free from conquest.

Weary months at sea brought the fugitives to the mouth of the River Bann. They made their home beside the vast inland lough and lived on into the future untroubled by violence.

I was to hear much less plausible tales on the continent.

Indeed much doubt surrounds the traditional stories concerning the discovery of the bones of the apostle James in Compostela. As for the Hebrew princess of Lough Neagh, it is not improbable that there were ancient contacts between the eastern Mediterranean, and even the more remote parts of the British Isles. Mesolithic hunters and Neolithic farmers did not know the art of smelting metal, but bronze artefacts and weapons became widespread in the Mediterranean area over 4000 years ago. Bronze is an alloy of tin and copper. Copper was plentiful. Tin was sparse, but plentiful only in Britain. Traders from the Mediterranean conducted a regular traffic with Cornwall where it was mined. The earliest and most notable of the merchants to embark on this trade were the Phoenicians of Lebanon, the ancient allies and friends of David and Solomon, whose King Hiram provided the cedar and the skilled artisans for the building of the Temple in Jerusalem. It is entirely plausible that a Phoenician trading expedition for tin escorted the fugitive princess to a safe refuge at the Bann. Princess and goddess? The watery landscape has a mesmeric fascination and a gentle beauty.

A related legend concerns the family of local rulers who settled on the west coast of Scotland in Argyle and who later emerged as Kings of Scots. At their crowning these monarchs were placed upon an ancient stone. The Stone of Destiny was reputed to have been the pillow on which Jacob had slept and dreamed of angels ascending and descending a pathway to heaven in the old biblical story. Robert the Bruce was the first King of Scots not to be crowned upon this ancient possession of his family. It had disappeared at the time of the first invasion of Scotland by Edward 1 of England, though some say that the sandstone block beneath the ancient throne of England in Westminster Abbey is the Stone of Destiny, looted from Scone Abbey. Had the Hebrew princess brought this ancient talisman of her people to her loughside refuge in the north of Ireland?

Once over the river and the countryside to the west rises into the northern outliers of the Sperrin Mountains. It is bleaker and harder country. The bulk of the population in this part are Roman Catholic and staunchly Republican in their political affiliations. Everywhere the Tricoleur of the Republic flaunts gold, white and green against the sky. Papal flags with the crossed keys of St. Peter flutter from lamp posts. It was a Saturday evening and many families were attending mass. Cars were parked by the score outside trim churches, all with a Tricoleur fluttering its challenge.

Cold seeped into my bones and gnawed the knuckles of my hands. Sudden gusts of wind swept over the cold moorlands. Beyond the watershed of the Sperrins a growing stream carved a deepening valley down which the road wound towards Stroke City. Armoured patrol vehicles, soldiers and policemen wearing flak-jackets and carrying firearms were in evidence as I passed the Waterside and headed for the bridges over the Foyle and into the city. Housing schemes not unlike those of Glasgow and Dundee rise behind the town centre. Twenty five years earlier, Civil Rights marchers had protested at the poor housing endured by Roman Catholics. It was a justifiable complaint and huge rebuilding programmes were put into action by the Westminster Government. Perhaps it was being cold and weary, but I found the city by the Foyle cheerless, even though everyone I spoke to in shop, petrol station or pavement was friendly. It was growing late. The grey skies promised a swift dusk and there were another 40 miles through County Donegal, past Lough Swilly and the city of Letterkenny before Gartan Lough. I still had another hour or so in the saddle.

The road out of Stroke City has the same excellent engineering as elsewhere in Northern Ireland, and the same lamp posts, road signs and street furniture. Post boxes are painted red, but in 3 short miles I came to the border-post with the Republic where postal boxes, telephone booths and much else besides are painted an ubiquitous green. Barbed wire, steel posts, concrete blocks and a jagged steel barrier that can be raised from the road surface stood as one of the achievements of the Troubles and a blot on the landscape. A smiling policeman waved me through. He carried a carbine and wore a flak-jacket.

Despite the fortifications this border seemed less of a cultural and geographical divide than the crossing of the River Bann. There are sizeable concentrations of Protestant communities to the west of the Bann around Fermanagh and the Foyle, but their proportion of the population has dwindled in relation to the growth of the other community. Despite the four centuries of Protestant predominance, the western counties of Fermanagh, Tyrone and Londonderry seem to have less in common with the eastern coastlands of Antrim and Down than they do with neighbouring districts in the Republic. Much of County Armagh, the sixth county of Northern Ireland, has been a virtual no-go area for British troops for many years, unless they used a helicopter.

Ulster is the name of the old nine county province. When Ireland was partitioned after the First World War, Cavan, Monaghan and Donegal were included in the new Irish Free State, which was later to become the Republic. The six remaining counties were constituted into the new state of Northern Ireland with its own semi-autonomous parliament at Stormont. The name Ulster derives from a tribal confederation which flourished in those centuries when Roman legions garrisoned Hadrian's Wall. They spoke a language that was akin to Welsh and called themselves the Ulaid. The lands of the original Ulaid were east of Lough Neagh whose wide waters shielded them from the Gaelic tribes of the Sperrin and Donegal mountains with whom there was often war.

In the mid 4th century A.D. the stronghold of the Kings of the Ulaid at Cavan Fort was captured by Gaelic tribes from the west of Ireland. Some of the earliest stories in Irish literature refer to the defence which Cuchulain, the champion of Ulster, offered to the invaders, and these stories which portray the Gael as the oppressor and aggressor gave to the future the Red Hand of Ulster as the heraldic symbol of the province which modern Loyalists have adopted as their own with which to oppose the Republican Tricoleur.

I had never been to Donegal and it had been many years since I had visited the Atlantic coast of the Republic. The past is indeed another country and in that Ireland of the 70's there had been few cars. Country people used bicycles and donkey carts. They lived in tiny cottages under thatched or corrugated iron roofs that were wreathed in peat smoke. Paraffin lamps glowed in windows because the electricity grid did not always reach into the ruralities. Shops were general stores selling everything from bacon to string and hardware Butter was sold by the pound and loaves were double sized because of the many children in Roman Catholic families.

The Scottish Hebrides had been similar in the days before roll-on roll-off vehicle ferries became commonplace. Motor traffic was thin in the islands. The Hebrides had changed and shops in tiny island villages were filled with deep frozen, tinned and plastic wrapped items that were identical to the products that filled the shelves in any suburban supermarket. I expected the same influences of motorway culture to have flooded into Donegal.

After the wave from the smiling policeman a broad ribbon of recently constructed road swept west to soon follow tidal Lough Swilly to Letterkenny. In Northern Ireland the lines of the tarmac were white, yellow only being used to signify no parking in urban areas. In the Republic the road markings were yellow and road signs followed different conventions. At a junction where a traveller needs to give way to oncoming traffic instead of the familiar "Give Way" sign was one which said "Yield". I yielded where necessary and soon found myself entering the straggling outskirts of Letterkenny. Many people were leaving the evening mass at the 19th century cathedral and crowds thronged the narrow streets. Pubs and clubs glittered with neon and young people were enjoying a night on the town. Helpful and kindly people gave directions for Gartan Lough. I explained that I was going to Gartan because of my link with Iona.

A few days earlier John Smith, the leader of the British Labour Party, and a staunch advocate for an Edinburgh parliament, had suddenly died. His remains had been taken to the island that was for centuries the burial place of Scottish kings. Iona had received a huge amount of attention from newspapers and the television. As soon as I mentioned Gartan of Columba and the link with Iona a hush descended. It was followed by outpourings of appreciation for the decency of this Presbyterian politician. It would have been easy to have remained that night in Letterkenny and joined what promised to be good company, but saddle sore and with thirst unquenched I headed into the hills for Gartan Lough.

There has been a rash of new building in Letterkenny with concrete and plate glass giving a continental flavour. People seemed more carefree and without that sense of foreboding and watchfulness that pervade Northern Irish towns.

Light was beginning to fade on the narrow, winding road that was as enfolded with round drumlin hills as the River Bladnoch. There was an election in the offing for the European parliament that shuttles between Strasbourg and Brussels. Photographs of posing candidates had lined the roads of Donegal and alongside the posters of the constitutional parties were the colours of Sinn Fein, the political wing of the I.R.A. Throughout the Troubles the I.R.A. has used Donegal as a base and they have had considerable support from a vocal minority.

I arrived at the small village of Church Hill above Gartan Lough as the sun was setting over a landscape that was a mirror to Argyle and the wilder parts of Galloway. I parked the bike, and cold fingers fumbled to remove the helmet, while stiff limbs prepared to enter a welcome-looking pub. As I did so there was a cacophony of sound from down the road; of raucous shouting, wild singing and blaring car horns. A cavalcade of vehicles came into view with people sitting on top of cars and waving Tricoleurs. My heart sank. A Sinn Fein rally, or so I thought. Cheering, waving faces appeared at doors and windows. I resolved to do without a pint and slip quietly away, when it became apparent that these people were not cheering the I.R.A. The local football team had just scored an important victory. They were cheering honest sport. The bar was a long low room flickering with firelight. Later that evening there would be music. Conversation filled the room and time passed. Too late I realised that daylight was almost gone and in gathering darkness I made my way down to the shores of the little lough.

The tent had been designed and made by a friend. It used the motorbike as a frame. It did not have a flysheet and was erected in seconds. Inside the rucksack was the same down sleeping bag that had crossed America with me all those years ago. It was a comfort to gain the inside of the tent and close the zips against a deepening chill. Wind gusted down the lough to swirl among the branches of the low trees and flap against the tent. Candlelight flared to drive back the dancing shadows of the night and I opened the small bottle of Bushmills I had bought as a consolation for not visiting the Antrim distillery. In Ireland whisky is spelt whiskey, and the Bushmills seemed to contain the bottled sunshine of the Corrymeela coast. Its malted barley from a harvest long since reaped brought welcome warmth.

I was glad of the wind outside. Without it I would have been at the mercy of midges, the voracious insects that can make a misery of camping. My head lay near the engine of the Yamaha as it slowly cooled in an irregular ticking of contracting alloys.....and then sleep was overwhelming on a thin mattress of long grass.

In the chill, small hours I woke to heavy rain beating a tattoo inches from my head, hurled against the thin, clammy, nylon skin by a howling wind. Swift showers were sweeping down the lough. I was glad to be in the lee of the solidity of the bike, and I had made sure the side stand was wedged firmly on a wide stone. I did not want the weight of the machine falling on top of me.

No walls, no roof; and I huddled in a tiny island of dryness, protected by a thin envelope of material whilst water percolated everywhere outside. It was also cold, very cold. I heard later that the temperature had dropped nearly to freezing. It was to be June in a few days, but I was still at 55 degrees north. There are no vineyards or fig trees in Donegal.

Light crawled slowly into a leaden sky. It was too cold for sleep, and since the rain had stopped I was up as the first skylarks filled the sky with their song. There were encouraging patches of blue and shafts of low sunshine speckled the hills. I danced around on the wet grass, less from exuberance and more in an attempt to generate body heat and stimulate the circulation. I would have appeared like an oversized leprechaun to any observer. The camping gear had to be stowed and packed away before the next shower of rain and I piled on every available item of clothing. Breakfast was an orange and a few oatcakes. It was frugal fare, but sufficient even though a hot drink would have been welcome. I had not brought a camping stove with me. The need to travel light was paramount. My pack was heavy enough as it was, but on many another morning of the journey, waking early in the wilderness I thought longingly of steaming mugs of coffee.

There was little chance of finding an open cafe for several hours yet. It was only six o'clock on a Sunday morning in Ireland and I was miles from the next settlement of any size. The last hot food had been on the ferry the previous afternoon, but my grumbling stomach and head faded into insignificance as I began to take in my surroundings. I had arrived the night before in the dark, having stayed too long in the warmth of the pub after the chilling dash from Larne, but now I heard swans beating great wings as they came in low to land in long splashes on the lough. After the showers of rain the air smelt of bog myrtle and pine while the wild notes of lapwing and curlew did not disconcert the browsing rabbits, though the crunch of my boots on the gravel of the road startled them into thickets of briar and gorse. I carefully avoided the big black slugs that were savouring the fresh dampness with groping antennae. The few trees were stunted and deformed by the incessant westerly winds, and the steep hills of coarse grass bracken and thorn scrub rose above poor agricultural land where fields with rough, dry stone walls alternate with patches of scrub land and thorn with the bare rock showing between. It was no different from the hill country of home.

Gavin Maxwell was born in the Machars of Wigtownshire and later rose to fame with *"A Ring of Bright Water"*, his book about otters. He was one of the pioneers of environmental concern and he often commented on the divorce that urban life had created between nature and modern humanity. *"I am convinced that man has suffered in his separation from the soil and from the other living creatures of the world"*.

On that Sunday morning in Donegal I felt little separation and by Columba's lough there was a blessing.

Lovely though Donegal was, it was not what it had been in Columba's day. Centuries of human hunger had gnawed away at it, destroying forests for charcoal and timber, and driving sheep and goats to eat the seedlings.

In Columba's childhood, groves of oak, ash, birch and elm were home to beavers, elk, the wolf and the bear; but without trees to enrich their fertility thin soils had soured. The bleakness of so much of Ireland and Scotland is not irreversible and developments in Norway illustrate how sensible afforestation with a mix of species not only produces valuable timber, but the growing trees also provide shelter in which patches of arable and pasture can produce increased yields. Wind tearing off the ocean can lacerate fields. Trees protect, and this enlightened policy is making barren areas of Norway bloom for the first time in centuries.

I walked along the shore of the lough and came to an incomplete building. It looked handsome with stone and slate and large double glazed windows. The central section stood complete. The wings on either side were half built. A considerable budget was being devoted to this exercise. European Union money was creating a visitor centre with a small museum and a display outlining the life and achievements of the first Abbot of Iona. Columba is credited with bringing Christianity in the 6th century to the wild Picts of northern Scotland, the people who had so successfully defied the Romans. Columba and his legacy guided the Irish colonists in the south western Highlands until they eventually were united with the Picts to form the Kingdom of Scotland in the 9th century. He is remembered as a peacemaker in Scotland, reconciling the Gaelic colonists of Argyle with the Picts, and the Cymric tribes of Strathclyde, Ayr and Galloway who were kin to the defeated Ulaid of Ireland.

Columba was born a prince of the most notable family in

Ireland at that time, the O'Neils. Their descendant a millennium later was the Earl of Ulster who defied the armies of Elizabethan England in the long, stoic years of Ireland's last defence before the foundation of the Protestant colony.

In their early days the O'Neils had been a successful dynasty of pirates and sea rovers whose exploits against Roman shipping in the Channel had been legendary. In Ireland they had risen to a predatory dominance among the competing families and tribal groupings of Celtic society. Leadership among the Celts did not automatically pass from father to son. The succession took into account the claims of cousins and uncles: claims that not only depended on bloodline, but also on personal qualities of courage and wisdom.

This custom caused rivalry and sometimes fratricidal strife broke out at the time of a succession.

Columba's father had been of the royal kin closest to the throne. He died young and his widow took Columba far from Tara of the High Kings to the safety of Gartan lest his boyhood be threatened by one who saw him as a future rival. The quiet lough in its remote valley was well suited to be the refuge and eyrie of the royal eaglet. Out in the lough I could see several small islets of boulders raised like platforms above the waters. These were not natural features, but the handiwork of the tribal people who lived in Columba's day. They built these artificial islands as safe refuges. Strangers could not approach unawares over the submerged causeways, and escape could be swift in a coracle, a light leather boat, to the hidden rushes of the shore, and away into the secret paths of the forested mountains with loyal clansmen to hinder a pursuit.

Columba lived here as a threatened infant in the early 6th century. These were years of relative peace in both Ireland and among the competing nations of the island of Britain. The Anglo-Saxons from Germany and Denmark who had destroyed the Roman province in south eastern Britain had been contained by the Celtic west of Cornwall, Wales and along the Pennines to the northern Cymri of Galloway and Strathclyde. The one main legacy to survive the time of conflict spanned by the legendary but not mythical King Arthur of Celtic Britain was the survival of the church from the defeated Roman province. In Cornwall, Wales and Galloway it thrived. Ninian's Whithorn was one of many similar centres.

Early traditions tell of a man of Britain named Patrick who sowed the seed of the church far and wide over a long lifetime in Ireland. Columba was born into a culture that was undergoing profound change as the stories of the Hebrews and the new stories of Jesus began to spread among them. There were unique insights in Hebrew religion, and study of the sacred texts spread the skills of literacy wherever settled gatherings of Christians became established. The stories of the Hebrews began with the poetic tales of creation, exile from Eden, the murder of Abel by Cain, and the progress of the first generations to the cacophony of Babel and the Flood which only the Ark survived.

Their religion truly began when Abraham broke the ancient and barbarous custom of human sacrifice that has been so widespread throughout the planet in the history of human religious experience. Abraham did not sacrifice Isaac to placate divine forces that were thought to be hostile, and if bribed with human blood would give luck.

Thereafter the nomadic tribes of the Hebrews had been driven by famine to enter Egypt where they became an enslaved people. They escaped under the leadership of Moses and set about trying to construct a society which gave protection to the poor, the orphan and the stranger. They had been strangers in Egypt suffering the worst and wanted a better way of life in the future. The yearning for social justice pervades the Hebrew experience.

Infiltrating into Palestine from the desert they established their land of milk and honey. Years of greatness followed under David and Solomon, when they mastered the technology of iron, but soon came conquest by Assyria, Babylon, Persia, Greece and Rome. Even so, the voices of the prophets continued to articulate the values of compassion until the life of the carpenter from Nazareth began to change the world.

This rich tapestry of stories travelled the length and breadth of the Roman Empire, and when the power of the Caesars ebbed back to the Mediterranean there was left an evolving, thriving community in the distant islands of the west, in far northern latitudes. The Church of the Romans had taught the threefold nature of God, the Trinity of Father, Son and Spirit, and this struck a chord with native religious understanding.

These new and powerful ideas were not ringing in emptiness. Britain and Ireland had been home to the respected wisdom of the Druids for many centuries. The basic belief of Druidry was in a Trinity. Three golden rays of light were the Druid emblem representing three aspects of divinity emanating from the one, ultimate divine source. These were know as Beli, the creator as regards the past; Taran, the controlling providence of the present; and Yesu the coming saviour of the future. The oak was their sacred tree and groves of oaks were their temples. The mistletoe which grows upon the oak with its three white berries was held sacred in its representation of the Trinity, but it was particularly associated with the coming of Yesu and was known as "All Heal". Druidry in these respects anticipated Christianity and pointed to a future saviour under the very name by which Christ was called.

Julius Caesar was the first Roman general to visit Britain during his two unsuccessful campaigns in the 1st century BC He did not like the Druids because they united the tribes to drive him out of the island, but in his journal he wrote *"the Druids teach that by no other way than the ransoming of a man's life by the life of a man is reconciliation with the divine justice of the immortal gods possible".* Caesar was referring to the Druid practice of human sacrifice. When the first Christians told the saga of Christ on the Cross, of death, resurrection and a future return in might and majesty as the King of Life to heal all ills the new gospel found ready echoes and acceptance in the Celtic world.

The story-telling of Patrick had started an avalanche of change in the Ireland in which Columba lived. When his infancy by Gartan was over he was sent to study with a priest called Finnian who revealed to him the mystery of letters. Finnian had studied for many years at Whithorn and he raised the young Columba to manhood. This O'Neil princeling was eligible for the High Kingship had he so chosen. Instead he embraced the unmarried life of a priest.

By the time he was 40 years old Columba had made Ireland a dangerous place for himself. The High King Diarmid found the growing influence of the Church and of Columba a threat to his royal authority. Increasing resistance from the traditional forms of Druidry resented the new Church as a usurpation, and the clan warfare of Donegal and the Sperrins of the O'Neils had spilled into open conflict with the Ulaid. Finnian lived among the Ulaid, and when the two priests quarrelled bloodshed among their clan supporters shamed them both. So it was that Columba went to the oak groves of Derry beside the Foyle and set sail for Scotland.

The new visitor centre would tell much of this story. A year or so earlier there had been an opening ceremony with Eurocrats in attendance. On the previous day an immense, concrete reconstruction of a Celtic cross decorated with interlaced knotwork had been delivered. It was to be positioned within the vestibule as a key feature of the display. Try as they would, the workmen could not get the cross through the double doors. The space was apparently much too small. In exasperation and in search of inspiration they retired to seek the solace of a small refreshment in the nearest licensed house. Returning after a suitable interval to the object which was impossibly jammed in the doorway they gave it a tentative and reluctant heave. Effortlessly it slid into the interior and was installed. The astonished workmen declared it to be a miracle wrought by the blessed saint, for by no other means had they got the overlarge cross through the undersized door!

Asking Columba for a similar blessing on my journey I returned to the bike.

A LONG WAY TO TIPPERARY

CHAPTER THREE

" I have striven not to laugh at human actions, not to weep at them, nor to hate them, but to understand them."

Spinoza 1677

"It's a long way to Tipperary, it's a long way to go"

Gartan, Gweebarra, Sligo, Athlone,Cashel and Co. Tipperary.

The narrow road wound along Gartan Lough. Beside it stood a small Presbyterian chapel. Protestants had once been numerous in Cavan, Monaghan and Donegal of the old nine county province of Ulster. Few now remain and the simple stone and slate building with clear glass illuminating the interior seemed little frequented in comparison with the many Roman Catholic churches I had seen glistening with new paint under the ubiquitous Tricoleurs and papal flags. Roman Catholicism in Ireland is assertively associated with Republicanism in this most visible of manners. Protestant churches on the other hand had been seen as agents of the imperial British state.

High mountains closed in as the River Bullabo became a

tumbling burn. When I crossed the watershed the road turned for the south. I was heading for Gweebarra Bay. Throughout the next undulating 20 miles the road passed few dwellings. Fencing was sparse and sheep wandered everywhere. It was a delight to see little of the barbed wire which disfigures so much of Scotland, but young lambs would wander aimlessly into the path of the bike and vast potholes occurred with a frequency that did not encourage serenity.

Sheep have eaten this landscape barren of trees over the centuries. I travelled through a green desolation where once there had been forests and a myriad of wild creatures. Even the people of the land seemed to have abandoned the struggle. Cottages and farmsteads stood empty and roofless in patches of nettles, nesting places for owls whose silent wings prowl the moors. The Donegal mountains were like the Scottish Highlands, a disaster area where fragile and marginal ecosystems had finally collapsed under the pressure of remorseless human hunger. Like the Highlands, also, there was a pervading sadness for the life that had gone when the bulk of the Gaelic speaking inhabitants had left for the cities. The Highlands had known a terrible ravaging after the defeat of Culloden in 1746 when the last free Celtic tribesmen of Europe were broken by the imperial power of London; and Highlanders had suffered again in the 19th century when sheep ranching destroyed their age old farming communities.

Donegal and the Irish west had other tragedies to mourn, but the result was the same, an empty landscape with never the smudge of chimney smoke beneath the sky. The catastrophe of the Potato Famine of the 1840's drove many poor Donegal families to face the cold welcome of Industrial Scotland. Many did not even reach the harbours on the coast, but died famished by the roadside. Hunger returned in the 1870's and many more Irish families were driven overseas for New York and Liverpool.

These famines have left a terrible legacy of bitterness.

Hunger has always limited human numbers, but when the Protestant colonists secured their land grants in the most fertile areas many indigenous families had to move to the more marginal lands to subsist as best they could. They kept more cattle and sheep in their need than these thin soiled areas could support and the remaining tree cover was destroyed. Widespread famine would have come to Ireland sooner had it not been for the introduction of a new crop which became very popular in the 18th century.

At first the potato seemed a deliverance. This fibrous and nourishing root was easier to grow than thin crops of oats or barley. Less labour and land yielded far more food. As a consequence throughout the 18th century the population of Ireland doubled. Disaster struck when a succession of mild winters and damp summers spread potato blight. This fungus destroyed the food supply on which the people had come to depend for the bulk of their diet. The onset of tragedy was as swift and as horrific as drought in Ethiopia.

There are those who see the Famine as the catalyst which has created modern Irish Nationalism. It certainly left the legacy of an abiding hatred for the London Government which had done so little to alleviate the suffering of the starving.

Of course it was not only Roman Catholics who were ruined by the blight. Four generations ago my father's family were driven by hunger from their small-holding in the Ards peninsula of County Down to find work as best they could down the dark and dangerous mines of Ayrshire; but many of the larger Protestant farms of the east grew cash crops like linen for sale to the mills of Belfast and were little affected. The memory remains that the barley and oats of Antrim and Down did not find their way to fill the ache of hunger in Donegal. Famine leaves a sour memory of fear and anger.

There was another legacy too. Destitute Irish refugees were mocked by the prosperous certainties of England. Jokes abounded about the hilarious stupidity of the "bog Irish" and so insult was added to injury. It is a slander, for the Irish enjoy quicksilver conversation and have a joyful sense of the absurd.

Scotland once knew a famine as terrible as Ireland's great tragedy. Estimates vary, but the empty granaries of the "Ill years of King William" throughout the 1690's diminished the population of Lowland Scotland by more than a third. Strangely, this is not one of the more well known episodes of Scottish history, but the impoverished aftermath of the famine was the context in which the ancient independence of the Scots Parliament was subsumed into Westminster in 1707. Famine achieved what centuries of warfare against Rome, the Vikings and England had never managed, the apparent surrender of the last flicker of political independence in the north of the island of Britain.

The prosperous certainties of England mocked the Scots for their poverty and the archetype of the mean Caledonian was manufactured to stand alongside the thick Paddy. *"How was copper wire invented?" "Two Scotsmen quarrelling over a penny."* The Welsh were not immune either. *"Taffy is a Welshman, Taffy is a thief,"* but the Celtic legacy is more than that of an idiot, a miser, or a kleptomaniac.

The causes of Scotland's famine were different from potato blight, that tuber being as rare a delicacy in a Scots ferm toun of the 17th century as was the swede. A catastrophic sequence of wet summers had destroyed the home harvests of barley and oats. Scotland had traditionally imported Baltic grain in times of shortage. Barrels of salted fish were traded from Aberdeen, Dundee and Leith for Polish and Lithuanian harvests, but warfare closed the northern seas. The vast armies and navies of Sweden and Russia were locked in a titanic struggle. Peter the Great was making his impact on history. In the south the seas were also closed. England and Holland were locked in war with the France of Louis XIV. Scotland starved for long years. There is still a lingering folk memory of the cannibalism to which some surrendered in their desperation. In Ayrshire the cannibal family of Sawney Bean (Alexander Bain) were long remembered for their barbaric hunger.

I was glad to leave the desolation of the Derryveagh Mountains and the oppression of their memories. At the coast vistas of white shell sand heaped into enormous sand dunes. The surf was thunderous, driven onto the headlands by the stiff north-westerly breeze. This was the same blend of ocean and rock as the Hebrides. Raven and buzzard tumbled together through the sky; gannets dived into the sea; cormorants perched on rocks and stretched their wings. Rocks and islets shimmered in the sun. This is the half submerged edge of the continent. In the spring and summer, during the calm days of anticyclone, the sweet scent of the land wafts out to ships at sea.

The wind was now at my back and not in my teeth. As though liberated from a heavy burden the machine easily loped down the tarmac. The road from Letterkenny had been narrow and pot-holed, but the coast road leading south to Sligo had recently been undergoing major construction. Winding bends would suddenly be superseded by wide new roads built to the standard specifications of the European Union and with cash from Brussels. Huge amounts of money have been spent in recent years on road building in the Republic. Throughout the journey to Cork I was to see everywhere the evidence of this massive influx of spending power. Until very recently only the nations of the United Kingdom and Germany have been net contributors to the funds administered by the European Union. Spain, Portugal, Greece and the Republic have been the main beneficiaries. France, Italy, the Benelux and Denmark have guarded their prosperities and paid less than they have received. Throughout my adult life Scottish oil revenues had been siphoned off to subsidise the activities of Westminster and Brussels. I did not resent the newfound prosperity of the Irish west. Indeed I was glad of it, but I realised how little European money had come to Galloway in comparison.

Donegal town passed by under it's trees. It had been a busy port with a safe anchorage. Ballyshannon at the mouth of the River Erne soon followed where the furthest western extremity of Northern Ireland comes to within two or three miles of the Atlantic. Protestants had once been very numerous in the fertile lowlands around the Upper and Lower Loughs of the River Erne. There was still a sizeable population in Enniskillen where the IRA had once attacked a Remembrance Day parade and caused horrific carnage. The Troubles have not been a war of open conflict but a cold and calculating shedding of blood in stealthy ambush and assassination.

I had once before visited friends at a township called Derrygonelly which is a few miles beyond the present frontier with Northern Ireland and upriver from Ballyshannon. It was in the early years of the Troubles and it was that visit to Derrygonelly in County Fermanagh which had first brought the reality of the Troubles to my doorstep in Galloway. A friend called Aidan came from there. He worked with a Dutch charity which organised foreign holidays for the children of both communities. One night there was a knock on the door of the flat they used as a base in Stroke City. His flatmate opened the door. Seconds later his brains were splattered over walls and ceiling by a pistol bullet. No mercy. Friendship between Roman Catholic and Protestant youngsters was not to be encouraged. That was the message of the bullet. Aidan fled for Larne and the Galloway ferry.

When I opened the door to him and drew him into the

safety of my home he broke down and wept in shock, revulsion, and outrage. The murder had only been hours before. My friend was a Roman Catholic. I was not, and we did not know which side of the fence of bigotry had fired the bullet.

I pressed on for Bundoran, a town with enormous views over Donegal Bay to the mountains I had crossed that morning. I had already covered over 50 miles since Gartan Lough. It was more than time for breakfast.

I stopped at a little café offering fried food and a view over the bay. There were two other customers, young men looking as cold and windswept as I felt. They were over from Belfast to enjoy surfing in the massive Atlantic waves. Sausage, bacon, tomato, beans, eggs, toast and coffee restored the inner man.

There are many young men in Bundoran, because the Dublin government maintains a military base here. The Irish Army has a distinguished record of service overseas with the U.N. but it has not been successful in stopping I.R.A. activists from crossing the border to cause mayhem and murder in Northern Ireland.

I studied the map of the roads for the south. Cashel was the destination for that night. I would be staying with friends, archaeologists who had spent many years unearthing the earliest secrets of Whithorn. They had recently moved to County Tipperary in search of fresh archaeological challenges. As the old marching song from World War I declared *"it's a long way to Tipperary, it's a long way to go"*. I still had nearly 250 miles to cover through the heartlands of the Irish interior. I had not intended to travel such a long distance in any one day, but the breakdown of the James had lost a day's journey, and the ferry for Brittany left Cork on the day following the next. I would be needing to wind up the twist grip of the throttle, but the following wind would ensure a brisk pace.

As I sped southwards I passed through towns and villages enjoying a sleepy start to an Irish Sunday. People wore their Sunday best and leisure and lassitude were in the air.

The wild outline of the Dartry Mountains came into view. It is here under the sweep of Ben Bulben that the great Irish poet William Butler Yeats lies buried. His epitaph *"cast a cold eye on life, on death, horseman pass by"* echoed in its mourning of the years the epitaph of another poet, Keats, on his gravestone in Rome, *"here lies one whose name was writ in water".*

The early Christians contradicted such fatalism with the teaching that the immortal soul is made only little lower than the angels, is greater than pulse or breath, and will rise up on wings like eagles, shining like the dawn. So Columba taught, and Patrick and Ninian before him. Yeats was a sophisticated Dubliner who was a passionate advocate for Irish Home Rule. I wondered how he would have viewed the squalor of the more recent Troubles in Northern Ireland............. *"greasy fingers grubbing in a dirty till"*, no doubt, for the "godfathers" on both sides have found affluent lifestyles for themselves.

Yeats had been one of the idealists of the Irish Nationalist movement which had campaigned for Home Rule from Westminster. He had been a passionate supporter of the armed struggle against British troops in Ireland and he became a member of the Senate in Dublin. In his last speech to the Senate this lyrical poet chose an unusual theme. He chose to speak about the plight of the Protestant minority in the newly independent Irish state in which the Roman Catholic church was so predominant. He castigated his fellow senators for their indifference to the fact that social ostracism, vandalism and violence had forced more than half the Protestant population to flee their homes. Many settled in Northern Ireland and took with them tales of the brute bullies who had ruined their lives in the south.

Viewing Ben Bulben I was struck by the lattice of straggling hedges and dykes that rose high up onto the flanks of the mountain. In the early 19th century, before the Potato Famine, the people of the land had tried to cultivate even such unpromising ground in their efforts to feed their children.

Beyond Ben Bulben lay Sligo town and the plains of Roscommon, Athlone and Offaly. The great mass of the Mayo Mountains stretched away into the wilderness of Connaught. I turned my back to the Atlantic and with every mile away from the coast the wind warmed and softened. Excitement rose with the thought that every day that followed would bring warmer air, or so I hoped.

Much of inland Ireland drains into the great River Shannon, which like the Bann swells out into placid loughs. The Shannon is very different from most Scottish rivers whose swift descents make them impracticable for long distance boat journeys. The Shannon meanders through wide plains and marshes. The currant is deep and slow and the river is navigable from its estuary at Limerick to beyond Lough Ree to the north of Athlone where a canal links the Shannon to the loughs on the River Erne. A considerable tourist industry has developed in recent times along the ancient watery highways of inland Ireland. The bosky banks and quiet islands along the Shannon had been home to many communities of the Celtic Church in Columba's day.

From Lough Arrow the route I had chosen followed the flow of the great river and I gazed at islets with round towers that had for centuries been sanctuaries of peacefulness.

The early Christians of both Britain and Ireland were not utterly isolated from the Mediterranean. Distant Egypt influenced Celtic Christianity as much as Greece or Italy. Many of the pigments of the inks used in the interlaced decoration of Celtic manuscript scripture came from Egypt. The land of the

Nile was the earliest home of Christian monasticism. There, monks withdrew from the crowded ribbon of irrigated farmland into the quiet of the desert and the wilderness of the marshes. Egyptian monks developed the devotional practice of standing up to their necks in the water of the Nile whilst reciting psalms. The Irish monks imitated their Egyptian brethren by standing up to their necks in the somewhat chillier waters of the Shannon. It is even reported that Columba did the same in the frigid sea of Iona.

I had thought Galloway and Ulster green in the new growth of May, but beyond the Iron Mountains and into the Leitrim lowlands the Emerald Isle was an astonishment as new fronds and ferns and reeds and leaves stretched out to cover the barrenness of winter. Expanses of sphagnum moss stretched to the horizon. This is acid, rushy country with willow and alder scrub, but occasional rises of limestone were islands of fertility in the sodden boglands. Wildfowl abounded and ducks, heedless of the highway code would wing down the road in trajectories that threatened collision with the motorbike and its rider. The north wind kept insects to a minimum, but in sheltered woodlands clouds of flies eddied across the road and bumble bees promised a more significant impact.

Wide areas of these boglands have been developed. Peat is mined in massive quantities to generate electricity. Its is also compressed into briquettes for the domestic hearth and huge quantities are shredded, dried and wrapped in plastic to be sold to suburban gardens throughout the European Union.

The effect of stripping peat is not dissimilar to the dereliction caused by open-cast coal mines in central Scotland. The result is the same churned up mess pulled this way and that by mammoth machines. However, when the mining and the peat extraction stop the ground is restored to pasture.

A great deal of the peat which covers so much of Britain

and Ireland developed little more than 3000 years ago at much the same time as Moses led the captive tribes of Israel out of Egypt to the accompaniment of volcanic storms and tidal waves. Intense volcanic activity was not restricted only to the Mediterranean. Mount Hecla in Iceland exploded to veil the sun in dust for long years in northern latitudes. In the cold, damp, dark chill which resulted only mosses thrived in the shadow to embalm the ground in an acidic pickle that stopped dead vegetation from rotting. The peat banks grew and buried entire networks of Bronze Age fields, villages and tracks.

This catastrophic deterioration in climate would have brought a famine more terrible than the Potato Famine or the "Ill Years". The long continuity of those who had built the stone circles and raised the standing stones and burial mounds of Atlantic Europe came to an end under this volcanic cloud. Marginal lands in northern latitudes are intensely vulnerable to even slight fluctuations in annual temperature. Even modern methods of mechanised farming are puny before the forces of the weather and the compound effects of 20th century pollution from the Machine Age could prove to be as damaging to marginal environments as was the volcanic dust from Iceland 3000 years ago.

Athlone was the largest town I had encountered since Stroke City. The roads were clogged with traffic. Horse racing had attracted huge and flamboyant crowds, for the Irish have a passion for the sport. New Euroroads were being built in the outskirts and the roadworks had caused a snarling, static traffic jam that reeked of combusting petrocarbons. Every fibre in me wished to flee to the countryside. My two slender wheels soon negotiated the mess of lorries and cars and regained the greenery.

Athlone is dominated by the vast dome of the cupola that crowns its cathedral, but more recent developments were less attractive to the eye. A rash of advertising hoardings and flickering neon signs stretched along the road out of town. Brash new bungalows with cement walls, cement tiles, cement balustrades and cement pseudo-classical statuary stood beside their concrete drives to shout out their owners new prosperity, but other housing showed how patchy the new wealth is in its distribution. Derelict looking houses were inhabited.

Planning laws and concessionary repair grants given by local authorities in Scotland enable many old properties to be refurbished into dry, well-insulated dwellings enclosed within the old stone and slate. In Ireland's Republic much of the older housing stock seems to lie abandoned or near derelict.

After Athlone lay the wide lands of Offaly and County Tipperary. Posters extolling the virtues of professional politicians lined the route as the day of the Euro elections loomed. The same professional smiles and self confident features only changed when I crossed constituency boundaries. In the Republic there are three main political parties. Sinn Fein of the I.R.A. has very little support away from the borderlands. It was not contesting these constituencies in the Irish heart land. The Labour Party, Fianna Fail and Fine Gael were the main antagonists slugging out the slogans by the roadside.

Labour is the smallest of the three parties. It seeks to promote the usual social democratic policies that are echoed by the other left-of-centre political parties throughout the European Union. It is also the political grouping which is most distanced from the Roman Catholic Church with which socialism has often had an uneasy relationship. It has a secular emphasis and has a concern for a more equitable distribution of wealth than the market provides.

Fianna Fail and Fine Gael are the other two political antagonists, but their identities were moulded in the Civil War which established the legislative assembly in Dublin called the Dail, and Irish independence from Westminster in the years after the First World War.

The competing imperial rivalries of Europe had culminated in the mechanised slaughter of the fifty months of the First World War. The old rivalries of the religious wars of the 17th century had been eclipsed by the Germany that Bismarck made. Rebellion against Westminster had always prospered in Ireland when England was embroiled in continental wars like those against Napoleon, Louis XIV or Philip of Spain whose Armada had come to grief in 1588 and abandoned the O'Neil Earl of Ulster to the tender mercy of the Tudors. It was no different when U-boats were plundering and British regiments were being destroyed in Flanders. Civil disobedience in Ireland flared into insubordinate defiance and the spontaneous growth of armed militias. There was little actual fighting in the island apart from a savagely repressed uprising in Dublin in 1916, until the armistice was signed in 1918 to end the continental war.

In 1914, before the outbreak of the First World War, the Liberal Government had been attempting to pass an Irish Home Rule Bill through the Westminster Parliament. The Liberal Party had tried since the time of Gladstone to steer Home Rule legislation through Parliament in every administration they formed. In 1868 Gladstone had said *"my mission is to pacify Ireland"* and to do so he intended to devolve power to a Dublin assembly. In this he was opposed by the Conservatives, and Randolph Churchill had said *"Ulster will fight, and Ulster will be right".* Northern Protestants would not happily accept the authority over them of a legislature that would inevitably be dominated by Roman Catholic southerners.

The attempted legislation of 1914 was bitterly opposed by the Protestants of Ulster as Randolph Churchill had predicted, but the murder of an Austrian Archduke by a Serbian assassin in Sarajevo pushed Irish Home Rule off the Westminster agenda.

It was not only Irish Home Rule that suffered. The Liberals

also intended to introduce legislation for Scottish Home Rule. It was hoped that the Edinburgh and Dublin parliaments would evolve into self governing dominions in the British Empire, as was the case in Australia, New Zealand and Canada, but the First World War utterly changed the landscape of the future.

By 1918 Roman Catholic Ireland was weary of waiting and the machinery of insurrection sprang into action. Rural police stations were burnt out. Garrisons in the towns were under virtual siege and civil government collapsed.

The dominant principle in the peace negotiations that ended the continental war was the right of small nations to self-determination and freedom from the imperial ambitions of more powerful neighbours. The German, Austro-Hungarian and Turkish Empires were dismembered. Another World War would have to pass against Hitler before the French and British Empires unravelled in other continents, but the Irish rebels demanded self-determination. Poland, Czechoslovakia, Yugoslavia, Hungary, Finland, Estonia, Latvia and Lithuania had all gained their freedoms. Now it was the turn of Ireland.

Public opinion in the United States supported the rebellion. Public opinion in Scotland, Wales and England was too preoccupied in their million dead and the millions of maimed to give overmuch attention to Irish problems, but the Protestants of Ulster mobilised militias of their own. The prospect of rule from Roman Catholic Dublin galvanised them and awoke ancestral memories of fear, fire and pitiless Gaelic foemen.

As the insurrection spread the initial response of Westminster was to deploy in Ireland brutalised veterans from the continental fighting. These men were volunteers. They had become addicted to war and they enjoyed its cruelties. Many British newspapers denounced the atrocities of these Black and Tans.........black and khaki because they wore a mixture of police and army uniforms. Their brutality was counterproductive because it united the massive majority of the population behind the insurgents.

The militias of the Ulster Protestants were not challenged in the north, but ugly fighting elsewhere disquieted public opinion in Britain. London began to negotiate with the rebel factions. Fine Gael was the rebel grouping that reached an accommodation with London. In the face of the implacable opposition of northern Protestants, Fine Gael agreed to a partition of Ireland into two states, a Protestant dominated Northern Ireland which would still send M.P.'s. to Westminster, and a Free State ruled from Dublin with commensurate powers to those of the Australian, New Zealand, South African and Canadian Dominions.

Fianna Fail on the other hand denounced the partition and demanded a United Ireland; and so began the second phase of the Irish Civil War. The armed forces controlled by Fine Gael eventually overcame the hard-liners of Fianna Fail, killing more of their erstwhile brothers-in-arms than had the execrable Black and Tans.

The Free State of Fine Gael was later to be overthrown in democratic elections when the defeated survivors of Fianna Fail regrouped around the magnetic personality of a veteran of the fighting with a Spanish ancestry called Eamon de Valera. Once in power it was an article of faith for Fianna Fail that Northern Ireland was an artificial statelet with no moral status. It was on the primacy of that declared principle that they had fought and lost their bloody civil war. Under de Valera the Free State severed its last links with the British Crown and became a Republic, renouncing also membership of the British Commonwealth. The constitution of de Valera's Republic lays formal claim to the territory of Northern Ireland. These moves only further entrenched the resolve of northern Protestants to have nothing to do with Dublin.

In recent years Fianna Fail has distanced itself from the atrocities inflicted by its lineal descendant, the I.R.A., but the identities of these two main political parties of the Republic were moulded by the anguish of a Civil War long ago.

Yet the Republic was fundamentally changing. The crowds I had mingled with in Letterkenny and Athlone had been mostly of young people. Half the population of the Republic is under the age of 25 and this new generation is of an independent and secular frame of mind. When the Troubles broke out 25 years ago Roman Catholic Ireland had one of the highest birth rates on the planet. The people then were obedient to the teaching of their clergy against contraception, but priests no longer dominate society in the south as they once did. The birth rate in the Republic is now one of the lowest in Europe in proof of that. On many other issues the Irish young pay little attention to the strictures of the Roman Catholic Church, but it is middle-aged and elderly politicians who dominate the Dail and the hierarchy of Roman Catholicism still wields immense political influence. The question needs asking "for how much longer?" A social revolution is under way as the new, secular generation loose their deference before episcopal pronouncement.

Athlone had buzzed like a wasps nest. Deeper into the countryside the posters and slogans of modern politics became fewer.

It was mid-afternoon and high, grey cloud had spread across the sky. In the lowlands of the Shannon the horizon had enclosed a smaller world, but the countryside began to undulate in County Offaly and hills brought distant views of blue dales and moors not unlike Yorkshire. The landscape had a gentler feel than the sparse hard lands of Galloway and Donegal. Trees grew taller with resplendent foliage overhanging the road so that I travelled in speckled sun and shade. Market towns like Birr, Roscrea and Thurles carried the sheen of an older prosperity than that brought by the European Union.

When Protestant England rose to an unchallenged Ascendancy over Ireland in the 18th century the prosperity from this fertile landscape went to build the great houses of Protestant landowners and to support their lifestyles of conspicuous consumption. Often the revenues of great estates went to absentee landowners who spent the profit of their rents away from the district that produced them. Gladstonian Liberals attempted to alleviate the worst suffering of the rack-rented peasantry, and money from the London Exchequer enabled many Irish tenants to buy their farms in late Victorian times. The Irish Civil War was the final factor which destroyed the hold of the Protestant gentry on the Irish countryside.

There was little arable in the fields of Offaly and the soil was relatively unscathed by the giant machines that rip, rend, comb and clip the fields of Galloway. Birds and wildlife thronged the hedgerows as a result.

The new roads carve through the landscape and the miles disappeared and clicked up on the speedo. The weight of the rucksack dug into my shoulders and it was not only my fingers on the handlebars that had grown numb. Cashel grew nearer. The plan was that I should go to a suitable hostelry in the town and phone my friend, the archaeologist. He would then arrive to lead me through the labyrinth of lanes to where he lived. There I would find more comfort than the tent at Lough Gartan.

The name Cashel means simply castle, with an Irish accent. A great plug of hard rock rises out of the surrounding plain to provide a natural fortress. This geological formation is similar to those which provide foundations for the castles of Edinburgh, Stirling and Dumbarton in Scotland. Cashel was the centre of the kingdom of Munster and had been just as pivotal in history as the three northern strongholds.

The Rock of Cashel came into view and was so astonishing

a sight that I brought the bike to a halt to gaze with open-mouthed admiration. The three Scottish castles glower over their surroundings behind austere battlements and barracks. Cashel had bastions also, but within its circling walls rose graceful arches and the stone traceries of gothic windows.

> *"Loud above the grassland*
> *In Cashel of the towers*
> *We heard with the yellow candles*
> *The chanting of the hours"*

.... in the words with which the poet Austin Clarke remembered his visit.

In the 12th century Cashel had ceased to be the powercentre of the Kings of Munster and became instead the site for the building of a great cathedral and abbey. I would visit the Rock of Cashel in the morning. Its story could wait until then. The warmth of a snug bar and a glass of stout were more pressing matters. The wide streets of the town were devoid of traffic. I discovered on entering the pub of my choice the reason for the empty streets. The football team of the Republic was playing against Italy in one of the opening matches of the World Cup being staged in the United States. The pubs were full of people watching the game on T.V. Having made my phone call I subsided into a soft chair. The noise was indescribable when the Irish scored and glee was unbounded when full-time brought victory. The manager of the team was an Englishman and many of the players were English by birth and residence, but they were Irish by sympathy and they had at least one Irish grandparent. This was the first World Cup in two decades at which a Scottish team had not gained the finals. Time and again the Scots had snatched defeat from the jaws of victory and failed to get beyond the first round. They returned to a bickering press and national gloom at their failure to beat the best in the world.

Despite their early victory the Irish were to do little better than had the Scottish teams, but they were welcomed home like heroes. It was an interesting contrast between the mentalities of the two nations.

Archaeologists as a breed tend to be as windblown and tanned as any farmer. They spend much of the year digging holes and sifting rubble on open hillsides in all weathers. It was good to see the weather-beaten face of my friend as he entered the bar during the uproar that followed the football. We soon left the noise for green tunnels of trees. Dave's home was an isolated farmhouse a mile away from a small cluster of low houses. It was good to arrive. The little Yamaha stood outside the door clicking as it cooled.

After supper we strolled through the evening to the little village. Its shop doubled as the pub. Warm domesticity and simplicity were in stark contrast to the bustling establishment in Cashel. No television or juke box cluttered the wood-panelled room. There was little choice in beer. Only stout was on draught, with a few bottled beers on the shelf beside a giant, upturned bottle of Paddy's Whiskey.

We settled down with froth on our lips to renew old acquaintance and drink a cup of kindness.

My friend's new project was at Portlaoise where his skill at deciphering the clues of the past was being devoted to a meticulous excavation of a 12th century castle. This had been built for Strongbow, an Anglo-Norman baron called Richard Fitzgilbert who had honed his military machine in the Welsh borderlands before invading Ireland. Strongbow was supported in his enterprise by Henry II whose empire included England, parts of Wales and much of south western France. Strongbow also carried a letter of accreditation from the Pope supporting his war of conquest. A visit to the rock of Cashel would help unravel the reasons for that papal support, but it is an irony of history that the first major invasion of Ireland from England should have been embarked upon with papal blessing. Strongbow's mounted knights brought the same to Ireland as his Norman forebears had brought to the English shieldwall at Hastings in 1066.

Stout and a whiskey more sour than Scotch joined with the gallons of fresh air from the journey to have me nodding over my pint during one of the long silences of friendship, but the party was only just beginning.

Dave had married an Irish girl from a farm near Cashel. We were about to leave when her brothers and a group of friends burst into the bar. Hilarity and joyful nonsense made the minutes speed away and the world was viewed through the bottom of a glass. I was happily drowning under their hospitality when the conversation turned to Northern Ireland. I was asked for my opinion.

I tried to wriggle off the hook of their curiosity. At Loughinisland in County Down there had been a massacre in a pub. Six were killed and more were maimed by Loyalist murderers whilst they watched the World Cup football. This atrocity was in response to an I.R.A. assassination in Protestant Belfast. I sighed with apprehension and hesitantly and with some embarrassment began by talking about Solomon when he was confronted by two mothers each claiming the one living infant. The judgement of the Hebrew wizard was to instruct his guards to cut the child in two and give each woman half. Of course the real mother could not accept the murder of her son and the impostor was exposed. I then caused a hush by saying that if Solomon's sword were to cut Northern Ireland in two both parts would survive and thrive.

The conundrum of Northern Ireland is no less puzzling than the paradox Solomon solved. Irish Nationalists lay claim to all the six counties. Ulster Unionists are adamant that they will not submit to rule from Dublin and the hated influence of the Roman Catholic hierarchy. Perhaps the new, youthful, secular Ireland will change attitudes on both sides, but I told them about the murder of the friend of my friend from Derrygonelly and the experience of Corrymeela in dealing with traumatised victims. I said that in my view any legislation towards a United Ireland would have to wait on the long process of reconciliation which would have to come first.

The ultimate goal of a United Ireland has so often been treated as an article of faith and an inevitability of history taught to all school children in the Republic, but in the quiet of rural Tipperary I saw only anxious and gentle concern for the tragedy in the north.

Warming to my theme and fortified with another glass of Paddy's I said that the vast majority of people in Scotland want to by-pass Westminster in their dealing with Brussels and that a Scottish parliament had become a necessity. This was greeted with a warm rumble of approval which turned to perplexity when I pointed out that if two legislative assemblies were to have divided authority in the island of Britain (and perhaps three if the Welsh so chose) it would be no more of a disfigurement of geography for the island of Ireland to contain a Border and two separate legislatures reflecting two very different cultural identities of mutual antipathy.

I then proposed that there should be a Re-partition, and that County Down and County Antrim should form a New Northern Ireland. They would be severed from the rest of the island by the River Bann and Lough Neagh in whose truncated autonomy the Loyalist community would be free to design their own future. Future generations could make their own decisions, but 25 years of murder must be ended and a frontier of water would not allow terrorists to percolate through. Barbed wire and a Berlin style wall would not be needed.

Many of my Tipperary companions had never visited the

north. They merely wanted an end to political violence and vowed that none should start that night in the pub!

The conversation turned to local gossip and mined the rich seam of human frailty and vanity that is common to us all. In a whirl of laughter we said good-bye and wandered into the empty night.

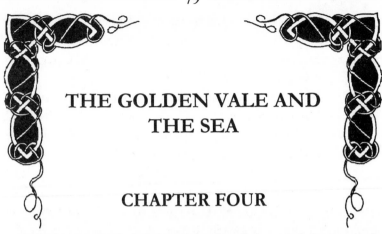

THE GOLDEN VALE AND THE SEA

CHAPTER FOUR

*"Death green of yew, huge green of oak, tall deer, quiet does, trapped
trout, sweet sloes and honey, black winged beetles, small bees, fine white
gulls all sea singing"*

6th century description of the Irish countryside

Rathduff, Cashel, Cahir, Mitchelstown, Fermoy, Cork and Crosshaven.

I woke to an empty house. Dave had already left for his
castle at Portlaoise and his wife was away with her parents. All
was quiet, save for the ticking of a clock indoors and the sounds
of birdsong and animals at pasture outside. I sat in the sunshine
for a long interval of recovery after the mirth of the previous
evening before I dared to grapple with the motorbike.

After a bath, clean clothes, draughts of coffee and slices
of hot toast the effects of the fatigue and exhilaration of the
previous day were soon restored. The routine of collecting
belongings and packing gear was swiftly completed, but my first
problem of the day was to discover exactly where I was. Rathduff
was the place I had slept and the little village with the friendly
pub was called Fethard. Cashel was somewhere in a radius of

seven miles or so, but without a map of sufficient detail I was as lost as I had been at Corrymeela when I had forgotten the location of my room. Trial and error, mostly error, brought Cashel into sight after a meandering 15 miles.

It was already late in the morning when I arrived and the town was a hive of activity. It was a contrast with the deserted streets of the previous day during the football match. I made my way to the Rock of Cashel and was confronted by rows of enormous buses, many sitting with their engines running and the fug of diesel obscuring even the robust scents of agriculture. The pavements were speckled with ground-in discarded chewing gum. Cashel thus bore the true hall-mark of a modern European tourist venue. Kiosks sold ice-cream and souvenir knick-knacks. Blocking the entrance were several dozen middle-aged Germans who sprouted expensive-looking cameras. I turned tail and fled. I did not wish to leave my luggage unattended in such a busy place, and my rucksack was too bulky to wish to jostle with it in a throng of noisy people.

I wandered a field length away from the Rock and gazed back at it. Several cows regarded the intruder in their midst with a similar interest, and their warm breath misted the air.

Cashel had been of ancient significance in the centuries of pre-Christian Ireland. Patrick was reputed to have preached here in the 5th century. A footstep carved into the stone of the bed-rock was attributed to the saint by legend. In all likelihood it was older and was associated with the rituals which inaugurated kingship in Celtic society. The new king placed his foot in the indentation and took vows and pledges before his people in a powerful symbolism that was echoed a millennium later in the folk tale and fable of the glass slipper of Cinderella.

Cashel had been the chief stronghold of the Kings of Munster until the 12th century, when Strongbow attacked with murderous effect from his power-base at Portloaise. Strongbow had the support of the papacy for his campaign against the Irish princes through the pretext of bringing the native expression of Christianity into a closer conformity with Roman usage and custom. The technology of warfare which the Normans had mastered was the most devastating since the legions of ancient Rome. The Irish, like the Scots, had held most of their own against the Vikings, and King Brian Boru of Ireland had inflicted as sharp a defeat as Bannockburn upon the Scandinavian invaders at Clontarf in 1014. A century later and the Normans appeared invincible as they ploughed through brave armies of Irish foot soldiers. An infantry that had held the Vikings was cut down by armoured cavalry on great horses. Called destriers, these destroyers flailed through ranks of axemen and stubborn swordsmen with steelshod hooves like sledgehammers.

Welsh archers with 6 foot bows of yew could drive arrows through chain-mail, and in ambush on armoured columns in their steep valleys they defended their freedoms for a few more centuries; but it was the Scots who evolved a method whereby infantry could defeat the mounted knight in pitched battle. Heavy steel spikes were fitted to 15 foot shafts. If ranks stood steady, three deep, a hedgehog of long spears would impale horse and rider. This was the same strategy that Greek hoplites had used to resist charioteers 2000 years before Bannockburn. This technology of warfare was available to the poor farmer who could cut his own ash stave and have the village blacksmith hammer his scythe into a spear head, but a war horse and armour was the preserve only of the rich. The Normans were rich.

They were descendants of bands of Vikings who had settled in northern France and forced the French into paying them protection money. They were masters of the sea in their sleek ships, and on land they had learned the cavalry skills of the French. Their artificers clothed them from head to foot in forged iron. They were the terrible spearhead of the first Crusades which captured Jerusalem and plundered the wealth of the Levant. In Sicily they had driven out the power of Islam. In France and England they had risen to dominance and their weight was to fall heavily on the Celtic west of Brittany, Ireland, Wales and Scotland; but it was the Anglo-Saxon people of England who knew first the horror and humiliation of conquest at their hands. Wherever they conquered they forced the defeated to build them castles, first of wood and earth, and then of stone.

In response to Strongbow's military victories the Archbishop of Armagh went to Rome to discover how the Irish Church could conform more closely to what the Pope required. If Archbishop Malachi could bring reform then papal support for Strongbow would lessen and a compromise could be reached with these terrible invaders. Part of this compromise was to turn Cashel from a fortress into an ecclesiastical centre.

Even seen from the fields around it, the cathedral is a splendid building. It is one of the earliest examples of Romanesque influence on architecture in Ireland, but beside the continental arches and vaulting rise traditional round towers in the irrepressible native style.

During the years of the Protestant Ascendancy these magnificent buildings were allowed to fall into the same dereliction as the Cathedral of Galloway in Whithorn.

The day was of clear fine weather and the distance to Cork and the ferry port for Brittany was little over 100 miles. I had resolved to cover the distance as quickly as possible so that I could browse along the headlands of the south coast for a good place to spend the night, and so I followed the main roads. County Tipperary is lush and fertile. Great, sweeping mountains rise up above rolling meadows in the aptly named Golden Vale. At Cahir below the Galty Mountains I had hoped to see one of the best-preserved castles of the Anglo-Normans which straddled the crossing of the River Suir. When I arrived I discovered that the same bus load of German tourists had got there before me. I decided not to bother with ancient monuments and press on for the coast, but some stonework I had seen in Cashel lingered in my mind as I dodged speeding lorries on the Euroroute which channelled a torrent of traffic towards the industrial city of Cork.

These stones had not been carved by mediaeval craftsmen, or heaped into immense buttresses, arches and crenellations. They were merely rough hewn rubble piled into low walls less high than my shoulder to create a reconstructed 17th century cottage for the interest of tourists. Lime-washed stone, a thatched roof, tiny windows and an earth floor covered with rushes and herbs sufficed to provide our ancestors with homes. A chimney hearth was the chief improvement from mediaeval times, and the interior was sparsely furnished. Bone, wood and copper provided the few utensils. This simplicity contrasted with the enormously complicated machines for living that modern Europeans have come to expect. Vast quantities of steel, concrete, glass, timber, plastic, metal, ceramics and other building supplies were rushing along the tarmac beside me on their way to be constructed into what modernity requires, but older generations had built their dwellings out of what nature had provided close at hand.

I have often heard archaeologists claim that the rubber boot is one of the supreme achievements of human technology. When November rain and darkness turn the world to mud, life in a thatched cottage with wet, cold feet was probably something other than picturesque; but our ancestors survived with an utter simplicity of domestic possessions. In the modern world we have so much that we do no value what we have and we constantly dispose of a litter of plastic and metal. I envied the past its freedom from waste until I remembered the sporadic famine, the warfare, the disease, the depredations of aristocrats and the resulting poverty which blighted so many lives.

Scotland had often suffered invasion, but the dewy dens and forested denes of Galloway and the Borders, and the glens and moors of the Highlands provided bastions into which few interlopers were rash enough to enter. Ireland has areas of wilderness, mountain and moor, but away from Connaught these upland refuges for rebels are small in extent, and are surrounded by plains in which invaders planted their castles. Rebellion could flare in a great uninterrupted arc in Scotland from north to south, but in Ireland rebels could be cut off, isolated from one another, and destroyed in turn.

During the Napoleonic Wars the Irish rose in rebellion, even though the French fleet had failed to land a promised army. At this time many northern Protestants made common cause with the rebels. Presbyterian dissenters can lay claim to have been the most persistent and the most successful rebels in these islands. In the 16th century they rose to destroy the power of Mary of Guise, Queen Regent of Scotland, and then that of her daughter, Mary Queen of Scots. In the 17th century they had been a crucial part of that process which contradicted the royal pretensions of Charles I and James VII and II. In the 18th century their idealistic descendants in the American colonies fought to create the infant United States. They saw the French Revolution as a continuation of the same striving to build a more egalitarian society that was free of feudal overlords, and so they were prepared to throw in their lot with southern Irish Roman Catholic insurgents. Isolated and unsupported, these northern rebels were either cut down with sabres or strung up on public gallows. The mythology of Fianna Fail extols the United Irishmen of the north, but the lack of co-ordinated support they received from the south made this the last occasion when northern dissenters made common cause with southern rebels.

Government regiments brought an awful retribution to the mutinous south. They marched with portable gallows which they erected in every town and village from which to hang the fruits of their victory. A favoured punishment was to smear the head of a suspected insurgent with pitch and set fire to it. The Terror which followed the French Revolution killed far more on the continent, but the barbarism with which the revolt was destroyed in Ireland is long remembered.

Another consequence was that Westminster swallowed the Irish Parliament in Dublin, and the diagonal red of the St. Patrick cross was added to the Union Jack. So it was that the Ascendancy kept its monopoly of power into Victorian times after Napoleon had met his Waterloo.

I had been winging south for many miles on broad Euro roads. Ribbons of yellow paint on the tarmac had enclosed me in a cocoon of rushing air, but it was warm southerly air and it was a delight not to be hunched with gritted teeth against the cold. Suddenly the Euro road stopped on the edge of the jumbled streets of Mitchelstown whose handsome buildings were from the time of horses and carts. A tangle of road works showed where a by-pass was being constructed, but in the meantime the little town was being torn up by incessant lorries in the heart of it. Every building was encased in dust, and the old street surface was collapsed and deformed by crushing wheels.

Beyond the Knockmealdown Mountains lay the vale of the deep Blackwater River. It was as dark with peat as its name suggests. Tired of the grind of machinery I longed to drift down its length to the sea in a small, open boat. Perhaps one day I will do it and return, for I was beginning to love the unknown south of the island. Clean Antrim behind its towering cliffs and silver waters had long had a hold on my heart, and here I found its counterpoint.

I stopped in Fermoy in the hope of finding a pie or bridie, without success. The name of this old town beside the Blackwater made me mindful of Patrick Leigh Fermor. In the war against Hitler he captured a German general in Crete and gained a certain notoriety when a successful film dramatised the event. He also walked through Europe before the war broke out and reached Constantinople. The record of his journeys provide delightful reading and had probably done much to provoke my own journeyings away from domesticity.

Leaving Fermoy it was not far to Cork and though the countryside was beautiful life on the road was much as it would have been on tarmac near Edinburgh or Glasgow. With every mile the traffic thickened.

Cork is the most populous and prosperous city in the Republic after Dublin. Oil refineries, chemical works and industrial complexes have developed to surround the old harbour area at the heart of the city. Many of the older parts of Irish towns were built with the austere understatement and graceful proportions of Georgian architecture. Cork is no exception, but compared with Bath or Edinburgh this magnificent architectural legacy is ill-cared for, perhaps because the flavour of these older buildings is that of the British Empire. Protestant merchants and seafarers built its prosperity and the Royal Navy made it a powerful base from which to patrol the western approaches to the Channel.

Wide anchorages and wharves could accommodate entire fleets and in World War I convoys from America thronged its waters as they did during World War II in Loch Ryan. However, Eamon de Valera denied these strategically vital port facilities to the Allies during the Battle of the Atlantic against Hitler's navy. Many thousands of sailors died in these waters as a result and the Dublin Government was reviled by more that the Ulster Protestants for their refusal to offer help. However, tens of thousands of ordinary Irishmen volunteered to fight in the ranks of regiments of the British Army against Nazi racism.

Cork harbour is created by a network of wide and winding

rias. These are river valleys and their tributaries which were drowned by rising sea levels after the last Ice Age. I was to see similar inundations of the coasts of Brittany, Galicia and Cornwall. Northern landscapes have been sculpted by huge sheets of ice that were up to a mile thick. Glaciers grind a straighter course. Rivers erode strata in irregular curves. Winding southern rias give a different coast to that of a northern sea loch. Away from built up areas great trees overhung the mud of low tide.

The roads through Cork city were pot-holed and traffic was fast, but I eventually cleared the city centre and negotiated suburbs and their supermarkets to follow a tributary ria to the village of Crosshaven where it joined the main ria from Cork to meet the sea at a narrow entrance between tall headlands. Immense fortifications had been dug into these hills by the Royal Navy. In World War II they stood useless and empty while U-boats sent hundreds of ships and their crews to a watery doom.

I had intended to camp that night, but the environs of the city were too busy to find a quiet spot. Furthermore, the old fortifications were infested with rats and so the decision was made to find accommodation for the night.

Crosshaven is much favoured by the sailing fraternity and many people from the city come to stroll around its beautiful marina. Palm trees were exotic reminders of the mildness of winters on this southern coast. I booked into a clean and freshly painted B & B which also contained a bar and restaurant. The proprietor was a pudgy, bulbous type propping up the bar downstairs. His teenage daughter seemed to do all the work. She had a tiny baby and appeared exhausted by all that was expected of her. My room had a delightful view over the harbour, but it was no bigger than a cupboard. I strolled down the road to sit in the sun outside the other pub in the village and gently watch the world go by.

After the night before I resolved to content myself with my own company. Excitement rose with the thought that in the morning I would take ship for the continent. In Ireland I had spoken my mother tongue, and the coinage and bank notes were in similar denominations to those at home. Even in the Republic life was not so very different from the United Kingdom, although the cost of living and of beer was considerably more expensive, but I had a great sense that ordinary people had gained a liberation from much that blights life in Britain. Despite wide disparities in wealth, for I had seen much poverty amongst the more recent glitz of the Republic, they had built a less class-ridden society than in the other, bigger island. The hand of the descendants of the Norman barons who had conquered at Hastings in 1066 still lies heavy on England, Wales and Scotland. Their titled descendants still own huge estates. In Scotland 500 estates cover half the country. We have been brought up in a culture of deference, to cringe and feel inadequate before the braying accents of the gentry. The Irish threw off this deference in their War of Independence. There is another inherited deference in Ireland though, and there are those who would argue that it is as corrosive of social well-being. Deference before the hierarchy of the Roman Catholic Church has created an ecclesiastical aristocracy, though the younger generations pay them less heed than their elders.

Ireland's tragedy is in its culture of violence. It has been said that Scots *"took to whisky as they took to religion, with violence"*, but I was glad that Scotland has produced a civil society where political violence is always denounced as criminal. I was glad that Scottish Nationalists had not resorted to murder or mayhem in our campaigns for a Scottish Parliament. Friendship, co-equal friendship with England, will build a better future than the enmity of bloodshed. There had been enough of that down the centuries, and would the imperialisms of Spain, France or

Germany have been better neighbours in these islands than England?

That night in Crosshaven I was a stranger sitting in the shadows, and weariness left me silent. I read a newspaper article which exposed the scandal of a Saudi businessman who had invested £1,000,000 in a dog food firm owned by the Toiseach, the Irish Prime Minister, in an apparent attempt to purchase Irish citizenship so that he could reside and operate anywhere in the European Union. There were other scandals in the tight little circles of Dublin politics. Power corrupts and there was a stench coming out of the Dublin Establishment that was little different from the sleaze surrounding the Westminster Government.

A television flickered in the corner and the unmistakable features and voice of the Rev.Ian Paisley began to fulminate on the screen. He was heard in a silence of contempt followed by belches of derision. In his demonisation, unattractive though he may be, I was suddenly reminded of the gulf, the chasm of misunderstanding that exists between the two communities of this island.

Ulster Unionists are often portrayed as Britain's Boers. They are seen as bigots, their religion narrow minded, their politics aimed at maintaining Protestant domination in an apartheid that saw Roman Catholics oppressed for half a century, but there is an arrogance within Irish Catholicism, too, which regards Protestants as heretics and inferiors, their religion as merely negative or anti-catholic. A lack of curiosity about each other and a mutual sense of superiority have perpetuated Ireland's problems.

My shoulders slumped and I was tired, tired of Irish contradictions as much as fatigued by wind, weather, and the long miles since Larne; and so after an ill-cooked meal from the poor wee Cinderella I sought my bed and sleep.

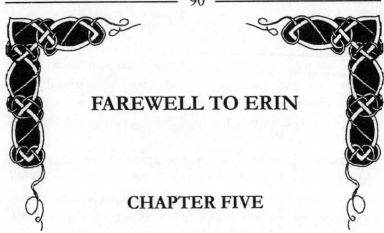

FAREWELL TO ERIN

CHAPTER FIVE

*"Yonder is the sea, great and wide wherein are things creeping
innumerable, both small and great beasts.........There is leviathan".*
Psalm 104

Crosshaven to Roscoff

A few lazy miles lay between Crosshaven and the ferry
terminal. I passed through extensive new industrial areas where
electronics and computer factories predominate. There has been
much foreign investment in Cork during recent years by
multinational corporations keen to have a base within the
European Union. The Dublin Government has been very active
in attracting these multinationals with tax concessions and
financial inducements because unemployment is as high in the
Republic as it is in much of Scotland. The result is the same.
Ireland exports people as does Scotland in a wide diaspora
searching for jobs in Birmingham, Hamburg, Sydney and
Chicago.

After the shiny plate glass and steel of the utilitarian
computer factories came the grubbier sprawl of oil refineries,
chemical works and the steel structures used for handling cargo

of bulk commodities that clustered round the waters of Cork harbour. The ferry terminal is situated on a spit of land. Landscaped mounds and wide fields of grass had been reclaimed from industrial wasteland. The new-sown grass was studded with daisies and poppies.

The terminal building was also new and in the same bland style as the computer factories. Ferries sail from here to Wales and Brittany. Men in overalls scrambled around with paint brushes putting last minute touches to flagpoles and some old cannon brought up from the old Royal Navy depot. The flags of every member state of the European Union fluttered in the breeze. Furniture was being unloaded from vans and a man staggered past under the weight of a decorative plant in a tub as he peered through the foliage. The building was to be opened officially that week by a clutch of Eurocrats and everything had to be as perfect for them as possible. In 18th century Russia when Catherine the Great visited the countryside entire villages were constructed and populated by well nourished families to persuade the Empress that all was well in her realms. The same syndrome seemed to be at work at Cork ferry port.

The ships that serve the crossing between Stranraer and Larne have black hulls and red smoke-stacks as they butt through the storms of the North Channel, but the ship which was moored beside the terminal rose above her surroundings like a huge wedding cake, a confection of white with only the red and blue of the French Tricoleur fluttering at the stern to provide any colour.

I waited for the signal to embark with a clutch of other motorcyclists. Two men arrived on immense touring machines that were as new as the terminal buildings. They wore fancy leathers that would have cost more than my bike and they chatted to each other through microphones in helmets like those worn by cosmonauts. They turned out to be genial souls when their head-gear was removed. They had motored down from Belfast that morning and were hoping to be in Italy in two days. I discovered that they were serving officers in the Royal Ulster Constabulary. Northern Irish policemen get lots of overtime. I did not begrudge them the money that had purchased their finery or the temporary anonymity of a foreign holiday. Much maligned in the south as a militia of religious bigots, their jobs involve high levels of stress and they have "earned" increasing respect in recent years for even-handed restraint under great provocation. 25 years ago they had an uglier reputation.

Next to arrive was a disreputable machine in matt black with bits of fur and leather tied all over it. A young English lad with crew-cut, purple hair was off for a romp through France with his Irish girl friend. I was to meet up with them later that day and good company they were too.

In Stranraer the cold edge to the wind had driven me down into the heated interior of the Galloway Princess. In Cork I baked in warm sunshine. The white ship I had boarded was called the Duchesse Anne after a descendant of the old Celtic princes of Brittany. When she married the King of France in the early 16th century the ancient independence of the Bretons began the long process of erosion by Paris. French dynastic alliances intended to do the same to Scottish liberty when Mary Queen of Scots was married to Duchesse Anne's grandson. Mary's husband died young and so she returned to her northern kingdom. The eventual union of crowns in a United Kingdom had almost been between France and Scotland, and not England and Scotland.

The Duchesse Anne sparkled by the dockside under a bright sun in a sky unblemished by cloud. There was not a breath of wind. Having found a quiet corner on the top deck I settled down to enjoy the sunshine. May had been cold and windy in Galloway. It had been a long, hard winter since I had last bared my pallid skin.

Other passengers who had arrived by coach and car soon began to throng the deck and I found myself surrounded by French voices. My ears began to attune themselves to the music of their language. They were grave and courteous as they greeted each other with formal pleasantries and the double or treble kiss of an embrace. Scots and Irish tend to greet friends with a casual nod of the head and a volley of jocular insults, offering the occasional handshake for people they do not know so well. Their politeness to each other made the French seem very foreign.

Cables were cast off and with Gallic enthusiasm great blasts of the ship's siren announced to the world that the Duchesse was leaving.

The Irish coastline diminished to a low line on the horizon. Farewell to Erin.

On the continent I would soon pick up on the old pilgrim roads that stretch to Compostela. I hoped to learn more about the mediaeval Roman Catholic Church which had left such a legacy of mistrust and fear in the Protestant community of Ulster.

Whilst the I.R.A. has waged the actual campaign of terror its sister organisation, Sinn Fein, has been the propaganda machine. Sinn Fein propagandists are very quiet though about another civil war in which Irish Republicans were very active.

During the Spanish Civil War thousands of volunteers paraded before de Valera as they marched off to fight alongside Hitler's Condor Legion and the Italian fascists that Mussolini despatched to help Franco topple the elected government in Madrid.

There are those who argue that Irish Republicanism became tainted and morally damaged by this contact with continental fascism.

I dozed and watched the wake of the ship until with unbelieving eyes I saw three whales lift their great bulk above the waves. Minutes later the leviathans dipped below the surface. The passengers in the ship stood enraptured by the display. These waters off the southern shore of Ireland were the clear green that can sometimes be seen in the sides of mirrors and as dusk fell the turbulence of the wake began to swirl with luminescence.

Two young men started to play music. Flute and penny whistle intertwined with alternating guitar and mandolin in joyful renditions of Irish jigs and reels interspersed with slow airs. A cap lay on the table in the hope of small change. These young men were originally from London, but they had been living in the Republic for several years. With their music and laughter they intended to busk their way through a continental summer.

The sun set into a glassy ocean and the colours of the spectrum dazzled the eye.

As night fell a chill spread through the air and dew covered everything. I intended to sleep on deck and soon my fellow passengers abandoned the night air for the brightly lit interior of the ship. I was alone beneath a sky in which stars were growing and planets were shifting.

The Duchesse was to berth at Roscoff at 6 a.m., French time. That was 5 a.m. in Wigtown time. It would be an early start and there would be a long, hard day of travelling in the morning. .

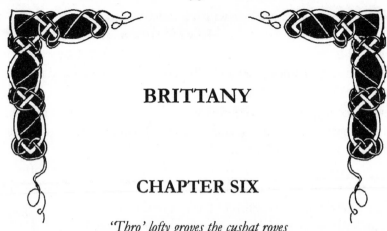

BRITTANY

CHAPTER SIX

"Thro' lofty groves the cushat roves
The path of man to shun it;
The hazel bush o'er hangs the thrush
The spreading thorn the linnet".
Robert Burns.

Roscoff, Quimper, Loctudy, Quiberon, Carnac, Locmariaquer

A cold dawn welcomed the first day in June. Softer colours than sunset grew in the eastern sky and the constellations of the night faded away. No skylarks heralded the new day as they had done at Gartan Lough. Only seagulls twitched their feathers, soaring over the Duchesse and uttering raucous cries. I was observed by bright yellow eyes from above whilst I packed my gear.

On this maritime morning I could swiftly find a cup of coffee. In Scotland and Ireland coffee is brown, hot, wet and often very little else. In the cafeteria of the Duchesse there was glorious French coffee and crisp croissants for breakfast. I had changed my Irish money with its delightful motifs of curlew, deer, dolphin and salmon, and my morning mind had to grapple with the intricacies of the garishly printed colours of French bank notes. I knew that French prices could severely damage the limited funds I had for the journey. With this in mind I intended to sleep in the countryside for the next couple of nights. In preparation for the austerities ahead I took full advantage of the hot water on the Duchesse.

After necessary ablutions there was time for another coffee, for the smell of the percolating brew was irresistible. Smug at my relative lack of bibulousness on the previous evening I watched my bleary fellow passengers emerge into the new day. I said farewell to some of my chance met companions of the night before and was embraced and kissed in return by a couple of friendly gents from Normandy. The culture shock of the experience was considerable

Is it true to state that English people and French people have a mutual antipathy? England and France were rivals down the centuries, and although there is a strong element of friendship between the two great nations, as a result of the alliances against the Kaiser and Hitler, Anglo-French relationships are not always easy. Scottish people on the other hand feel at home in France. Perhaps this is a lingering consequence of the Auld Alliance which was first signed in 1296. Each would give the other mutual support in time of war with England.

This alliance brought the total disaster of Flodden upon Scotland in 1513 when the French embroiled the northern kingdom in an unnecessary war with the England of Henry VIII, but a century earlier things had been very different.

At Agincourt an army of Welsh and English archers had smashed the chivalry of France. In the decades that followed only Joan of Arc stood against the defeat of her country. Her staunchest friends were 10,000 Scots under the command of Sir

John Stewart and the Earl of Douglas who had crossed to the continent to aid their stricken ally. Joan repeatedly urged on her compatriots with the phrase *"faire comme les ecossais"*.... *"do like the Scots"*.

When the warfare was ended Scottish troops were awarded the honour of becoming the Royal Guard of the Kingdom of France. Scottish and French gentry and royalty intermarried and Scots in France were awarded all the privileges of French nationals.

The 15th century was a culinary and architectural golden age in Scottish history as a result of this friendship and apart from on the rugby field this fondness for Scotland is still tangible. Often the phrase *"non, je ne suis pas anglais, je suis écossais"* would soften stony attitudes.

It was with some trepidation that I made my way down onto the vehicle deck ... I had driven cars on the continent before, but never a motorbike. Driving on the right was always disconcerting and I would need my wits about me.

The coast near Roscoff is called the "Cote du Granit Rose". Much of the Armorican peninsula is of low, swelling hills of granite. The scattered townships and settlements of the Bretons are built with blocks of this enduring stone. Rugged walls beneath roofs of slate were reminiscent of home. The more southerly climate of Brittany is mild and equable compared to the savageries of Scottish weather, but foul conditions can bring raging storms to the Cote du Granit Rose. In consequence Breton farmhouses have few windows in the northerly walls. They would not have looked out of place in Galloway, but the fields of onions, asparagus and artichokes were exotic in their strangeness. The northern coastlands of Brittany are famed for their fertility and the Breton "Onion Johnny" with strings of the vegetables draped around his bicycle and his shoulders was a common sight in Scotland before the days of the ubiquitous supermarket. These

Onion Johnnies populated my childhood with their black berets, striped jerkins and strong-smelling cigarettes as they sold their produce from door to door.

After I had negotiated the ferry terminal, which was built in the same concrete, steel and glass Eurostyle as at Cork, I became lost in the narrow streets of the old town. There had been no passport control and I was waved through by a sleepy policeman in his kepi headgear. It was disconcerting to see the pistol at his belt and I was reminded of the smiling policeman on duty at the fortified border post near Stroke City. The streets were deserted, but the smell of baking bread accompanied me out of town as I found the road that followed the estuary upstream to Morlaix. The huge towers of an ancient church dominated the flat landscape.

In Ireland few ecclesiastical buildings were older than Victorian or Georgian times, and Scotland is little different. Tearing winds, frost, rain and mouldering dampness continually attack old walls and timbers, but it was iconoclastic Protestants at the time of the Reformation who destroyed so much of the architectural legacy of mediaeval Scotland and Ireland. Brittany never embraced the Reformation and the resulting continuity bequeathed to the present many church buildings that have been embellished throughout the centuries. 11th century Romanesque naves were enlarged with Gothic aisles in the 14th and 15th centuries, and these composite mediaeval jewels grew neo-classical spires in the 17th century. Whilst 16th century Bretons stood loyal to the old Roman Catholic customs with which they had little complaint, the Reformation created in Scotland one of the first literate peasantries upon this planet. The Presbyterian General Assembly decreed that there should be a network of parish schools, burgh academies and universities. Scots were to be literate so that they could read scripture for themselves. Roman Catholic clergy, on the other hand, did not encourage the laity to read the bible in the vernacular. The result of this was that most Bretons remained illiterate until the 19th century. This lack of literacy resulted in a wonderful plethora of sculptures which tell bible stories in visual form. These Breton "calvaries" can be found in churchyards and beside lonely cross-roads and they are eloquent in their silence.

The stories of the Hebrews began their work early in the lands of the Armorican peninsula. When Ninian and Patrick were busy in the north during the 5th century the same process which was to so profoundly affect Druid Ireland was already at work among the kindred Celts of Brittany.

Despite the well known saga of Asterix and Obelix insisting to the contrary, the Armorican peninsula was subdued by Julius Caesar in the middle of the 1st century B.C. The Armoricans had been a great sea power whose ships dominated the Bay of Biscay and the waters commanding the western approaches to the Channel. Julius Caesar described their vessels in these terms:-
"their keels were flat .... the bow was perpendicular and the poop was so contrived as to bear the force of large and tempestuous waves. They were altogether built for strength. The ribs and beams were made of timber a foot square and fastened with iron bolts an inch thick. Instead of cables their anchors were made fast by iron chains; they also made their sails with hides ..... strong enough to serve ships of so great a burden and sustain the force and violence of their tempestuous seas".

With vessels such as these the Armoricans had ventured from their peninsula north into the isles and southwards to the coasts of Spain. They were an integral part of the cultural and linguistic community of the Celtic peoples who populated the Atlantic coastlands of Europe. Rome absorbed them into an administrative province that was governed from distant Tours in the headwaters of the Loire. This remoteness from centres of imperial power did not save Armorica from assault by marauding bands of German tribesmen when the legions of Rome were broken along the Rhine in the 5th century. Famine and plague followed the bloodshed. St. Patrick is reputed to have travelled through Brittany. He wrote that wide areas of the countryside were no longer inhabited and that rich agricultural lands were reverting to wilderness.

German tribesmen came to Britain also. Anglo-Saxons from the lands around the Elbe were first employed as Roman mercenaries in the effort to drive back the Picts. The descendants of these mercenaries multiplied in the eastern coastlands until in the mid 5th century they rebelled against Vortigern who was the ruler of the Romano-British. After initial defeats the Britons rallied round a leader called Ambrosius who was succeeded as war leader, or Dux Bellorum, by the legendary King Arthur. It was in Britain that a Roman province put up the longest and the most successful resistance against barbarian invasion in all of western Europe. It was not until the middle of the 6th century after a terrible plague had undone the legacy of Arthur that the Anglo-Saxons began to pen back the Celtic inhabitants and surviving influences from Roman civilisation into what became the enclaves of Cornwall, Wales and Scotland. The most important influence to survive the wars between Celt and Saxon which created England was the Christian Church. The other main consequence of Anglo-Saxon expansion was the forced migration of much of the old population of Roman Britain. Few Celtic words were absorbed into the language of the Anglo-Saxons. Many scholars think this suggests there was little pity shown to the conquered and that population movements in consequence were profound. There was a continual migration from Britain to Armorica. The incomers spoke the same language as the original inhabitants, and battle-hardened veterans from the fighting in Britain defended the peninsula with great success against the barbarian tribes which roved at will throughout France.

The Britons of the island had provided the legions of old

Rome with excellent archers and horsemen, and the peninsula became known by the name of these migrants who had defended the land and made it their own.

Seething tides of barbarians isolated the Bretons from the Mediterranean Church of Rome. It was with Cornwall, Wales and Ireland that ecclesiastical links grew and prospered. The Celtic flavour of the spirituality which nourished the people was not without the reverence before the forces of nature that had been inherited from Druidry, but their "sancti" or holy men and women were remembered for their ordinary human kindness and spiritual happiness as much as for supposed supernatural abilities.

Beyond the old seaport of estuarine Morlaix the road followed wooded valleys into a region of granite uplands covered with heather and pine woods. The road climbed to Montaigne St. Michel. It was still very early, but the sun was already warm and banishing the dew. The moorlands of Galloway and Donegal had been the dun brown of winter, but on Montaigne St. Michel fresh green shoots were everywhere flourishing. From the top of the hill I looked out over the Breton landscape whilst skylarks kept up there frantic singing despite the attentions of predatory hawks. Mist wreathed much of the lower ground and extended its tendrils over placid lakes.

This was not my first visit to Brittany. A decade earlier I had played on beaches with my infant children on the south-western coast of Cornouaille near the resort of Benodet and nearly three decades earlier I had spent an adolescent month at Quiberon. I hoped to revisit both places and so the road from Montaigne St. Michel lay due south. I resolved to wind up the throttle and head for the old cathedral city of Quimper. I had once sailed up the ria from Benodet with my family to explore the town . This time I approached from the north on the broad dual carriageway of a Route Nationale.

It was mid-morning when I arrived and parked the bike in the main square behind the cathedral. Market stalls were being set up by gesticulating traders, and cafe tables cluttered the pavements. I sat down and ordered some refreshments as I stretched my cramped legs. The conversation at the surrounding tables was that of English people with the extenuated vowels of the "Sarf East". Regimental blazers identified my companions as D-Day veterans who had crossed the Channel to take part in the 50th anniversary of the landing in Normandy. It was hard to think that these aged gentlemen had once outfaced the Nazi S.S. and brought more than hope to a subjugated continent.

The British Army had attacked the northern beaches and eventually swung through the Pas de Calais and into Belgium and the Netherlands. The Americans advanced into Brittany after breaking out of their beach head, but the Germans had a large garrison in the peninsula because Lorient and St. Nazaire on the south coast had been major U-Boat bases from which the Nazis had inflicted carnage in the Atlantic. It was not until August that the German defence in Brittany crumbled, and even then an enclave around Lorient held out until May 1945. Their besiegers were the Free French of General de Gaulle. The Bretons have a long and distinguished history in the sorry saga of warfare. De Gaulle visited Quimper in 1945 and he said that after the fall of France in 1940 it was the Bretons who were the most indomitable in defeat. Despite only contributing 1/10th of the population of the French Republic, Breton soldiers, sailors and airmen had constituted 1/3 of the numbers of the Free French who did not surrender but went into exile to continue the fight against Hitler.

I entered the cool of the cathedral and stared up at the high vaulting. Organ music danced fugues within my head and I went in search of a priest. I had with me a pilgrim passport for Compostela. I needed a cleric to sign the document as proof of my passage and I was given directions for the residence of the priest on duty. I was eventually ushered into the presence of a tall, ascetic looking man. Pere Louis Jestin was delighted to oblige when told of my adventure and the nature of my request.

I must have looked rather a wild and dishevelled figure as I stood before him. Nevertheless the Breton priest was much amused by my Presbyterian pilgrimage to Compostela and we talked of the great antiquity of the Breton church. Roscoff had once been the base of a Roman legion and the immense church building that had dominated the landscape around the ferryport was dedicated to Paul Aurelian who had come to Brittany from south Wales during the last great migration of the mid 6th century. Paul Aurelian had been taught by Maucennus of Whithorn. There were ancient links between Galloway and Brittany. With exquisite courtesy the interview was concluded and he saw me to his door, giving as he did so a blessing on my journey with the parting comment that it was an ancient tradition among Celtic peoples to wander the face of the earth far from home.

Quimper lies about ten miles inland up one of the long, flooded rias which interrupt the southern coast. I intended to revisit the marvellous beach that had been the playground of my infant children and so I took the road for Loctudy. On the outskirts of Quimper I stopped at a small supermarket and purchased sausages, cheese, fruit, biscuits and a tin of scallops. The scallop shell was the traditional symbol of a Compostela pilgrim just as a palm branch was the symbol of a Jerusalem pilgrimage. I had a huge Solway scallop shell fixed to my rucksack, but the idea of scallop for a pilgrim lunch seemed most suitable.

It was not long before I reached the old fishing village of Loctudy. It is named after one of the old Celtic "sancti". Tudy came from Cornwall to Breton Cornouaille. The cluster of the old village is built on a low spit of land at the mouth of a wide inlet. We had once spent a magical evening of hilarious celebration sitting at tables in the village square. We had dined outside and as dusk fell the western sky was lit up by the most spectacular electric storm. Thunder boomed off the Atlantic. Much of the conversation that night had been about electricity. The Paris Government of the day had decided to build a nuclear power station at Polgoff not far away at the Pointe du Raz. It was an unpopular decision in the locality and there had been violent demonstrations against it. In Scotland we had lost the fight to stop Torness nuclear power station, and as a result the Scottish coal field had been destroyed. I sat in the sun at Loctudy and ate my scallops using a shell taped to the tin as a spoon and watched the tide ebb through the narrow mouth of the ria. On the north coast of Brittany, at St. Malo, has been built a powerful barrage which utilises the power of the tide to make electricity. Tidal power stations avoid the Chernobyl-type risks of the nuclear industry, but Plogoff is the European norm and St. Malo the intelligent exception.

The south coast of Brittany has long beaches of brilliant white sand ground from the granite headlands by the crash of Atlantic waves. Many thousands of holidaymakers from England, France and Germany come here during July and August. New developments of holiday homes have been built everywhere. The tourist industry has brought considerable financial benefit, but it has also resulted in an influx of incomers who have diluted the distinctive Breton flavour that I remembered from earlier visits. The past is another country, but the place names on the map were those given by the migrants from Britain at the end of the Age of Arthur. The Breton identity down the centuries was one of the legacies of the long defence of those who had cherished the last fragment of unconquered Roman civilisation in the west.

Quiberon was nearly a hundred miles to the east of

Loctudy and it was time to get the bike moving. Unaccustomed heat beat down as I followed coast roads until the great city of Lorient blocked further progress and I had to use a busy Route Nationale to bypass the built up area. It was a relief to return to the peace of pine forests sweeping down to wide beaches and soon the long peninsula of Quiberon drew in sight. Driving out to the tip of the peninsula would add 30 miles to the journey, but my pilgrimage was as much an exploration of the past as a physical journey to a remote Galician cathedral.

After D-Day strong German forces retreated into the concrete bastions that had turned Quiberon into a Nazi bolt hole. The eastern shore of this finger of land is sheltered, but the west side is exposed to the full fury of the ocean. The house I had stayed in overlooked the rocks of the Cote Sauvage. Looking for it I came across an old whitewashed church which on an impulse I decided to enter. My eyes adjusted to the shade after the bright sun and I noted the model of a wooden sailing ship that hung from the ceiling. In the 18th century there had been a terrible battle between the Royal Navy and the French fleet off Quiberon, but there were other memorials to the human capacity for self destruction. On the wall behind a statue of the Madonna were dozens of plaques bearing the word "merci" and with the name of a person inscribed. Dates and places from the First World War clustered at the centre, whilst at the peripherary were the names of soldiers and sailors who had survived the second great conflagration. It was all so simple and so poignant that I was moved to purchase a candle and leave it flickering as a memory of a moment of prayer. I thought with an inappropriate glee of the disapproval with which a candle to the Madonna would be viewed by some of the Galloway ministers I had known who held to an extreme Calvinist theology. As I placed my candle I noticed the largest of the plaques. It simply said "merci, August 1944-May 1945". The parishioners of this little church had been held hostage by the German garrison for a terrible nine month gestation through starvation into liberty.

I could not find the old house we had stayed in all those years ago because of the rash of holiday homes that had grown up in the interval. The afternoon had been almost too hot for comfort, but banks of grey cloud were building up in an ominous fashion out to sea and the wind was growing in strength. It was time to find somewhere to camp.

To the east of Quiberon lies the Gulf de Morbihan, a wide and shallow inlet of the sea studded with islands of pine trees. Two short peninsulas like arms enfold gentle waters. Years ago there had been a ferry linking the two arms which I hoped to use to avoid the congested traffic around the city of Vannes at the head of the gulf. It was my plan to catch the ferry that evening from Locmariaquer at the head of the western peninsula and spend the night at the little fishing village of St. Gildas de Rhuys. Gildas was one of the most notable of the travelling Celtic clerics of the 6th century and he wrote pungent chronicles recording the events of the world in which he lived. Gildas originated in Scotland and spent much of his life in Wales before coming to Brittany, but in between Quiberon and St. Gildas de Rhuys lay a stretch of countryside in which is situated one of the most dramatic monuments to human achievement. The standing stones of Carnac dwarf even Stonehenge, Avebury or Callanish. Long lines of carefully positioned stones, some as high as five metres, march in parallel lines over miles of countryside.

The small stone circle of Torhousemuir in Wigtownshire was a later outlier of a culture in which Carnac was an influential focus. 7000 years ago Neolithic farmers began the building of the complex that also includes massive underground burial chambers. Forest, field, garden, shore and sheltered waters would have provided as plentiful a larder as Lough Bann, but the stones of Carnac reflect the power, wealth and numbers of these earliest

European farmers in the west. Thousands of miles later in a remote town in Cantabrian Spain I would find some clues to the mystery of the origins of the people of Carnac, but the road drew me on towards Locmariaquer.

When I arrived it was to discover that the ferry to St. Gildas de Rhuys had long since been discontinued. Locmariaquer is surrounded by a network of small fields that are enclosed by tall hedgerows. I would have little difficulty in finding a burrow for the night.

Whilst I was wandering the streets of the little town my nostrils were assailed by the savoury smells of cooking coming out of a small hotel. I succumbed to unendurable temptation and was given, at a reasonable price, one of the most memorable meals of my life. *"Etes vous anglais?"* *"Non, je suis ecossais"* and I rather suspect that had I replied in the affirmative the meal would have been slightly less superb.

First came a great platter of oysters, mussels, cockles, winkles, prawn, spider-crab and half a lobster. That was just for starters, and was followed by spiced lamb, salad, cheese, fruit and coffee to the accompaniment of local cider and apple brandy. A great contentment followed which only turned to consternation when I saw drops of rain begin to fall. It was time to get the tent up.

In gathering darkness I found a quiet hedgerow and quickly erected the olive green fabric of the tent and crawled into the interior. It was much warmer than it had been at Lough Gartan or on the Duchesse. Sleep was almost immediate in the pattern-less noise of raindrops.

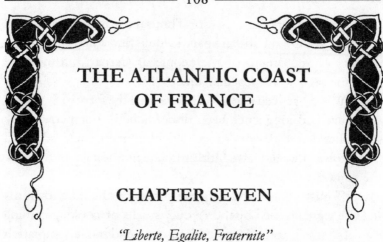

THE ATLANTIC COAST
OF FRANCE

CHAPTER SEVEN

"Liberte, Egalite, Fraternite"

Locmariaquer, Noirmoutier, La Rochelle, La Palmyre.

I thought to myself that this must be one of the strangest mornings of my life. I was sheltering under an overhanging bush beside an old stone wall. I was next to naked and the rain was lashing down all around. A web of ivy gave good shelter, but my arrival had disturbed a wren whose home it was. Dawn was an imperceptible lightening of greys and there was no colour in a sky of low, scudding clouds. I was not cold. The rain was deliciously warm, but it had finally breached the defences of the tiny lightweight tent which had been abandoned for the bush at first light.

During lulls in the rain I had recovered my belongings from the wet interior of the tent. Everything had been packed in plastic bags and eventually I managed to dress in dry clothing.

Roscoff to Locmariaquer had covered 250 miles of coastlands with headlands, vast beaches and deep rias. The Breton countryside had waved with stands of barley already come into ear beside orchards budding into fruit. In cottage gardens I had seen fig trees and lines of beans already in flower. Back in Wigtown the beans in my garden were hardly showing above ground, and the warmth of the rain on my naked skin had reminded me that I was far to the south of Scotland

The route planned for the second day of June would take me south for 300 miles to the estuary of the Gironde. It would follow the coast as closely as possible and avoid the great city of Bordeaux by taking a ferry across the Gironde and travelling into the pine forests of Gascony. It was going to be a long hard day in the saddle and the weather conditions were not going to help. The motorbike was given the once over and the chain was tightened in preparation for the long miles ahead. The rain began to slacken and soon the damp sleeping bag and the soaking tent were packed into a rucksack that was heavier than on the previous day, but before the long hours on the machine my body needed the exercise of a morning walk.

The lanes behind Locmariaquer were full of wonders. A long, grassy mound gave a panorama eastwards to the gulf and west to where Quiberon blocked the horizon. My viewpoint was not a creation of geology. Its stones and tilth had been piled by human hands and covered a burial chamber in which generations of the people who had raised the standing stones of Carnac had been buried. It was more than 100 metres in length and beside it lay fallen and broken into three fragments a huge stone that had stood over nine metres in height.

Awe at the achievements of these people who had lived in a world without metal fell on me as I gazed over the expanse of the landscape of Carnac which had been sacred to them. I had slept with the ancestors and it was with care and quietness that I absorbed the morning before the roar of the motorbike broke the hush of the fields. The first hour of the journey was tangled up with rush-hour traffic as commuters made their way into

Vannes. It had been a prosperous town in Roman times and like any sizeable 20th century community it sucked commuters into its vortex before exhaling them at the end of their working day.

Brittany ends at the River Vilaine which flows to the sea in a deep valley over which the road soars at a giddying height on a single concrete span. A blustery wind gave some anxious moments before I gained the French side of the river. The rain diminished into occasional showers and the sun burst through the clouds.

In Scotland and Ireland, and also in Wales, there are powerful national identities that are quite different from England and which insist that they are not English regions, even if populations all speak variations of the language which evolved out of an amalgam of Latin, German and French, and which was spoken by Chaucer and Shakespeare. The English language has become the "lingua franca" of the modern world and in the last 4 centuries it has replaced Gaelic and Cymric (Welsh) in the Celtic areas of the British Isles. Most Bretons still spoke their version of Cymric into the 19th century when the educational system of the French state and the impact of commerce had the consequence that the Breton language withered, but there is still a great sense of an identity which is different from the rest of France. I had seen the black and white stripes and cross of the Breton flag fluttering in every town and village and the traditional music of Brittany includes bagpipes. They are proud of their links with Ireland, Wales and Scotland, but there seems to be little in their political life or their relationship with Paris that is the equivalent of the yearning for home rule that was expressed in Edinburgh in December 1992 or the fervour of nationalisms which disfigure Ireland.

Modern Brittany has prospered under successive French governments. Farming and fishing have thrived, but one of the main engines of Breton growth has been the burgeoning tourist industry. Fertile and with an equable climate, Armorica has become one of the playgrounds of the continent, but the episode of violent resistance to Plogoff power station is a reminder of the distinct heritage of Breton identity.

The names of the villages beyond the River Vilaine are French and not Breton. The nature of the coast changes to a brackish marshland of tall reeds that swayed in the wind. I began to see a sight with which I would become familiar on the long roads to the Gironde. Deep excavations are used to rear oysters on an industrial scale. Oysters are in voracious demand in France and the oyster beds create much employment. Canals and a network of sluices and ditches bring tidal sea water far into the marshes.

The Vilaine was a broad river and its bridge was high, but the estuary of the Loire was spanned by a structure as massive as the bridges over the Firth of Forth. It rose hundreds of feet above the water to allow ocean-going ships upriver to St. Nazaire and Nantes. Gusts of wind attacked the bike and it was with considerable relief that I reached the southern shore. I needed time to regain my equanimity and allow adrenaline levels to sink, and so I parked the bike and watched the broad river, yellow with sediment, roll down to the sea. The Loire flows through the rural heartland of France and I was watching its topsoil being lost to the future. Mechanised agriculture and the continual turning of the earth are destroying the soil of France in the same manner as in Scotland.

The turbulent currents of this great river limited its use for commercial navigation inland from Nantes, but in the past the Loire had been a highway for the light leather boats of Celtic clerics as they made their way to the episcopal city of Tours that had once been a Roman provincial capital. It had been at Tours that a soldier in the garrison called Martin divided his cloak with a sword to give half to a shivering beggar. Thereafter Martin began to develop the first communal monastic settlement in western Europe during the 4th century. The ideal of communal living was based on sharing, exemplified by the gesture of the founder in dividing his cloak. Individual greed was to be tamed by simplicity of life and the contentment of enough.

Implicit in the life of Martin and those who followed was a strong critique of the society of a weakening Empire in which the rich were very rich and the poor were mired in utter deprivation. It was said that *"humankind is divided into three classes, the rich, the poor, and those who have enough......abolish the rich and you will have no poor.....for it is the few rich who are the cause of the many poor"*.

One of the spokesmen of this movement was called the "Sicilian Briton" and he declared with great humour that *"the understanding of truth is not a function of wealth, but of thought"*.

The emphasis which Martin and his followers placed upon the need for social justice echoes the continual theme of the prophets in the Old Testament and the compassion and pity which the earliest Christians showed to each other in their communal living which is recorded in the letters of the New Testament.

Some ecclesiastical historians refer to the decades after the Emperor Constantine converted to Christianity as the "Dawn of the Age of Hypocrisy". Flattering courtiers would seek baptism as a way of finding imperial favour and not in the motivation to worship God by establishing a just society on earth. Comfortable, self seeking complaisance with the status quo has marred the centuries of the Church despite the continual counterpoint of those inspired by the biblical message of the need for social justice.

"One man owns many large mansions adorned with costly marble, another has not so much as a small hut to keep out the cold and heat. One man has vast territories and unlimited possessions, another has but a little

stretch of turf to sit upon and call his own. Inequality of wealth is not to be blamed upon the graciousness of God, but upon the iniquity of men". So wrote the Sicilian Briton. This shadowy figure is thought by some authorities to have originated in Wales and his legacy was an inspiration to the monastic communities which flourished throughout the Celtic world in imitation of the achievements of Martin and his friends at Tours.

In the middle of the 5th century when Ambrosius and Arthur began the fight back against the German invaders of Britain the last Roman authorities in western Gaul surrendered their power to the invaders. A group of clerics from the Loire fled into exile. They settled at Kirkmadrine in Galloway where they looked out over Luce Bay to Whithorn where Ninian had established the earliest Christian community in the north. They would have brought with them the ideals of Martin and the Sicilian Briton which have nourished Scottish Christianity ever since.

The inhabitants of Tours and the Loire may have had to sue for peace and bend the knee to the German invaders, but not the Bretons of Armorica who continued a successful resistance. The Bretons had few dealings outside the battlefield with those who came to dominate Tours and an inevitable distance evolved between the Church of the Bretons and that of the German occupied towns of the old Roman provinces of Gaul. On the north coast of Brittany at Dol began to evolve a monastery whose influence rivalled Tours. An associated legend insisted that the devil had been defeated by the archangel Gabriel at this place, and a fiery Welshman called Samson became the leader of the community at Dol of the Bretons.

The story of Michael vanquishing the devil is often associated with a Christian centre developing in what had previously been the sanctuary of a pagan religious cult. A few miles south of the estuary is a village called St. Michel-Chef-

Chef. Had the new Christian cult overwhelmed some revered site of pagan Rome or Druid Celt at the mouth of the Loire?

I returned to the bike to resume the journey. Factories and shipbuilding yards had lined the river near St. Nazaire. 50 years ago this had been a U-Boat lair and a British force had attacked German shipping upriver and rammed an old destroyer called the Campbelltown into the U-Boat pens where it exploded killing hundreds of Germans. The ubiquitous Gildas had been here too, paddling his coracle up the Loire to visit Tours.

Further south the marshlands grew wider in a flat, wild countryside above which eagles circled. Oyster beds glinted through the reeds and the world smelled of salt and mud as it did beside the Solway. I was travelling southwards beside the Baie de Bourgneuf. Offshore lay the tidal Ile de Noirmoutier. Noirmoutier means black monastery. At the southern end there is a new concrete bridge over a deep channel, but the traditional route to the island follows a strip of tarmac that is only negotiable at low tide. The tide was rising and it would have been most unwise to risk the three mile crossing, but I wished to visit the island and rest for an hour or so near the site of an old Celtic monastery at La Blanche, and so I took the bridge and gave myself as long a detour as Quiberon had been on the previous day.

Ile de Noirmoutier greatly resembled the Isle of Lindisfarne on the Northumbrian coast from which the Celtic church had worked among the north-country English. Both are offshore lengths of sand-dune that have been piled by tide and wind in the wake of shelves of rock, but the sand-dunes of Noirmoutier are huge and overhang the canals and lagoons of the oyster farmers. At La Blanche I hoped to spread the sleeping bag and tent to dry in the mid-day sun.

On the bridge from the mainland, zephyrs of wind played their usual unkind tricks and a ferry was preparing to leave the slipway below for the Ile d'Yeu several miles further out to sea. I passed concrete block-houses like those on Quiberon. They had been built by the slave labourers of the subjugated peoples of the Nazi Reich. Many had died of cruelty and neglect in building the defences of Hitler's Atlantic Wall which had been so conclusively breached on the beaches of Normandy. It was with gratitude that I thought of the old men with white moustaches and "Home County" tones that I had met in Quimper.

On modern Noirmoutier the block-houses were surrounded by the neat little concrete boxes of holiday homes that have sprung up all around them in recent years. In Brittany houses were built with stout walls and steep slate roofs. Red tiles on less steep roofs were the traditional style south of the Loire, but many of the little holiday houses on Noirmoutier were built in the flat-roofed style of the Mediterranean with rounded Spanish arches and whitewashed walls. I watched as builders threw up another batch with thin walls that were only one brick thick. They would make adequate hutches in summer, and in winter most would stand empty when holidaymakers had returned to the cities of Europe. Compared with the caravan sites that disfigure Galloway these little houses were comely and inviting even though most of them were still shuttered and closed after the winter months.

The main settlement on the island is an old township built beside a venerable harbour basin which is linked to the sea by a canal. There were many boats, both pleasure craft and fishing vessels tied up alongside the town, but taller than their masts were the towers of a mediaeval castle which loomed over everything. Beside the castle rose the main church of the island, much of which had been rebuilt in the 19th century. Even before I entered the old buildings I was aware of a mounting sense of disquiet. When I looked around the church I discovered that it had been the scene of an ugly episode in French history.

The French Revolution of 1789 was one of the turning points in European civilisation. The "ancien regime" of the Bourbon kings had become utterly corrupt and unable to govern a society that was being transformed by manufacturing and mercantile developments in the burgeoning cities. In the countryside the peasantry seethed with resentment under the burden of the rents which they were forced to pay to their landlords. Aristocratic families lived in a grandeur of which the lifestyle of the Anglo-Irish gentry was but a pale imitation. They flaunted their wealth in the teeth of the poverty of the people. The Roman Catholic church was also the object of public scorn. This widespread unpopularity was an inevitable result of the huge estates of the church which extracted from the peasantry rents as heavy as on aristocratic estates.

These problems were compounded by taxation under the "ancien regime". Its burden fell on those sections of society least able to bear it. The aristocracy and the church were exempt from most taxation and the Bourbons had been profligate with the wealth of France as they built palaces like Versailles and indulged in an expansionist foreign policy that had resulted in a long sequence of wars against the Hapsbourg emperors in Vienna and the Protestant powers of Holland and the United Kingdom. As a result the demands of taxation in France grew heavier and heavier on the poor.

The forces of resentment built up like unseen stresses in a geological fault-line which reached crisis point and exploded into a sudden earthquake of change. Famine in the poor districts of Paris enflamed the situation and bourgeois attempts to control the eruption of violence were not successful. Inspired by philosophers like Voltaire and Rousseau, French intellectuals, exalted the cult of Reason over the primitive superstitions of the church, but the mobs which burned the chateaux of aristocrats with the same enthusiasm as they attacked ancient abbeys did not listen. They wanted vengeance. In the cities this resulted in the erection of guillotines in the central squares. The revolutionary regime in Paris began a reign of terror. The King and Queen of France were executed before huge crowds. Queen Marie Antoinette met her death with quiet dignity, and Europe was outraged. English revolutionaries under Oliver Cromwell had beheaded Charles I in the 17th century, but they had not harmed his queen. The brother of Marie Antoinette was the Austrian emperor. Foreign armies invaded France only to be repulsed by fierce levies of revolutionary citizens singing the bloodthirsty anthem of the Marseilles.

However, not every part of France backed the revolution or its attack on the ecclesiastical establishment. These foreign invasions of Prussian and Austrian armies had encouraged the peasants of the Vendee to rise up against the revolutionaries of Paris. I had been travelling through the coastlands of the Vendee since leaving Brittany.

The people of the Vendee were loyal to their clergy, and the Royal Navy supplied them with arms, but revolutionary armies moved to crush them. Outnumbered and outfought they were forced to retreat to Noirmoutier where hunger made the army of the Vendee surrender. These peasant soldiers had their wives and children with them, but their conquerors were without pity. Thousands of the defeated men, women and children were penned up in the castle and the church. They were left without food and water for many days until the survivors were taken out in batches to meet the bayonet and the bullet.

Those who have visited Auschwitz say that a terrible atmosphere of horror clings to the place and that even birds shun it. The castle and church on Noirmoutier had the same effect on me and I felt nauseous and weak. Inside the church I had read an inscription on a memorial which stated simply that this atrocity of mass-murder had been committed in the name of "Fraternite".

The Russian revolution was also accompanied by great barbarity. There is something in the human psyche that leads to terrible cruelty when individuals and groups are utterly convinced of the absolute correctness of their own viewpoint. Intellectual arrogance has no humility and not a flicker of doubt. Bolshevik commissars who stripped the Ukraine of food to leave millions to die were little different from the S.S. who ran the death camps. Religious fundamentalists of every persuasion are just as capable of atrocity as political zealots like the followers of Robespierre or Lenin or Hitler. The burning of "witches" and heretics throughout the centuries is proof of that.

As I left the church with a bowed head and crushed in spirit I was struck that in France the revolutionary Tricoleur of Republicanism was steeped in hostility to the Roman Catholic church, whereas in the Republic of Ireland it was quite the opposite. It was an irony to think that in 1798 Roman Catholic Irish insurgents were content to welcome a French army whose commander had supervised the butchery of the Vendee.

I was as glad to leave Noirmoutier as I had been to leave the desolation of Donegal, and for the same reasons. History in these places had become a tragedy!

For many miles beyond Noirmoutier the coast consisted of pine forests on rolling sand-dunes with a sprawl of holiday facilities accompanying them. At Les Sables d'Olonne I left the coast to run inland along straight roads overshadowed by poplars. Fields of grain stood yellow and ready for the harvest. Dust rose up from a countryside that would be burnt brown by the midsummer sum. Fields of sunflowers were busting into bloom when I began to see vineyards with increasing regularity. I was entering the great wine growing country which exported its vintages through the great port of Bordeaux. This was the countryside of Claret.

I had turned inland to avoid the industrial city of La Rochelle, but I was soon caught up in the afternoon rush-hour of commuters leaving the city. The French drive fast and with the aggression of gesticulating hands and grimacing faces. It was not a pleasant interlude as I breathed diesel and tried to keep my distance from speeding lorries.

La Rochelle had been one of the most important trading towns along the Atlantic coast during the 17th century, and as I struggled through the traffic I began to pick up on a strand of history that helps to explain persistent attitudes in Northern Ireland to Roman Catholicism. During the 16th century Protestant preachers like John Calvin had gained a great following in France even though the renowned reformer chose to take up residence in Geneva having been forced to flee from Paris by threats of violence. Many of the magnates of the aristocracy sided with the Reformation and for similar reasons to those of the German princes who had supported Martin Luther. The Reformation offered them the wealth of the extensive estates of the old church which had been the recipient of so many bequests over the centuries. In Scotland the "Lords of the Congregation", the military leaders who backed John Knox, apportioned out among themselves the lands of the mediaeval church. Kings in Sweden and England did likewise. However it would be quite wrong to attribute the success of the Reformation only to the self-interest and greed of aristocratic families. The main centres of Protestant thinking and idealism were in the manufacturing and trading towns where literate craftsmen and merchants studied the flood of books which were emerging from the new printing presses in a torrent of ideas which swept away the intellectual stagnation of the mediaeval world.

"To every action there is an equal and opposite reaction". This is not only a law of physics. The impact of the Reformation caused the reaction of the Roman Catholic Counter-Reformation, and

France was not immune to the contagion of the wars of religion which raged throughout the continent.

The assault on Protestantism in France erupted when their leadership were taken unawares during a time of truce. The St. Bartholomew's Day massacre of 1572 killed over 8000 Protestants in the streets of Paris in one night. Bitter warfare followed. One of the most effective leaders of the French Protestants was Henry of Navarre. A pragmatic man, he agreed to change his religion when offered the throne of France, saying "Paris is worth a mass". He established the Bourbon family as monarchs as a result, and by the Edict of Nantes he promised toleration to the Protestant communities. This enlightened man was eventually murdered by a Jesuit priest and thereafter Cardinal Richelieu and Cardinal Mazarin embarked on a long campaign to erode Protestant liberties and power.

La Rochelle had become a centre of Protestant thinking and it was placed under siege. The population were starved into capitulation, even though English ships and a small army tried to come to their aid by occupying the offshore island of Ile de Ré. French Protestants called themselves Huguenots and after their defeat tens of thousands were driven to emigrate to northern Germany, Holland, England and the north of Ireland where they helped to establish a thriving linen industry. Every tide brought woeful refugees to northern shores who planted in the hearts of their host communities the terror of the Counter-Reformation which had indulged in multiple cruelties, massacres and the perfidy of broken treaties. In 1688 the tolerant Edict of Nantes was revoked by King Louis XIV. A few die-hards held out in the mountains of the Cevennes, but Protestant power in France had been broken. Nevertheless, the cat of free-thinking was out of the bag of Roman Catholic control.

The persecution of the Huguenots climaxed at the same time as the Protestant Ascendancy gained the victory in Britain and Ireland. The same punitive laws which Louis enacted against the Huguenots were used against the Roman Catholic Irish after their defeat at the Battle of the Boyne by the army of "King Billy" in 1689. La Rochelle had fallen decades earlier, but the 30,000 Protestant fugitives in Londonderry had survived their siege. In both Ireland and France it was the same for the vanquished in a hideous equilibrium of state-sponsored intolerance.

The harsh persecution of religious dissidents in France during the 17th century does much to explain the avalanche of hostility that poured over the old ecclesiastical establishment in the years after 1789, and it does much to explain the lingering attitudes of Ulster Protestants whose ancestors narrowly escaped the same fate as the Huguenots of La Rochelle.

I had purchased a road map of France and Quimper. It was printed on both sides of the paper and it was with great satisfaction that after La Rochelle I needed to use the side of the map which covered the south of the country. I had travelled over 300 miles since the morning and fatigue weighed heavily upon me. At Rochefort I had to negotiate another huge bridge over the estuary of the Charente and then I escaped from the busy traffic that had plagued the journey since La Rochelle.

The coastline south of Rochfort was very similar to that near Noirmoutier. Offshore lay Ile d'Oleron with the inevitable pine woods, marsh and oyster-beds, when round a curve of the road I was suddenly confronted by the walled citadel of Brouages that rose above the reeds. It was from Brouages that Champlain set out to establish the colony of Quebec and the French presence in Canada. Inside the 17th century battlements and emplacements for cannon was a perfectly preserved town. Time had allowed it to moulder quietly until large quantities of Eurochash had been devoted to restoring the buildings in recent years. New bistros and shops showed that it was becoming popular with tourists, I could have found a quiet nook for the night at Brouages, but I preferred to find a spot nearer the sea and so I drove on through a wasteland of oyster-beds across a causeway to the pine forests of La Palmyre which overlook the mighty estuary of the Gironde. Beside it even the Loire would have been dwarfed.

It was twilight when I turned off into the woods to park the bike in a clump of bushes.

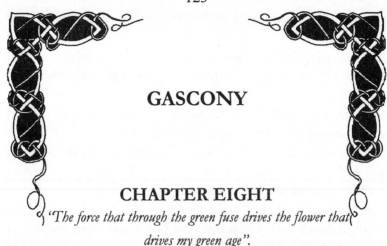

GASCONY

CHAPTER EIGHT

"The force that through the green fuse drives the flower that drives my green age".

Dylan Thomas

La Palmyre, Le Verdon, Villandraut, Castel Sarrasin, Lavour

Slumber in the pine forests of La Palmyre had been long and untroubled, but waking had been to a strange world.

I had parked the bike and put up the tent in a clump of bushes in the last fading light of evening. A comfortable litter of pine needles had mattressed the ground and spreading branches had been a canopy overhead. Through the trees there was the glint of the waters of the Gironde swirling towards the sea in a sheen of moonlight, whilst there was the roar and hiss of distant waves breaking onto sand banks. A dreamless oblivion followed.

It is a delight to wake slowly in a tent and listen to the morning chorus with which birds greet the return of light. As I travelled further south I had expected to hear new noises from species that do not thrive in the north. I had heard the unexpected rattle of the woodpecker in Brittany and in the Vendée I had seen eagles darker than the golden eagle of Scotland. I hoped to hear the song of the nightingale, but on that morning in the forests of La Palmyre I listened to my ears with mounting astonishment.

Strange animal voices filled the air. Unknowingly, I had spent the night only a few hundred metres away from the perimeter fence around one of the biggest zoological parks in all of France. Lions were roaring, camels were groaning and spitting, and flamingos were hooting with a cacophony that soon had me wide awake. I luxuriated in warmth as I munched a leisurely breakfast. I had travelled 600 miles since arriving at Roscoff. It was good to be lazy as I listened to the unexpected voices of Africa.

However, once I got started I knew there would be rigours enough on this day for I hoped to reach the ancient city of Lavour before sunset. Lavour is situated in a strong defensive position of a high bluff above a loop of the River Agout to the north of the great southern city of Toulouse. I expected to have to cover over 300 miles before I reached my destination.

On an old farm in the hills behind Lavour lived a family of great friends. They had visited us several times in the Machars of Wigtownshire which they had found an exquisitely exotic location, and they had journeyed with us through the Hebrides in the astonishment of a midsummer anticyclone. I told them it was different in midwinter. We had travelled once before to visit them as a family and had been overwhelmed by hospitality. The friendship had begun some years earlier when my wife had accompanied a group of disabled people from Stranraer as their interpreter to a festival in France that had drawn together similar groups from throughout the European Union for a celebration of music, dance and theatre.

The group from Stranraer were dressed in tartan and waved

the saltire flag of Scotland as they joined the international throng in the old streets of Figeac. They had taught the crowd to join in the chorus of the *"bonnie, bonnie banks of Loch Lomond"* and the ancient and genial amity between Scots and French had resulted in a growing friendship between our two families.

Dominique worked with disabled people in Toulouse. They used horses and carts as a therapy to enhance the quality of the lives of these disadvantaged people. In the summer months they embarked on great journeys through rural France behind the swish of horses tails.

We had invited Dominique and his colleagues to come to Galloway for the opening of the first section of the Whithorn Pilgrim Way at Whitsun in 1993. With the help of some very kind local farmers we had arranged for Clydesdale horses to pull carts for the French visitors between Glenluce Abbey and Whithorn. It had rained but nothing had dampened the happiness of those few days. Village schools had lined the pavements to cheer the cavalcade. Pipers had played the Marseilles and our visitors had returned to Toulouse with memories that would last a lifetime. The huge gentleness and the furry hooves of the Clydesdales had given great pleasure to people for whom life had not always been kind.

I knew that when I arrived that evening at the farmhouse of La Serre I would receive a warm welcome. Dominique was not only a horseman of great skill, he was also a "chef de cuisine". I chewed the stale remains of yesterday's baguette and thought with anticipation about supper.

The trees obscured most of the sky. I took a walk to find a viewpoint from which I might discover what the weather promised for the day. A wind was rising from the north and when I reached the dunes at the edge of the trees I saw heaps of black clouds building up and billowing into the sky over the sea. Fists of wind began to shake the branches of the pines and I made my way back to the motorbike.

From the tip of La Palmyre it was 10 miles up the estuary to the town of Royan where I would catch a ferry to the southern shore of the wide river. I arrived just in time to see the small vessel leave the harbour. It would be an hour and a half before the next sailing and so I wandered around the streets of this smart holiday resort. In July and August the town would have been full of holidaymakers, but on what threatened to be a stormy day in early June the streets were quiet. Concrete and glass were the favoured building materials. On the sea front, gardens and palm trees lined the boulevard. Out at sea the sky had turned an alarming hue of yellow and gusts of wind whipped the shallow waters into a fury of choppy wavelets. It grew dark and I realised that no ordinary shower of rain was about to hit the town. Anxiously I was searching for shelter when my eyes alighted on a little kiosk which sold refreshments. Beside the kiosk was a lean-to canvas extension with clear plastic windows that gave a broad view over the river. I hurriedly parked the bike and gained the interior before an avalanche of wind hit with the power of many solid objects. Huge hailstones bounced off the pavement and I sought consolation in hot coffee and fresh buttered bread while the canvas cracked, rattled and twitched around me.

The ferry journey promised to be entertaining. I was sure the wind was gusting to Force 8 on the Beaufort scale. When the worst of the hail had passed over I made my way to the harbour to await the ferry. Other cars and vans arrived, but I was the only motorcyclist rash enough to be out on a morning like this. My bike attracted the attention of some cheery young Germans in a battered Volkswagen van. They were travelling to Gascony for a surfing holiday. I told them I thought the waves would be big enough. They agreed.

South of Brittany the coast of France had predominantly been of low marshlands and damp pastures, but beyond the

Gironde the coast stretches to the Pyrenees in an unbroken line of sandy beach. Behind the shore lie the dunes and pine forests of Gascony. Some of these dunes are huge at over 100 metres in height. The name of this distinct region derives from the French way of saying Basque. Like Brittany, Gascony had a semi-detached relationship with the rest of France. The Kings of England had ruled Gascony for 300 years until the middle of the 15th century when it was incorporated into the Kingdom of France and English influence was banished. The Gascons and the English had been firm friends and allies to each other as they resisted the encroaching power of Paris. The inhabitants of Bordeaux had been loyal until the end to the English alliance and there were still many influences from this relationship visible in the landscape. The architecture of Gascon churches was very similar to England. Tall tapering spires evoked the style of Salisbury cathedral.

The Norman conquest of England in the years after 1066 replaced a Viking and Anglo-Saxon warrior aristocracy with one which spoke French. English peasant and yeoman families grew to associate that language with the cruelties of the new baronage. The feudal aristocracy of conquered England was cousin to the landowning hierarchy of France. King Henry II authorised Strongbow's invasion of Ireland, but he also married an heiress with title to the wide lands of Gascony. His third son was Prince of Brittany and his eldest son was the Crusader, Richard the Lionheart. Their power was great, even that of his other son, King John, who was so unpopular in England that the name was never again given to a monarch crowned in Westminster Abbey.

Trade between Bordeaux and London burgeoned and throughout the 13th and 14th centuries the links between Gascony and England grew ever closer. Armies of Gascons, English and Welsh campaigned with great success in Spain and France, but the balance of power began to swing away in the

15th century when gunpowder was introduced to the European battle-field. Time after time, at Poitiers, Crecy and Agincourt the English foot soldier had defeated the mounted knights of France. Archers poured deadly volleys of steel tipped arrows into French cavalry charges from six foot bows of yew. These bowmen were perhaps gaining an ancestral revenge for the miseries previous generations had endured after 1066. The descendants of the victors at Hastings spoke the language of their continental origins until after Bannockburn. The utter humiliation of the French speaking ruling class of England at the hands of the Scots is one reason among many others which helps to explain why the language of the common man in England again rose to become the parlance of the royal court. However, gunpowder nullified the power of the English longbow and it was near Blaye on the banks of the Gironde that the last Anglo-Gascon army was destroyed at the end of the 100 Years War in 1452. The population of England at this time has been estimated at 4 million, that of France at 12 million. The weight of French numbers had eventually ground down the English war effort into defeat.

I tied my bike to the bulkhead on the ferry with unusual care. The short voyage would be stimulating. Long lines of waves crashed in the shallows as the yellow and black tub wallowed through the tide-races. It was a turbulent and entertaining three miles before the ferry arrived at the little port of Le Verdon. The Nazis had kept their slaves busy at this strategic finger of land. Concrete gun emplacements and block-houses lined the beach and had been little affected by the passing of the years. Disembarking from the ferry I noticed the name of the road leading from the slip-way. It was called "Rue Rémy Normandin" and beneath the name was a simple inscription "Mort pour la France, 1944". Volunteers of the French Resistance had overwhelmed the German garrison, but not without cost.

The Gironde had been used by the Germans as an important naval base. British commandos had braved the turbulent tide races of the estuary in a daring night time attack on shipping in the harbour during the Second World War. They had journeyed from Britain in a submarine from which they had disembarked in canvas kayaks that were weighed down with limpet mines and equipment. They successfully pressed home their attack but many were drowned when their overburdened boats capsized. This attack became known as the raid of the Cockleshell Heroes.

Le Verdon had been for centuries the landing place for travellers from the north. One of the traditional pilgrim routes for Compostela led south from Nantes to Le Verdon before following the Gascon coast to Spain.

After the little port my route followed this pilgrim trail under towering trees that gave protection from the wind. Away from the coastal dunes the land was sandy, flat and infertile, but wherever undulations dipped close to the underground water-table a green fecundity was home to swarms of insects. I had to tie my scarf across my face as protection against the erratic trajectories of bees that seemed to be drunk with pollen. The ocean had been at my right hand since Stranraer, apart from the inland miles of Ireland, but soon I would be leaving the scent of salt water. I would not again see the Atlantic until after I had reached Compostela and so I followed a track to the beach to say farewell.

Deep water comes close inshore on the Gascon coast and the waves were blue and clear. I had thought I might take a swim since this was my third day without benefit of hot water, but the waves were enormous and grains of sand were hurled by the wind to sting the skin of my legs. It was a relief to regain the shelter of the trees and continue the journey southwards. In great gusts of ozone I had made my farewells to the ocean.

During July and August tourists throng this coast. The town of Royan had been chic and up-market, but many holidays along the Gascon coast are enjoyed in cheap and cheerful camping sites among the trees. I promised to remember to tell my daughter that camping sites with nudist beaches are called "La Jenny". Her brother would appreciate the information even if she did not.

For several hours I hurtled due south through air perfumed with pine resin until the straight coastline was interrupted by the wide inundation of the Bassin d'Arcachon. Here I turned to swing inland and head for Lavour through the broad and fertile lowlands of the River Garonne. I had come far enough south through lonely forests to avoid the congested traffic in the environs of Bordeaux. After the near solitude of the long run down the coast there were a few miles of lorries to endure. I passed over the six speeding lanes of the motorway which leads to Bayonne and the Spanish frontier. I was heading away from the direct road to Compostela, but I did not regret the diversion. I would be with friends for the week-end.

In the late afternoon I sat at a table under a striped umbrella outside a cafe in the little town of Villandraut. The entire scene seemed to have passed through the centuries unchanged since the days of English power in Gascony. The grey battlements and towers of an ivy covered castle rose above the red tiles on the roofs of mediaeval houses. Beyond Villandraut lay a different country, the lands which had once been ruled by the Counts of Toulouse, and so I said farewell to Gascony. After the week-end in Lavour I would cross the Pyrenees and learn more of the Basque people who gave their name to Gascony and to the Bay of Biscay.

The day had cleared, but the wind remained brisk out of the north west. I consulted the map and decided to use the motorway for Toulouse which ran near Villandraut. I reckoned that the wind would add an extra 10 m.p.h. to the cruising speed of the motorbike and that I could easily keep up with motorway traffic. There were still 150 miles to cover and I did not relish the prospect of finding Dominique's house in the dark. The motorway would save time.

Visitors to Britain have free access to the motorway network, as is the custom in northern Europe. In France it is the same as in Italy or Spain where a traveller must pay a toll to use each stretch of motorway. On a motorbike this cost £1. for every ten miles on the motorway between Bordeaux and Toulouse. It didn't seem fair, but it was great fun cruising down the tarmac after the intricacies of navigation through bumpy ruralities. Because it was late on a Friday there were few lorries on the road. As the evening shadows lengthened over fields of stubble that had already been harvested I laughed with sheer pleasure and happiness as the wind pushed me on. Vineyards and orchards surrounded elegant chateaux and old towns crowned hill tops. The churches near Toulouse were very different from the towers and spires of Gascony that had been built with hard, white limestone. In the old County of Toulouse churches were built out of red brick, and their most distinctive feature were tall walls from which carillons of bells were hung.

The shape of the bricks in the older buildings was flat and wide. I had seen the same type of brick in the ruined tenements of Ostia at the mouth of the River Tiber. Those tenements had been built when Ostia had been the seaport of ancient Rome 2000 years ago. Furthermore, the warm ochre roof tiles of the south of France have changed little from Roman times. The clay was rolled out flat and then shaped into a curve using the workers thigh as a pattern before being baked in an oven.

This architecture was indicative that southern France had known a great continuity from the old civilisation of the Roman

Empire. Northern France had been more completely overrun and settled by German tribes, but the populous towns and cities of the south had retained memories of an older identity. The language of the south had been significantly different from the speech of the north. Languedoc was much more similar to the Catalan of Barcelona which had descended from the Latin slang of the Roman Empire than it was to the "lingua franca" of the French north.

However, a greater threat to the culture of Languedoc came from the south and over the Pyrenees. I was reminded of this by signs on the motorway giving directions for a town called Castelsarrasin. The name of the settlement means the Castle of the Saracens, the warriors of Islam who crossed from Africa in the 8th century to overrun the Iberian peninsula before brimming over the Pyrenees to pour into France. The Saracens pierced north of the Garonne before the Frankish armies of Charles Martel drove them back over the mountains. In a churchyard at Fénioux not far from La Rochelle there is a strange octagonal tower. It was built as a Muslim minaret from which Saracen muezzins had called the faithful to prayer. It stands as the high water mark from the flood of Islam which once poured into western Europe.

The influence of the Saracens was felt throughout the Iberian peninsula and for a time the Pyrenees were the frontier between Africa and Europe, between the worlds of Islam and Christendom.

Soon after Castelsarrasin I left the motorway for the road to Lavour. It followed the course of the River Tarn which had emerged from its spectacular limestone gorges to enter the low country of the Garonne. This road had foundations which had been laid by Roman engineers two millennia earlier. It ran straight through a landscape of vineyards to deliver me to the familiar streets of Lavour.

Lights were twinkling in the windows of the farmhouse of La Serre when I arrived to a joyful reunion. With the help of some fine malt whisky which I had purchased a thousand miles to the north on the Duchesse, we renewed old acquaintance whilst I supped a stew of beans, sausage and unidentifiable segments of what I was assured was duck. Garlic, olive oil, haricot beans and garden herbs all blended to produce "Cassoulet", a staple and warming food of Languedoc. It was wonderful, so was the Hebridean malt.

Since Fethard in Co. Tipperary I had been a stranger. It was good to be among friends again.

THE MIDI

CHAPTER NINE

"Cups of kindness"   Robert Burns

La Serre, Lavour, St. Agnan.

The walls of the farmhouse of La Serre were built out of rammed earth and were nearly two metres thick. Bricks were only used to strengthen corners and the surrounds of windows and doors. Wide overhanging eaves supported a rippling tile roof that was held up by huge oak beams. The old farmers of the Languedoc built themselves substantial dwellings, but the house creaked as the strong wind buffeted around it.

The ground plan of La Serre is L-shaped. The two wings of the house half enclose a warm sheltered spot that catches the morning sun. It was there that the Raffin family breakfasted, dunking hunks of bread in great steaming bowls of sweet black coffee. Dominique's moustache was even bigger that the year before. It hung like a curtain over his lower face and projected out at the sides further than his ears. Seen from behind it looked as though his head had grown handles. His son had a motorbike and Dominique informed me that he had managed to get the next few days off work. He had resolved to accompany me over the mountains and into Spain. We would leave together on the Monday morning. It would be good to have a companion for a few days.

On the Saturday afternoon we made our way into Lavour to purchase provisions at the street market. Dominique knew that we would be camping, but he intended that we should eat well even if we were to sit and sleep on the ground. He chose charcuterie and cheese with care. We would buy fresh bread, olives, fruit, water and wine as we needed it. It was strange to have to pay more for water than it was for rough country wine. On the way back to La Serre we called on the local priest in the little village of St. Agnan. I wished to get my pilgrim passport signed and Dominique wanted to introduce me to a most unusual cleric.

The priest's house was centuries old and the rooms had high ceilings which provided a cool interior. A grape vine grew over a trellis outside to give shade and hens scrabbled and clucked in the village street in front of the church. Our host was a small, neat figure in carpet slippers. His eyes twinkled with merriment and mischief as he quizzed me about my journey.

Raphael Bastieri was at the latter end of middle age and his years had not been uneventful. An Italian by birth, he had entered the priesthood of the Roman Catholic church after the Second World War. He also had studied to become a medical doctor. This priest and physician had then become an accredited diplomat of the tiny Apennine republic of San Remo. These qualifications and skills enabled him to travel the world and he was fluent in many languages. Dominique has a very limited grasp of the English language, having only a smattering of what he called Frécossais, and so the subtleties and nuances of conversation were hampered by the limited vocabulary of my French. Father Rafael's travels had taken him to northern India. There he became involved in the tragedy which the people of

Tibet had suffered at the hands of the Communist regime in China. His skills as a physician were devoted to the needs of the weary refugees who had survived the journey through the highest mountains in the world to the sanctuary of India.

In a quiet voice Father Raphael described the torment of a nation. Tibet is an unusual place. It is the roof of the world, a high plateaux that endures the harshest extremes of climate. Tough tribes of nomadic pastoralists managed to subsist in the greener and more sheltered corners, and among them developed the wonderful expression of the divine in the human soul that is Tantric Buddhism. The shamanistic tribes of mountaineers listened with wonder to the teachings that had come up from India about a prince called Gautama who had renounced wealth and position to lead the life of a wandering beggar. Gautama grew into the Buddha and taught the gentle "Middle Way" that tamed the tiger of human passions and liberated the soul into the ocean of compassion that gives serenity and peace of mind in this world.

For two millennia the Buddhist civilisation of the high Himalayas had thrived and glorious monasteries rose above cities like Lhasa and attracted thousands of pilgrims. Pilgrimage is not only a Christian phenomenon and Father Raphael gave the traveller to Compostela a conspiratorial wink. Then, with a shrug of his shoulders that reminded me of the gesture given by the A.A. man in Northern Ireland, he described in an infinitely sad voice how the monks and nuns of Tibet had been slaughtered by the Chinese, but the Dalai Lhama, the spiritual leader of the Tibetans, had escaped and many of his countrymen have followed him into exile.

Father Raphael had spent many years working with these exiles and he had been instrumental in gaining for them a base in France. A large chateau near Lavour has become a Tibetan centre, "L'Institut Vajra Yogini".

In this there was a link with Galloway. In the lonely hills of Eskdalemuir above Annandale there is the largest Tibetan community in the western hemisphere. Three decades ago a scouting party of Buddhist monks travelled though Britain in search of a remote location in which they could set up an island of their own culture. Although only a rolling plateaux of little more than 1000 feet above sea level, the frosty nights and skies clear enough from pollution to show the galaxies were enough to persuade the monks to make Eskdalemuir their home. It regularly achieves the coldest temperatures in the British Isles and it reminded them of their homeland. Deep Himalayan mountain horns boom out over the hills of Dumfries-shire and the wise and pacific teachings of Tibet have found a well-respected welcome in Galloway.

There are many people who are tired of the wrangling between "Prod and Pape" that has disfigured European religion in more than just Northern Ireland. The history of Buddhism is not without its own doctrinal schisms and many of Gengis Khans blood-thirsty followers were Tantric Buddhists in name at least, and no less terrible than "Christian" Crusaders, but the dialogue between Tibet and Christianity is older than the flight of the Dalai Lhama. A thousand years ago there was the thriving Nestorian Church which had many populous and prosperous communities along the Silk Road between Persia and China. These Nestorian Christians established monastic communities in Tibet that for a time had many dealings with their Buddhist neighbours.

Father Raphael knew of the Tibetans in Scotland and he was enthusiastic about their recent purchase of the Holy Isle off Arran in the Firth of Clyde. This small island had once been the home of "sancti" in the Celtic Church. The Tibetans intended to restore this deserted island to its earlier role as a place of peace and meditation. We agreed that in small ways

France and Scotland have provided safe refuges for an ancient culture threatened by expansionist imperialism. The story of the Hebrew princess who had fled from threatened Jerusalem to find refuge by Lough Neagh sprang to mind and I shared it with my companions.

I wore around my neck and old silver cross from Iona. The Celtic Church superimposed the cross over the circle of the sun which had been the symbol of the three rays of Druidry. Father Raphael was interested in the design and we both lamented that the circle and the cross have been taken as the symbol of the new fascist groupings in Italy. He then showed us the cross which he wore. It was a Cathar cross used by a religious movement that spread throughout southern France in the 12th century. The Cathars were savagely suppressed as a heresy, but they have left their memories throughout Languedoc even though the dreaded Inquisition was created by the Roman Catholic church to destroy them. Father Raphael by wearing a Cathar cross was having his little joke with orthodoxy, but there had been little that had been funny about the Crusade which was launched to destroy the Cathars of Languedoc.

The beginning of the 12th century had seen the victory of the Crusaders in the Holy Land of Palestine. The capture of Jerusalem and the movements of hundreds of thousands of people had opened up western Europe to religious and cultural ideas from the Levant and the Balkans of eastern Europe through which the Crusader armies had marched. Roman Catholic orthodoxy did not welcome these new ideas which were seen as a diseased blight to be extirpated from the life of Europe.

Many of the Cathar teachings originated in Persia. The ancient religion of the Persians before they were overwhelmed by Islam was called Zoroastrianism after its founder who was a prophetic figure living like Moses in the latter part of the second millennium B. C. Zoroaster had denied the host of gods and demigods of polytheistic religious insights which the Hindus of India still find a divine parable. Instead he taught that the world was a battle ground between the two opposing forces of good and evil. The pain and suffering of material and physical life was equated with evil. Only the spirit could transcend the corruption of the flesh.

When tribes of these Iranian horsemen were eventually to coalesce into the Persian Empire their dualistic religion set them apart from cultures dominated by the many gods of India, Egypt, Assyria, Babylon and Greece. Only one people had a religion which appeared similar to their own. When the Persians defeated Babylon they encountered a subjugated community of exiles beside the banks of the Euphrates. These were the descendants of the Jews whom Ezekiel and Daniel had encouraged after the fall of Jerusalem. The Persians equated their God of light and goodness with the One God of Hebrew monotheism. This cultural empathy resulted in the Persians treating the Jews with great consideration and favour. The exiles returned to Jerusalem and Judah. The cultural and intellectual interchange which followed is evoked in the biblical story of the three wise men guided out of the east by a star to the manger in Bethlehem. The bearers of frankincense, myrrh and gold were Zoroastrian sages.

Christianity was viewed by later Persians as the suspect creed of the enemy Byzantine Empire of Constantinople, but it was the Christian Nestorians of Persia whose descendants along the Silk Road to China first developed the dialogue with Tibetan Buddhism. The far flung influences of Persian religious understanding also were to percolate westwards to surface among the Cathars of Languedoc.

Despite apparent similarities when seen in the context of polytheism there are profound theological differences between a religion which propounds a dualistic nature to the cosmos and one which attributes everything to a monotheistic source. In classical Zoroastrianism evil was held to be co-equal in power with good as the two forces were locked in an eternal equilibrium.

For Jews and Christians (Druids also) the power of evil was seen as a temporary rebellion against the creating force of the universe. The arrival of the Hebrew messiah, the second coming of Christ (the dawn of the age of Yesu) would herald the ultimate victory of good over evil.

These theological differences resulted in differing lifestyles. Cathars taught that physical life was utterly corrupted by evil. The spiritual path was a rejection of everything material in ascetic self denial. This contrasted with the complete physicality of Jesus on the cross and the material elements of the Eucharist utterly fused with the divine in a seamless unity which extended the sacred into the mundane.

There were other bones of contention. Cathar teachers equated the God of the Old Testament with evil and error and the God of the New Testament with truth and goodness. They also denied the validity of the Mass and held that the communion of the divine with the human was not restricted to rituals supervised by a Roman Catholic priest. The Cathars claimed to be custodians of esoteric and secret knowledge known only to initiates and they believed in reincarnation as do so many creeds from the east.

Among their itinerant preachers women were as active as men. In many instances it was the simplicity of the lives of the Cathar missionaries which attracted a great following. Their spirituality contrasted well with the worldliness of many of the magnates of the Roman Catholic hierarchy who had gained their elevated status by virtue of family links with the secular aristocracy. Gradually merchant and landowning families were attracted to the Cathar cause. Matters came to a head when the papal envoy to the Count of Toulouse was murdered.

This was a challenge which the Roman papacy could not ignore. A Crusade against the Cathars was sanctioned and an army of Frankish and Norman knights was mustered with the added lure of wide estates to be won in Languedoc. Behind the mail clad knights came the assiduous servants of a new ecclesiastical institution called the Inquisition. In effect they were the thought police of mediaeval Roman Catholicism and the shock troops of an ideological war. Their name became a byword for terror. I would learn more about the Inquisition in Spain where it was unleashed on the Jews and Muslims of Grenada.

The later name of the Cathars was the Albigensians because the townspeople of Albi nurtured a hostility against the Inquisition which resulted in the cathedral of Albi being turned into a fortress. Lavour had also been an Albigensian stronghold until its anti-ecclesiastical inhabitants were massacred by Crusaders after a desperate siege.

Father Raphael stopped speaking. The only sounds were the wind in the eaves and an old clock ticking in the hallway.

Father Raphael invited us to join him in the little church in the morning and we returned to Dominique's home in a subdued frame of mind, but somehow also strangely elated after the company of the elderly Italian.

At the turn-off for the road to the farmhouse of La Serre I noticed that balloons had been tied to trees and signs were up giving directions to a party. Dominique said that he had invited some friends round for the evening, several of whom I had met in Scotland. It was going to be a busy evening.

It was wonderful to observe the preparations that went into the feeding of several dozen people. Great bowls of salad, rice and vegetables appeared. Cheese, eggs and sausage were sliced and prepared while rounds of a local delicacy sizzled in frying pans. The French eat many of their magnificent variety of sausages cold and thinly sliced like salami, but this speciality of Lavour was of the type that is cooked and eaten hot. It was like a very good Cumberland sausage.

The old farmhouse was a capacious building and the paved area between the two wings gave a wide sheltered space. The visitors gradually arrived and I was embraced and kissed in a delightful routine. My friend Yves from Carcasson arrived and he lifted me off my feet in a huge bear-hug. His family were descended from the Huguenots of Guyenne and his father had been a pastor. We had last been together on a Hebridean holiday when we had visited rather too many distilleries. He had resolved to educate me concerning French wines and he came back from his car with an armful of bottles. Others visitors arrived bearing bottles and delicacies, cheeses, cakes and savoury loaves until every flat surface in the house was covered with a cornucopia of delights.

Before French people sit down to a meal they like to indulge in an aperitif. As a child I had enjoyed a penny bag of aniseed balls. It was no hardship to sip Pernod until it was time to begin eating. Everything was leisurely and informal. One course melded into another as dishes were removed and replaced to an enthusiastic appreciation. Special vintages of the grape were uncorked, sampled and compared until the conversation turned to Scotch whisky. I produced the bottle of malt from the Isle of Islay which I had purchased on the ferry and was astonished when four other bottles of Scotch were placed on the table by grinning bon viveurs who had an informed enthusiasm for one of Scotland's more notable contributions to the world of epicurean appreciation.

They said a good Scotch is comparable to a fine brandy and I did not disagree with them.

It had been the monks of the old Celtic Church who had introduced the art of distilling spirits in copper retorts to Scotland. Much of their output had been used to make herbal tinctures for their medical work, but mediaeval Scotland took to the art of distilling grain spirit with enthusiasm and skill. There had been a small and traditional trade in Scottish spirits with the Baltic until the long wars with Napoleonic France had starved Scotland of the produce of the grape and further stimulated demand for the home produced product, but the real breakthrough of Scotch as a quality product in great demand on the international market was caused by a disaster which almost destroyed French wine and brandy production. For long years in the middle of the 19th century vineyards throughout France were destroyed by a fungus called Phyloxera which spread as rapidly as potato blight in Ireland. It took many seasons before the new vines reached full productivity and Scotch grain spirit filled the gap in the market. Canny distillers in Scotland upped production and began to age whisky in barrels which had once matured brandy, sherry and port.

Scottish civilisation seemed to these French friends to consist of two main ingredients...........whisky and golf. They were probably right, but I belong to that persuasion which considers golf to be a good walk ruined by a small white ball!

Several of the guests who had stayed till late were to spend the night at La Serre. In the morning we all decided to attend the mass which Father Raphael would be conducting.

It was not a long walk to the church, just long enough to blow away the cobwebs from the night before. Crickets rasped in the dry grass at the side of the road and lizards darted across the tarmac.

The outside of the little church of St. Agnan echoed the style of the cathedral in Lavour where so many Cathars had died. It was built out of brick, but the octagonal tower and spire were of carved white stone. The interior was shabby with peeling plaster and flaking paint and it reminded me of Galloway kirks I had known in a similar state of neglect. However, there was an expensive tape recorder which filled the interior with music. Until quite recently there had been a numerous population in the French countryside, but the number of people gaining a livelihood in agriculture has sharply declined as mechanisation changed the face of farming. Father Raphael only expected a small congregation, and old peasant ladies in shawls were in the majority. They were survivors from an earlier age. A few younger families arrived, but the group from La Serre almost doubled the usual congregation.

I had often attended Roman Catholic services in Scotland and I was familiar with the liturgical movement of the mass as it began in sonorous French. On the previous Sunday I had had no wish to go to an Irish Roman Catholic church, not much liking the aggressive displays of papal flags and republican Tricoleurs around them. I had contented myself with the solitary and frozen ponderings that had given an internal dialogue and a Sabbath blessing by Columba's Gartan Lough; but in the shabby little French church I was soon enfolded in timelessness whilst Father Raphael preached on the body of Christ, on the seamlessness of the relationship between the physical and the spiritual realms. It had been that emphasis on which Christianity could not agree with the Cathar denial of any goodness in the material sphere of life. I did not go up to the table to take the wafer of the Eucharist. The Schism of the 16th century still leaves that legacy, but everyone else filed to the front, the children for a blessing and the adults for divine communion.

The Iona Community has long campaigned against the die -hards of both persuasions to bring about inter-communion, but official episcopal exclusion of Protestants from communion administered by a Roman Catholic priest was a reminder of the attitudes which had divided Europe and still divide Ireland.

I was to discover on the walk back to Dominique's house that many of the friends from the night before had not attended mass in many years. The last few decades have seen the influence of the Roman Catholic church dwindle in France in the same manner as has the Kirk in Scotland. Many of the young people of Lavour prefer the Institut Vajra Yogini. When the Dalai Lhama had visited Lavour in the previous winter Dominique had cooked food for over 300 people.

After the service the Sunday afternoon was a time of quiet until a game of petanc got under way. This French version of bowls involves much exuberant comment and eloquent gesticulation. Other people began the graceful exercises of oriental Tai Chi. It looked as though they were dancing through water in slow motion as the sun set on Lavour.

It had been a weekend full of wonders and so many kindnesses. In the morning Dominique would say farewell to his lovely wife and twin daughters before joining me on the road to the Pyrenees.

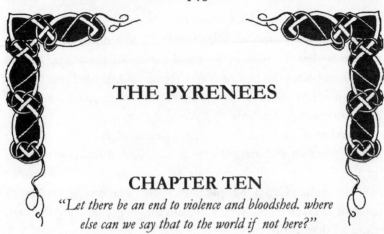

THE PYRENEES

CHAPTER TEN

*"Let there be an end to violence and bloodshed. where
else can we say that to the world if not here?"*

Auschwitz 27:1:95

La Serre, Lavour, Institut Vajra Yogini, Auterive, St. Bertrand de Comminges, Bigorre.

Our first port of call on the Monday morning was a small cafe in Lavour where Dominique had arranged to meet a friend from whom he would borrow a tent and rucksack for the journey. It gave me some time to renew my acquaintance with the old city.

The looming bulk of the cathedral dominates the skyline, but the waters of the River Agout in its deep winding valley down below are black. The traditional industry of Lavour was the manufacture of fine leather, but the toxic filth from the tanning of hides has poisoned the water for centuries. Pollution is not a new phenomenon and the extinction of most European wild-life was achieved long ago. The river is melancholy in its sterility and birds shun its lifeless waters. It reminded me of the lochs in the Galloway mountains that have died as a result of acid rain, but the Agout was black and impenetrable whereas the lochs cradled by Craigeasle and the Merrick are clear for fathoms. Not even algae mist the waters there, so acidic have they become.

The vast bulk of the cathedral loomed over me and seemed to squat on my heart. It had been built as a fortress against the Albigensians. The Inquisition had burned Cathars alive before the doors of this imposing edifice.

The Christian religion had begun as a Jewish heresy condemned by the orthodoxy of the Pharisees and the comfortable complaisance with the political status quo of the Saducees. As a result persecution of the early Christian community throughout the Roman Empire had been vicious in countless sporadic episodes over the first three centuries of the church.

A thousand years later and ecclesiastical institutions were behaving with the same cruelty as their early persecutors. Human viciousness is no new thing. Archaeologists who have studied the ceremonial monuments of Neolithic farmers from before the time of Carnac have found skeletons bearing the signs of terrible violence; of a flint arrow-head wedged in the vertebra, or a skull crushed and the body carelessly thrown into the midden of rubbish that accumulated when clans gather for mid-summer feasting. Head hunting was common in many parts of the world. Celtic warriors beheaded those whom they slew to nail their trophies to the gables of their houses and German tribes hung the bodies of captives from ceremonial trees that were bedecked with this hideous fruit in a continuous harvest. One of the most notable Celtic influenced missionaries to Germany, the indomitable Boniface from Northumbria was killed whilst trying to fell with an axe one such hideous totem tree. But the 20th century bears the stain of Auschwitz where cruelty was industrialised. When ancient Jerusalem fell to the Babylonians the slaughter had been horrific. The biblical story records the atrocity of the heads of infants being dashed against walls and kerb stones, but at Auschwitz there was the perpetual reproach of the thousands of silent children who each week and every month stumbled towards the gas chambers and the glare of the ovens.

I sat in the square beside the cathedral under the fronds of an unfamiliar mimosa tree and wept. It was the 6th of June, D-Day + 50 years. The ovens of Auschwitz were still to burn for more than another seven months, another thirty weeks, for more than two hundred days and nights after those old men I had met with beside the cathedral in Quimper had gone ashore on the beaches of Normandy. 50 years to the day after the liberation of Auschwitz a survivor who had returned to the place of his torture said *"let there be an end to violence and bloodshed. Where else can we say that to the world if not here?"*

1945 did not see and end to the mentality that produced Auschwitz. Stalin's Gulag and Mao's Chinese equivalent would continue to murder millions. Cambodia, Bosnia, Rwanda, Tibet, East Timor .... the list could be endless.

"Peace on earth. Goodwill to all". That had been the earliest message of the church. What was it in the human psyche, the human predicament, that produces the violence and cruelty which had once been perpetrated in the square of Lavour?

"Fraternite" had butchered the peasants of the Vendee in the same manner as the Cathars of Languedoc had suffered in the 13th century. Asia, Africa and the Americas had their own indigenous cruelties. Theologians propounded the doctrine of sin, but the natural history of evolution has its own explanations.

70 million years ago there had been the mass extinction of species at the end of the age of the dinosaurs. In the subsequent interval the genetic stock of small warm-blooded survivors of the catastrophe which caused the extinctions evolved to fill niches in the ecosystem as diverse as the blue whale, the bat, the cheetah and the giraffe. About five million

years ago in Africa groups of intelligent primates that were very similar to chimpanzees were confronted with a new evolutionary challenge when the rain forests of the continent contracted to a fraction of their former size. This was caused by an Ice Age so severe that sea levels in the Atlantic dropped to such an extent that the Mediterranean was cut off from the ocean. Primates like the chimpanzee had evolved to live in the branches of trees where they were safe from predators which prowled at ground level. That safety ended as the trees died and their inhabitants were forced to live as best they could without the refuge of tall branches. They supplemented a diet which had been based on the fruits of the rain forest by becoming scavengers and hunters of small game. The survivors of this trauma evolved into two distinct sub groups. Australopithecus Robustus was bulkier and stronger than the quicker and more slender cousin. Both learned to walk upright so that they could peer over the tall grasses of the savannah which was their new habitat.

Australopithecus was the direct ancestor of the humanity that had displayed such a capacity for cruelty throughout history. Bruce Chatwin and Konrad Lorenz have propounded the theory that the evolutionary experience of Australopithecus created the violence that lurks within the human psyche, but which is largely absent from the vegetarian gorilla and the orang-utan.

Homo Habilis was the next step along the evolutionary process from Australopithecus and was succeeded be Neanderthal and the latest mutation into Cro-Magnon. For a million years our ancestors have had a knowledge of fire and a gradually evolving weaponry that enabled them to hunt and snare even the biggest game until we had become the most terrible predator the planet has ever seen and one which adapted to every climate zone from the Arctic to the Equator. With flint, fire and fear the mass extinctions of entire species paralleled the spread of our ancestors. Mammoths, cave bears and aurochs are now but a memory like the more recent dodo.

The extinction of species is not unique to the activities of the human predator. Australopithecus Robustus was unable to survive because of the attentions of a fang-toothed lion which once roamed Africa. Dinofelis (the terrible cat) hunted by night. An Australopithecus cub would doubtless have been a tasty snack. Cats have excellent night vision, far better than primates peering anxiously through the gloom and stranded at ground level by climate change.

In the savannahs of Africa lightning-strikes often produce bush fires. The slender variety of Australopithecus found safety and an ability to see their surroundings on moonless nights by learning to cope with the fearful proximity of wild fire and ultimately in learning to tame it. However, there had been a legacy of fear and anguish, of having been the near helpless prey of Dinofelis.

Chatwin used the example of the modern leopard hunting a pack of baboons or chimpanzees, hoping to separate a young, weak, or old animal from its companions. The leopard takes a small proportion of its prey in this manner, but the jaws of Dinofelis had adapted to specialise in crushing primate skulls. So efficient did the terrible cat become that the larger variety of Australopithecines became extinct, and the slender cousins had been pushed to the brink of oblivion when their fear of Dinofelis overmatched their fear of fire, and the fight back of the hunted against the hunter began.

When threatened by a leopard chimpanzees respond with adrenaline fuelled aggression, of a fear-crazed rictus bearing fangs in a gibbering of saliva, a hopeless desperate defence, but as Australopithecine's became Neanderthal the tables were turned. Armed with fire, stones and clubs the early hominids destroyed Dinofelis. The legacy of this birthing of humanity is an ancestral fear knawing at the entrails of our subconscious minds. The original aggression that had been focused in an evolutionary crisis against the terrible cat was transferred to human competitors. Bands of hunters would fight for dominance over the best hunting ground. Agriculture created heavier populations and conflicts developed between rivals for control over fruitful harvests, but before the killing could begin humans had to bestialise their human enemy to dehumanise their competitors so that they could unleash the violence that had once destroyed Dinofelis. For the S.S. guards at Auschwitz the Jews were sub-humans, and in Lavour heretics were dead souls. Both groups were seen as unworthy of pity by their persecutors.

It was time to rejoin Dominique and return to La Serre to collect our luggage and prepare for life on the open road. A television flickered in the kitchen as we grabbed a last bite. All day there would be programmes about D. Day and the images of war.

There is something strangely soothing about driving a motorbike during times of turmoil and confusion. That morning by the cathedral had made the burden of history oppressive. I ached for the clarity of the mountains. We set off at a fair clip in a cloud of dust.

Dominique's machine was a Honda trail bike. - Its gearing would be good for the Pyrenees, but it did not have the legs of the Yamaha on the flat. Toulouse lay to the south of us in a haze of brown murk. We intended to swing in a great arc to the east and to the south of the city on quiet country roads until we came to the foothills of the mountains. Toulouse is an industrial and manufacturing conurbation much of whose modern prosperity depends on avionics, but it has a long history. It had been a great pilgrim city in the Middle Ages. The road from Avignon and Italy led through the city to join with routes from Paris and Germany on their way to Compostela like tributaries feeding a long river of travellers. Toulouse boasted one of the largest cathedrals in Europe. It had been built on the site of an old Roman temple dedicated to Saturn that had superseded the sacred groves of the Celts who had once dominated this region. The cathedral of St. Sernin also claimed to be home to venerated relics of St. James, but we would not visit the old shrine, islanded as it was in the centre of the city by a sea of seething traffic.

Dominique lead the way through a labyrinth of country lanes and then turned up the driveway to an imposing chateau set in towering trees. This was the Tibetan centre. A swelling oriental stupa had been build in front of the elegant 18th century building. Buddhists build stupas in which they place a relic, however tiny, of Gautama.

This eastern custom is not dissimilar from the mediaeval Christian tradition of venerating the bodies of saints. Bishop Victoricius of Rouen wrote in the 4th century "there are bodies that a bond unites with the whole current of eternity" It was thought that the currents which through their lives had linked them to the divine life force of the world underwent no interruption at their death. So intense had been the breath that inspired them that physical death brought them into a new dimension of being, namely sainthood. Pilgrims to a Buddhist stupa or a Christian shrine believed that healing virtue still residing in the bodily remains would flow into them, and that a whispered prayer would be conveyed to the ear of heaven. Unable to visit St. Sernin's I paused in prayer before the stupa to lift the heaviness that had descended on my soul. Afterwards I began to enjoy the sunshine of the morning.

Soon we were moving again through a landscape of rolling hills. In Scotland pasture land is dotted with grazing animals which are only housed in byres during the worst of the winter weather. In Ireland and Brittany I had seen animals in the fields but few were to be seen in the rolling hills of Southern France. Cattle are penned indoors throughout the year. One of the results is that the French countryside is not latticed with the web of barbed wire that has been strung across the face of Scotland but this aesthetic, visual benefit is bought at the expense of the happiness of the animals on French farms. Devout Buddhists extend their compassion and pity to animals as well as people.

We reached the town of Auterive which is twenty miles to the south of Toulouse. We had travelled fifty miles in our circumnavigation of the city through an undulating and fertile landscape that was yellowing into midsummer ripeness. The River Ariege flows out of the least populated part of France to run through the centre of town to its confluence with the Garonne in Toulouse. The Ariege was quite unlike the black waters of Lavour. It swirled faster than a man could run, but its colour was a milky, opaque green. This was the melt water of the high Pyrenees which were shedding their winter accumulation of snow and ice in the heat of summer.

After Auterive the hills began to rise, but apart from the colour of the melt water there had been nothing to suggest the proximity of the mountains until we breasted a ridge. Before us lay a wall of snow capped peaks, pinnacles and ridges. Visibility was very clear after the haze around Toulouse and for fifty miles east and west we gazed on the panorama of the mountains.

We had planned a route that would lead over one of the highest passes. From the coastlines of Biscay to the Mediterranean there are little over a dozen routes through the mountains that are passable by wheeled vehicles. The traditional roads used by pilgrims to Compostela lead through the Somport Pass and the Pass of Roncevalles, but these are now subjected to a continual stream of traffic on broad concrete highways that loop through the mountains or leaping bridges before diving into dripping tunnels in a high speed switch-back of diesel fumes. The Col de Pourtalet was one of the quietest routes and it lead through the wildest and most spectacular country where the

Pyrenees were nearly 3 times taller than Ben Nevis. The mountains of Scotland were old before the dinosaurs, and glaciers have ground them low, but the mountain range between France and Spain is, as are the Alps and the Himalayas, recent in geological terms. The continents of our planet are not static. The Indian sub-continent has drifted against Asia to force up Everest and the Tibetan plateau in the same way as the pressure of Africa against Europe has built the Alps and the Pyrenees. The peaks of these new mountains are jagged like fangs against the horizon. The route to the Col de Pourtalet passed through the town of Lourdes which in the last century has been transformed from a poverty-stricken textile town into the focus of a new enthusiasm for Roman Catholic pilgrimage.

We came to the headwaters of the Gironde which would eventually meet the sea at La Palmyre where I had awoken to the sounds of Africa only three days earlier....a morning chorus Australopithecus would have known. The river was the same icy green colour as the Ariege. We sped down a broad Route Nationale which followed the course of the river. I began to wish that we had an intercom radio like the two R.U.C. officers whom I had met in Cork. It was difficult to keep in sight of Dominique and I needed to signal that I was very low on petrol. My friend was used to the saddle on horseback, but he had taken to a motorcycle like a natural. Trying to overtake him I gave myself and a lorry driver coming the other way a nasty surprise. We had been grinding along the main road for a couple of hours and I needed a change of pace.

We pulled in for a recuperative coffee and consulted our maps. We would leave the Route Nationale and head for the old town of St. Bertrand de Commingues and thereafter stick to country roads as we made a more leisurely way to Lourdes.

This was the warmest day of the whole journey. Heat pressed down on my shoulders until I could not bear the weight of my leather jacket. I dispensed with my leather gloves too. This was a mistake. Leather can prevent lacerations if a biker takes a tumble, but the backs of my hands were soon tingling with sunburn. Too late I applied liberal quantities of protective cream. I was needing a break from the sunshine as much as I needed a rest from main road traffic.

Dominique lead the way through quiet valleys beside tumbling streams. Oak forest clothed the hillsides and the air was scented with the musk of the forest shadows. Bears and wolves once made this dangerous country for pilgrims. Their last survivors still linger in the mountains. At St. Just de Valcabrere we left our bikes and visited a church that had been built before the Battle of Hastings. Beautiful gardens and cypress trees surrounded the old walls and the custodian to whom we paid a modest entrance fee gladly signed my pilgrim passport. It was blessedly cool in the interior. I sat down to enjoy the peace of the place and to run my eye over delightful Romanesque architecture from the 11th century. A rounded apse at the eastern end contained a multitude of semicircular arches in which tiny slivers of polished alabaster allowed opaque shafts of light to illuminate the nave. Thick columns marched down the length of the church to support the massive vaulting of the roof.

Some of the detail on the carvings of the stonework struck me as incongruous. They were not in the style of the 11th century. On close inspection they bore the hallmark of ancient Rome. The church of St. Just had been built with stones quarried from a ruined Roman town in the vicinity. Lugdunum had been founded in the 1st century when Roman legions were completing their conquest of Spain and southern France. The settlement had prospered until attacked by German invaders called Vandals in 409 AD., and it had survived until marauding Franks from the north had destroyed it at the end of the 6th century.

Lugdunum had been a spa town which had built a

fashionable complex of bath houses. These utilised the warm sulphur springs for which the town became famous. Its location straddled the Roman road which led westwards for the passes through the mountains to Spain. This route later became the main pilgrim road from Toulouse to Compostela. In recent years this ancient route has been waymarked and signposted as the Camino de Santiago, the Way of St. James. In 1987 the Council of Europe decided that considerable funds should be devoted to the restoration of the pilgrim trails through France and Spain. In mediaeval times pilgrimage was the main focus of international understanding, and the Council thought that the restoration of the Camino de Santiago would be a symbol of a new internationalism that they hoped would flow through Europe. As we left Valcabrere behind we saw new signs proclaiming that the dusty little road was in fact the Camino de Santiago, the Way of St. James. Similar signposts bearing the logo of the star circle of the European Union would direct me to Compostela in the week ahead.

A few miles down the valley rises a rock, and like the Rock of Cashel towering gothic arches crowned it. Unlike Cashel the crown was not a ruin. The little cathedral of St. Bertrand de Commingues was the core of a mediaeval town that clustered on the top of a strong defensive position. It has become a very chic tourist centre selling the picturesque to armies of day trippers. St Bertrand had been a local bishop who had worked to provide the stream of pilgrims through his diocese with shelter and sustenance. After his death miraculous cures were attributed to the continuing beneficial power of the man, and his remains were thought to contain emanations of great virtue. His reliquaries were placed in a shrine behind the main alter. Martin Luther condemned the veneration of relics, but the Protestant tide did not sweep through here. The casket of St. Bertrand still rests where it did.

A prayer on a notice board read

"Seigneur,

Toi, la source jaillissante de tout amour humain,
accord nous la grace de devinir,
l'un pour l'autre,
un signe de ton invisible Presence,
un appel a' aimer sans retour,
un sacrement, un chemin
qui conduit vers ton Royaume de vie eternelle".

but a surge of tourists made the place clamorous and we soon left. Like Cashel the pavements of the old town were dotted with discarded chewing gum.

Soon after leaving we became utterly lost and after many detours we found ourselves back on the main road. We had been steadily gaining height for some time when the road dropped away to a deep valley thousands of feet below, Lourdes lay behind the next ridge on the other side of the River Adour. We descended into the valley beneath huge fir trees in a succession of hairpin bends. Dominique's trail bike handled the long pull out of the valley better than the Yamaha which wearily pulled me to the top. There we were awarded with a glimpse of the panorama of the Pyrenees that we had first seen after Auterive that morning. For the past few hours the high peaks had been obscured by the forested foothills through which we had meandered. We had travelled 150 miles since the morning and it was time to look for somewhere to camp. We had wanted to find a secluded spot that had uninterrupted views of the highest mountains. Sunset, moonrise and dawn would be spectacular. A small track led from the tarmac through a stand of trees. The convoluted patterns of the deeply indented bark and the lush, wide leaves revealed this to be a grove of walnut trees. It was a magical place of dappled sunshine and shadow. We hid our bikes in among the vegetation and began our hike to the ridge from which we expected to find an enormous vista. Sweat was running down my back as we toiled up the slope through rich pasture that was full of clover, daisies and a multitude of flowers rippling in the soft breeze. I half expected to hear Julie Andrews singing the Sound of Music, or for Heidi to come skipping by.

We found our place in a little hollow, gazing with awe at the majesty of the Pyrenees and then we promptly collapsed in heaps on the ground. Hunger had us soon unpacking supplies. We had good wine, cheese, olives and fresh bread had been bought by the roadside. Also I had a pewter flask with whisky in it. We had hardly finished our meal, which we had ravenously torn at with our fingers, when a heavy dew began to settle over everything. Having decided not to erect our tents and advertise our presence to the farmer, we wrapped our sleeping bags in the waterproof material and settled down to a sporadic conversation with long intervals of silence. We watched stars grow above distant snow fields while the lingering ribbon of fire along the western horizon glowed and went out, plunging the hills above Bigorre and Lourdes into darkness, until the rising of the moon bathed the world in silver light.

SNOWFIELDS IN JUNE

CHAPTER ELEVEN

"We don't see things as they are, we see things as we are"

The Talmud.

Lourdes, Col d'Aubesque, Col de Pourtalet, Jaca, Yeso and Monasterio Leyre.

I thought that I was a connoisseur of the many varieties of spectacular colour which greet the rising of the dawn. In Wigtown we gaze over the Solway to where the winter sun climbs behind the mountains of the English Lake District. New light outlines their serrations and bathes them in spectrums of colour that can glint off the winter snow, but sunrise in the hills above Lourdes began when the ice in the highest peaks of the Pyrenees captured the first rays of light before the sun was even over the horizon.

We had slept at over 3000 feet and it had been as cold a waking as at Gartan Lough. We did not rush to clamber out of our sleeping bags, but lay torpid, waiting for the warmth of the sun to banish the morning chill and the soaking dew.

This was our last morning in France and there was not a cloud in the sky. I had never been to Spain and Dominique had only once before crossed the frontier for a week-end in Barcelona. We had no knowledge of the Spanish language apart from a phrase book I had in my luggage.

The French and the Spanish have been uneasy neighbours and rivals down the centuries. During the years of Napoleon's power, French armies invaded Spain to place a Bonaparte sibling on the throne. The Spanish painter Goya recorded the horror of total war which followed.

After the execution of Marie-Antoinette the citizen armies of the Revolutionaries had been confronted by the regular troops of Austria and Prussia. The dominant weapon on the European battle field of that epoch was the flintlock musket. Well-drilled professional regiments stood in ranks three deep to unleash volleys of musket fire. Victory went to the side with the faster rate of fire. The half-trained levies of the Revolution could not be expected to match the speed or the clock-work precision with which Prussian Guards conducted the cumbersome process of preparing muzzle loading muskets for a disciplined volley. Instead, the French developed the technique of attacking in massed columns that charged through the gun fire to close with their enemies in hand to hand fighting. Before the charge of the columns to the rattle of drums and the blowing of bugles the French used skilled skirmishers and snipers to harass from a distance the deployment of the enemy ranks. Their tactics proved hugely successful.

When Napoleon attacked Spain the regular Spanish armies that were officered by aristocrats were swiftly destroyed, but there was a spontaneous uprising by the ordinary people against the invaders. The French responded with the same terror that they had inflicted on the peasants of the Vendee. Goya's brush and charcoal recorded the wholesale murder that resulted.

London despatched a small army to the Iberian peninsula to offer such help as they could to the Spanish insurgents. This expeditionary force was only a fraction of the size of the armies which Napoleon controlled and at first it was penned up in Portugal. Gradually though the French were driven back over the Pyrenees, outfoxed by the generalship of the Duke of Wellington.

British regiments responded to the charges of the French columns by evolving new tactics. Infantry were deployed in ranks only two deep, unlike the conventional three or four ranks. The British could pour a greater concentration of fire from their extended lines into the flanks of the advancing columns and shatter them before it came to close quarter fighting with the bayonet and sabre. Furthermore, Wellington also developed the use of light troops with long-range rifles to hold back the lines of French skirmishers. In cavalry though, Napoleon's cuirassiers and chasseurs were unmatched.

Dominique bore the physical stamp of a French cavalryman, with sunburnt features behind an overflowing moustache and the bow legged gait of a man who spent much of his life on horseback. Wellington had driven the defeated French over the Pyrenees before cornering them near Toulouse. Dominique's forefathers and mine had spent cold nights under the stars in these same hills as they sought to inflict death upon one another.

With a shiver down my spine that was the result of more than the chill of morning I threw off my covers and rose up to meet the day. I washed and shaved in the dew and we draped our wet sleeping bags and tents over a fence where they soon dried, steaming in the returning warmth.

It was before nine o'clock when we arrived in the streets of Lourdes. In the middle of the 19th century it had been a poverty stricken community where the traditional textile industry had fallen into decline. The modern town is hugely prosperous and has grown rich on the hundreds of thousands of pilgrims who flock to the complex of buildings that have grown around a modest cave beside a swift river of green water.

In 1858 a young girl called Bernadette Soubirons was looking for scraps of firewood along the banks of the river. Bernadette's family had been evicted from their home when her father lost his employment in a textile mill. They were bone poor and hungry, and they subsisted in a dark, one-roomed cellar. This unhappiness and circumstance of despair known throughout the planet was answered when the young girl began to experience in the little cave by the riverbank a sequence of beatific visions of the mother of Jesus. So intense was the spiritual experience that the life of not only Bernadette and her family but also of the entire town was transformed.

These visions were experienced in a sequence of astounding manifestations which were witnessed by the wider community in such a manner that the Roman Catholic clergy of the diocese were convinced of the veracity of Bernadette's experiences. Furthermore, wonderful episodes of the healing of physical and emotional hurts were reported by those who had kept vigil by the grotto.

Since the visions of Bernadette in Lourdes other adolescents have experienced similar revelations that have been accompanied by miracles and wonders. In Portugal and most recently in Croatia the same phenomenon have been reported.

Around the cave where Bernadette's life was transformed a huge complex of buildings has developed in wide parkland. A broad avenue leads between pollarded trees to the spires of a church built into the side of a hill. Closer inspection revealed that two churches one above the other are linked by broad stairways. Round the side of the rocky hill and close by the surging river is the grotto.

It was still early in the morning and only hundreds and not thousands of people had congregated. Wheelchairs were everywhere with nurses, nuns, monks and priests in attendance. It was poignant to see the hope and the fervour in the faces of the invalids as their helpers pushed them down the avenue towards the grotto from which came the sound of sweet singing and the smoke of incense. Voices spoke in every variety of language.

Dominique wanted to buy a candle to give to the Buddhists, but he was told very firmly by the officious salesman that the candle must be lit and burnt where it was purchased and not taken away. Others of his kind were renting wheelchairs and selling religious souvenirs for not inconsiderable sums. The click of money in tills grated against the sound of singing and I sought sanctuary in the lower of the two churches. This building was huge and had seating for 20,000 people.

On Iona, the blessed isle of the Hebrides, there is a saying that the veil between the eternal and the mortal spheres is gossamer thin. The crowds who flock to Lourdes were seeking the same contact with the divine, but the atmosphere was troubling my friend. I too was upset when a loud American family were noisily trying to arrange a group photograph around the harassed little priest who had crossed the Atlantic with them. *"This way, Father! No. A little closer. Father ..... this way ..."*.

I did not doubt the validity of Bernadette's experience. The bible continually repeats the theme of God's compassion for the poor. At Lourdes, in Portugal, and Croatia the experience had been very similar. The Queen of Heaven had spoken with poor children and transformed their lives. Miracles of wonder and healing had accompanied these visions. I was profoundly moved, but I felt a cultural antipathy to the mass produced experience of modern Lourdes in which I struggled to hear the still small voice in the hubbub which was growing in volume as more and more people arrived. Long cavalcades of wheelchairs blocked the roadway when we returned to our bikes and it was sometime before we extricated ourselves from the town.

The mountains beckoned and we flew down the road with growing excitement. The Tour de France is a cherished national institution. Every summer cyclists race the length and breadth of the country. The sections through the Alps and the Pyrenees are the most gruelling. One of the most challenging routes of all is over the Col d'Aubesque from Lourdes to the Col de Pourtalet and the Spanish frontier. Competitors in the Tour propel themselves to the top by muscle power and then plunge down hair-pin bends on lightweight machines with only the most minimal of brakes. Our motorbikes would climb to over 5,000 feet above sea level. After the little town of Aucun we began to wrestle with a spectacular ascent. The road was no wider than a single track road in the Highlands. The damage caused by winter ice and snow had not been repaired and in the higher reaches we could see where avalanches had torn through the trees. In the thin mountain air the sun broiled our skin. The day was without wind, but the muscles in arms and shoulders grew tense with clutching the handle bars when terrifying ravines dropped away into the depths. We were lucky. The previous week had been very windy. These minor roads through the Pyrenees would have been impassable on light motorbikes in strong winds.

We stopped at the highest point on the Col d'Aubesque, looking northwards over the lush valleys of France and into the haze over the lowlands of Gascony. When the noise of the motorbikes ceased the silence of the high mountains was intense. Harsh cries from above drew our attention. Five enormous birds were wheeling in thermal currents of rising air. They were far larger than any eagle. These powerful animals were the Pyreneean Griffin, the European vulture. They were searching for carrion. Sheep, goats, cattle and horses often loose their footing and fall to their deaths to provide the vultures with a good meal. They seemed to follow us for at least half and hour after we resumed our journey. Dominique thought that we must look like a potential dinner to them, and their presence undoubtedly helped concentrate the mind on the intricacies of the road.

The Col d'Aubesque means the Pass of the Basques. As we descended into the valley at the little town of Laruns we were still in modern France, but we were entering the land that had once been the independent Kingdom of Navarre which had straddled both sides of the mountains and held itself separate from both Spain and France until the 16th century when King Henry IV of Navarre became the King of France and Navarese independence ended in much the same way as the accession of the King of Scots to the English throne in 1603 began the long process of subjecting Scottish independence to the power of London. The Navarese say they took over France, though! Navarre south of the Pyrenees had earlier been forced to come to an accommodation with Madrid. Their political identity had been partitioned into the spheres of influence of two super-powers, but the cultural identity of the inhabitants of the region still remains distinct from either Spain or France.

The main influence on the language and culture of Navarre was that of the indigenous Basque people. Their language is unique in Europe and their origins are different from the Celts, Germans, Latins, Greeks and Slavs who rose to dominance over so much of the continent. Most European languages are closely related in terms of etymology and the people who spoke them came from a common stock, but not the Basques.

Much of what is now France and Spain had been a barren tundra of permafrost when glaciers shrouded Britain, the Alps and the Pyrenees during the last Ice Age but when the climate of the planet warmed 12,000 years ago the glaciers began their long retreat. Bands of hunters in pursuit of game followed into the lands that were awakening after the long frost. North Africa had been lush and well watered during the Ice Age, but as the glaciers melted the Sahara desert began its march to the Mediterranean. This was a slow process. Archaeologists and geologists have postulated that the great carved Sphinx of Egypt, which many think is much older that the pyramids, was subjected to the erosion of high annual rainfalls until as recently as 4,000 BC. The Atlas Mountains of North Africa teemed with game for millennia after the Ice Age, but the climate grew inexorably harsher and drier. In the east the bulk of the population was concentrated along the lush ribbon of the Nile and in the west the deteriorating climate caused migration from Africa into the Iberian peninsula. From there they spread along the Atlantic coastline of Europe. The early Mesolithic people who lived beside Lough Neagh are thought to have had this southern origin.

However, the people of the Neolithic arrived in Europe with the knowledge of farming as they colonised the continent from the east along the great highways of the Danube and the Rhine. Neolithic farmers grew more populous than the scattered groupings of Mesolithic hunters. The closest related languages to that of the Basques are found in remote parts of the Caucasus suggesting that the Basques are descended from these earliest farmers in the west.

2,000 years ago the Romans learnt to treat the Basque mountaineers with respect. German confederations of tribes like the Vandals, Goths, Suevi and Franks learnt to their cost that though they might control the lowlands of southern France and northern Spain the mountainous tract in between was forbidden. Even Charlemagne did not travel through the mountains with impunity and the Moors could not subdue the Basques to the power of Islam.

Larons was a small neat town shadowed by enormous fir trees. The route over the Col d'Aubesque had been narrow and difficult, but the road to the frontier from Larons has been the recipient of much Euromoney in recent years. After the town we made better speed as the new road followed a river into the mountains. The valley closed into a narrow and sunless gorge that was damp in the spray from tumbling waters. Further upstream massive dams harness the power of the river to generate electricity.

We climbed above the trees into a wilderness. Snow lies here for many months in the year and the road is frequently blocked in the winter. Concrete canopies and chutes have been constructed to protect against avalanches. In a landscape that was reminiscent of the Drumochter Pass in the Cairngorms we approached Spain. There was a cluster of cafes and kiosks that exchanged currency to mark the frontier. A policeman in an unfamiliar green uniform and dark sunglasses waved us through. Prices in France had been on average 20% higher than in Galloway. The peseta was not too healthy against the pound and life on the road in Spain was going to be a lot cheaper than in France.

A broad Euroroute led southwards where the blue mountains shimmered in a growing heat. The southern side of the Pyrenees was bleak and harsh, with only stunted stands of trees among hard yellow rock and mounds of rubble. The soil was thin and sour. Our descent out of the mountains was accompanied by rising temperatures. 40deg Centigrade is just tolerable when the bike is moving, but whenever we were stationary perspiration stung the eyes and dripped from my nose. It was exhausting. The small towns we passed through were deserted. Sensible Spaniards were taking their siesta.

It was early evening when we came to the old fortified city of Jaca above whose citadel floated the red and gold flag of Spain. Jaca is a garrison town full of young conscripts. Government wages and salaries have given a sheen of prosperity to the town. Squares were shaded by trees and fountains splashed. We stopped for an ice-cold beer which was served with a side dish of anchovies, olives and bread. The waitress spoke fluent English and laughed as we lay gasping in the heat. The road was called the Avenue of the Galician Regiment.

The garrison of Jaca had sided with the Fascist rebels under General Franco when they began their campaign against the elected government in Madrid in 1936. The Spanish Fascists had the backing of Mussolini and Hitler who sent thousands of German and Italian storm-troopers to support Franco. The Regiment of Galicia had sided with Franco and the Spanish Civil War was fought with a brutality that was an ugly premonition of what would happen to the rest of the continent in the Second World War. Spain gave Mussolini and Hitler the opportunity to test their new weaponry, especially the technology of aerial assault. Jaca was the border fortress of that part of Spain which had once been the powerful kingdom of Aragon, but the neighbouring Basques were loyal to the socialist government in Madrid. The old city of Guernica was the heart of Basque culture. It was the first town in Europe to be utterly destroyed from the air. Hitler's Condor Legion tested their equipment over the defenceless city and machine gunned the survivors of the resulting firestorm. Like Goya had before him, Picasso recorded the carnage that took place.

Jaca which had sided with the eventual winners of the Spanish Civil War prospered.

Having stocked up on supplies we set off westwards for Navarre. Mile after mile of new Euroroute gave fast speeds. Clouds of dust covered us in grit which stuck to damp skin so that our faces were caked in grey masks. The mountains became lower, but they remained stark and bare. Evergreen scrub covered much of the ground, but wide areas looked like an industrial waste land of slag heaps.

We were following the River Aragon which flowed to meet the mighty Ebro on its way to the Mediterranean. In the distance we could see the evening sun glinting on what looked like an immense lake. Slogans painted on the tarmac read "Yesa Non". It seemed like a contradiction, but the slogans were a legacy of a fierce campaign which the local residents had fought against the flooding of their valley to create the reservoir. We discussed the possibilities of a refreshing dip. The River Aragon was too swift and too cold-looking to be inviting, but the waters of the lake promised rest and refreshment.

A closer inspection of the banks of the reservoir did not encourage us to take the plunge. Half-drowned trees raised their branches above the green waters. A scabrous scum floated on the surface and I saw a snake swimming through the rank, flooded grass at the waters edge. The mountain melt-waters that fill this artificial lake ware full of oxygen and nutrients. Fish thrive and grow to a huge size. We watched giants bigger than salmon dart through the shadows of the depths.

High above the valley rose a tall building isolated in wild scrubland and forest. We turned off onto a small road to investigate. As we drew closer we could see the outlines of an ancient monastery. Most of the buildings have been converted to a very expensive hotel, but a small community of monks still use part of the cloistered enclosure. We turned away, for caked in dust from the journey and mired in mud from the banks of the reservoir we would have alarmed the prosperous clientele of the hotel. We headed further into the hills to search for a suitable camping spot. We found an ideal place surrounded by small pines and stunted oaks. It was the most glorious relief to remove my boots and hurl my socks into the depths of a thicket from which I had no intention of recovering them. As dusk fell so did the temperature to a more comfortable heat. The evening was sultry and heavy and we began to hear the distant rumble of thunder over the mountains.

Dominique supervised the preparation of our evening

meal. Huge slices of melon slaked our thirst and washed our faces. We had a bottle of vegetables in olive oil and some tins of seafood. Pickled tentacles were complemented by smoked mussels. Cherries and ripe peaches were followed by an orange as delicious as any I had ever eaten. Supermarket oranges in Scotland look handsome, but have very little taste. This Spanish orange was lumpy and misshapen but gorgeous to taste. We had not bought any cheese for Dominique had been less than kind when he had inspected the selection of Spanish cheeses on offer. His opinion of Spanish wine was also less than charitable, but I had bought a bottle of Rioja as medicine for his French culinary chauvinism. The strong red wine comforted us as we watched lightening flickering and flaring in the distance.

The bells of the monastery tolled the hour of Vespers and we prepared for sleep. The first preparatory doze inside the tent was disturbed by a strange tinkling sound that eddied and swirled through the scrub of the mountainside, but which grew ever closer to our camp. I heard the sound of stirrings from Dominique's direction and then the noise of the zip of his tent as he went out into the night air. I next heard a strange sequence of clicks and whistles followed by delighted and voluble outpourings of French endearments. Dominique was talking to several dozen horses. The animals each wore a bell round the neck like an Alpine cow so that the monks of the Monastery of Leyre could trace a missing horse.

A flurry of raindrops drove Dominique back to his tent. I wondered how long the downpour would be kept at bay by the nylon of my tent.

ARAGON AND NAVARRE

CHAPTER TWELVE

"I have seen dawns and sunsets on moors and windy hill coming in solemn beauty like slow old tunes of Spain".

John Masefield

Monasterio Leyre, Pamplona, Eunate, Najera, Santo Domingo de la Calzader.

It had not been easy forcing the tent pegs into the ground when we had tried to get our shelters up for the night. A surface smearing of glacial clay had been baked by a searing sun until it was hard and unyielding, but nothing had prevented slumber during that first night in Spain above the old monastery of Leyre. The thunder had rumbled off into the distance and we missed all but a brief flurry of rain. Sleep had been blessedly uninterrupted.

There was no sign of the horses in the morning, although the suspicion of a tinkle of bells was occasionally heard from higher up the slopes of the mountain. Dominique was in no hurry to emerge from his tent and I had the morning to myself.

The bells of the monastery tolled the hour of matins and we made our way on the dusty track down the hill to the venerable old buildings. Many coachloads of tourists come here every day and we hoped there would be public toilets and a wash-room that we could use. There were and we did.

We both struggled into clean clothes so that we were more presentable than the mud-stained, dusty scarecrows of a few moments earlier. I had hoped to explore the 9th century crypt and the 11th century basilica of the ancient church. Leyre in its time had been one of the most influential monasteries of Navarre. The Basques had been slow to adopt to Christianity, but Leyre had been home to a persistent community of monks whose witness over the generations had finally overcome Basque suspicions. One of the monks is reputed to have become so enraptured by the sound of a bird singing in the forest that he spent 300 years alone in the hills. Such stories of mortals being transported to other realms of existence where time was suspended were common throughout Europe. Rip van Winkle returned as though from the grave, and in Scotland there was a whole selection of tales about the "fairy folk" bewitching mortals and leading them to the hollow hills where time stands still. It was said that the monks of Leyre conversed with angels.

The monastery has another claim to fame. The Bourbon family which provided monarchs for Navarre, France and Spain had their origins in the mountains beside Leyre and the ancestors of kings are buried there.

Our first few hours in Spain had traversed the wildest parts of Aragon, but Leyre marked the western limit of the power of Aragon where the border marches of the Kingdom of Navarre marked the independence of the Basques.

We consulted our maps, and the names of the towns and villages we would travel through that morning had outlandish names which were quite different from the names of the Spanish Aragonese settlements we had journeyed through the day before. Yarnoz, Zabalegi, Imarcoain, Uuzue, Olcoz, Eneriz and countless unpronounceable names like them all spoke of their unique

Basque heritage.

From Leyre our road lead west through the not inconsiderable foothills of the Navarese Pyrenees towards the great city of Pamplona. Ernest Hemingway brought the city a certain notoriety by his description of the running of bulls through the streets on their way to face the unequal contest against matadors and picadors in the bullring. Pamplona was named after the Roman general Pompey whose legions campaigned against the Celtic tribes which dominated so much of Spain before the 1st century. The main Roman road and the later pilgrim route through the eastern Pyrenees still leads through the city. Pamplona in the middle ages had been a French speaking town. Settlers from the north were encouraged to colonise communities along the route of the Compostela Pilgrim Way to act as a bulwark against the Moors, in the same way as Protestants had been settled in Northern Ireland as a garrison. We would encounter many other "villa francas" in the north of Spain. Indeed, the pilgrim route is often called the "Camino Frances", the French road, because of its ancient appeal to northern Europeans.

One of the early chroniclers of the Compostela pilgrimage was a cleric called Aymery Picaud. He came from a monastery close to where the most northerly minaret had been built to mark the high tide of Islam near La Rochelle. His journey through Navarre had not been a happy one and he had little that was kind to write about the ferocious Basques he encountered in the early 12th century. "Ladrones", or thieves, was the least of the insults he heaped upon them.

The pilgrim passport I carried had been issued to me by the Confraternity of St. James. In earlier centuries such a document had been a necessary guarantee of safe passage, but brigands preyed on helpless travellers in many of the wilder stretches of country and the Basques had had an uglier reputation than most in this respect. Aymery was much happier when he could rest in a Villa Franca that had been established along the Camino Frances.

Having spruced ourselves up we visited the foyer of the hotel to enquire if it was possible to visit the monastery and if I could get my pilgrim passport signed. An extraordinarily beautiful girl with raven hair and olive skin was happy to help, but she told us in wonderfully accented English that the monastery remained cloistered and shut until later in the day.

Many of the larger buildings dated from the 17th century and had been built from huge blocks of a warm and golden stone that caught the morning sun to dazzle the eye.

The morning had been warm and sultry, but high cloud began to veil the sun. High, thin clouds are often the result of powerful winds at those altitudes and are a precursor of strong winds at ground level. I had once kept a small fishing boat on the Solway and it had been necessary to develop a weather eye for trouble.

As I was regarding the morning we met our first fellow pilgrims. A young couple from Bavaria were readying themselves for the day ahead. They were cycling to Compostela which was still more than 500 miles away. Muscle power alone would get them there. The Confraternity of St. James has re-established a network of hospices and refuges which provide free dormitory accommodation for bona-fide pilgrims who walk or cycle. Mere motorcyclists like ourselves were not eligible, but this network of support encourages many thousands to travel slowly and strenuously in the footsteps of earlier pilgrims. Travel with a motorbike and a tent has its own exertions, but I told our new Bavarian friends that I thought they would have to face a stiff headwind before the afternoon.. Contrary winds can double the effort on a push-bike. Wishing each other a safe journey and exchanging formal German handshakes we set off into the blue yonder.

Our route through Aragon had been through wild, harsh country and the miles to the west of Leyre were savage enough. Stark limestone cliffs rose on either side through a desiccated landscape in which occasional streams and pools in ravines provided flourishes of greenery. The countryside became gentler and more fruitful as we emerged into an undulating plain before we reached the outskirts of Pamplona. Seeing a fruit market we stopped to make a few purchases. Dozens of elderly women dressed in black were exchanging loud banter with the stall holders. They kindly allowed us to the front where with sign language we purchased the most marvellous selection of fruit. In the process we generated great amusement for the onlooking matrons. Grinning our thanks and nodding our heads we were about to leave when they noticed the scallop shells on our rucksacks. In the cacophony of speech and laughter that followed one phrase repeated itself *"Hola peregrino, hola"*, as we tried to explain that we were travelling to Compostela. They seemed genuinely pleased and
gratified that foreigners were maintaining an age old tradition. One old lady pressed an orange into my hands. *"Gracias, muchos gracias, senora, adios"*. *"Hola peregrino"*. It was my first ever dialogue in Spanish!

I thought about the word "peregrino" or pilgrim. It is a name shared with the peregrine falcon, the wandering hunter of the skies, and with the planets, the wanderers of the night. The word "peregrino" is also thought to be the origin of the Spanish term "Gringo" for northern Europeans which was later used in Spanish Mexico for white citizens of the USA.

We did not attempt to visit the historic centre of Pamplona, but made our way into the countryside as quickly as possible on the motorway from France to Madrid. Some Basques seem to find amusement in blasting with shotguns at signposts with

Madrid spelt on them. The Spanish government in recent years has devolved considerable autonomy to the Basques, but tensions remain.

The outskirts of the city were an ugly straggle of industry and commerce. Brick works, storage yards and electricity pylons disfigured the countryside, but worst of all was a huge cement works that ran beside the road for what seemed like miles. Everything was covered in an alkaline dust which would turn to grey slime when it rained.

The contemporary world has a voracious demand for cement. In previous centuries scarce and expensive mortar was only used to bind stones into walls. Modernity pours concrete everywhere. I thought of the little 17th century Irish cottage I had seen in Cashel and then I reflected on the hundreds of concrete bridges I had crossed on my journey since. Stone, timber and brick require the human skills of artisans to turn them into functional shapes, but concrete can be manipulated by giant machines and when reinforced by steel it can tower hundreds of feet into the air and span canyons. Its legacy is the blighted landscape on the outskirts of Pamplona.

The wasteland did not for long continue and we entered the heartland of the Basque countryside. It was a fertile and well-tended land. In Scotland scattered farmsteadings and cottages dot the ruralities, but in much of the continent farmers live in the towns and villages and travel out to work in their fields. In Navarre the countryside is largely devoid of dwellings. Animals are mostly confined indoors and there was little barbed wire in consequence. In Navarre, fields of wheat and barley stood ready for harvest in early June. Great round bales of straw lay scattered in stubble where the progress of giant agricultural machines had left the evidence of their passing, and vineyards laid geometrical patterns of parallel lines down the slopes of rolling hills whose summits were tufts of woodland. One young man was dressing the shoots of his vines with a long iron blade. I watched his hand rise and fall. When he saw me he waved and smiled. We waved back and shouted greetings as we sped by.

Near the small town of Eneriz we stopped at an old stone hostelry or "meson" for a long postponed cup of coffee. The last such cup had been in France and we both hungered for bowls of the brew. The interior was dark and cool with low oak beams above a stone flagged floor. Eyes peered out at us from the shadows until they decided we were harmless. "Hola peregrino". "Buenos dias senor".

I have visited pubs in Wales where when a stranger enters they ostentatiously switch to Welsh and exclude the newcomer from their conversation. These people were speaking the incomprehensible Basque language, but they were courteous enough to us and we were served with a truly excellent bean stew that was not unlike the cassoulet of Languedoc. It was good to eat hot food again after two days of cold food. Eventually we felt sufficiently restored to return to the bikes. As we stowed our luggage I felt my skin begin to tingle. Large white blotches revealed where mosquitoes had dined, and the rushes of marshland beside the road showed where they lived. It was time to go.

We had not travelled far when an unusual church in the fields beside the road caused us to stop and investigate. The little church of Eunate is octagonal and enclosed by an external cloister. It had been build as a burial place for those pilgrims who had not survived unscathed from the crossing of the mountains and the attentions of malarial mosquitos. We had the place to ourselves and I raised my voice in the echoing silence with a doxology in the metre of an old Scots psalm tune. The hairs on the nape of my neck stood upright throughout, so uncanny was the intangible atmosphere of the place. No less than at Carnac I felt myself to be in the presence of ancestors.

A few miles down the road we came to Puente la Reina, the "Bridge of the Queen" where the beautiful arches of a mediaeval bridge span a wide river. The town was well scrubbed and a testament to Basque industriousness. Geraniums and flower boxes decorated every street and we passed gracious, leaf-shaded squares. The town came into being when the bridge was built at the behest of a Queen of Navarre in the 11th century. The pilgrim road from Roncesvalles and Paris joins at this river crossing with the Camino Frances from Aragon that we had followed.

The afternoon grew increasingly grey and we had to face a headwind that was rising in force with every minute so that it screamed in our ears. The day before had been too hot for comfort, but the temperature had plummeted and gloves, scarf and jacket were necessary against the chill. The weather was rather like it had been in Donegal.

Aymeric Picaud had not enjoyed his journey through Navarre, but when he came to the town of Estela he wrote *"it was well supplied with bread, excellent wine, meat and fish and full of all good things"*. It was a "villa franca" and Aymeric felt safe among its more cultured inhabitants than he had among the terrifying Basques of the countryside. We did not stop in the old town, though we saw rising behind it the huge towers and buildings of the monastery of Irache which had played a notable role over the centuries in influencing the Basques with the gentle ideal of Nazareth.

Ignatius Loyola who founded the Jesuit order as the backbone of the Counter-Reformation against Protestantism had been a Basque soldier whose childhood had been spent among these hills. He had been horribly wounded, and in the long months of his agonising recovery he had had time to listen to the small voice within. The Jesuits who followed his example helped to recharge the spiritual dynamo of Roman Catholicism so that Austria, Southern Germany, Poland, Hungary and Croatia were recovered and Protestant regimes were driven back on the defensive. Jesuit missions to Japan and China in the 17th century were notable for the subtlety of their approach and their respect for the indigenous cultures they encountered.

As we left Estella we passed into a region where many of the hills on either side of the road were topped by crumbling fortifications. Villamayor de Monjardin was the most notable of these castles. In origin it had been a Roman fortification and then it was occupied by the Visigoths. The Moors in turn made it their own for two centuries until the Basques drove them out in the 10th century. These fortifications were a sign that we were approaching the western borderlands of Navarre where the little kingdom of the Rioja had once been a neighbour which posed little threat. However, the Rioja had been absorbed by the expansionist power of Castile to the west and the rivalry of the Castilians and the Basques had been intense.

The border lay near the broad valley of the River Ebro. Logrono, the main city of the Rioja lay across our path and the landscape changed. Much of the soil of Navarre had been a yellowish grey, but in the Rioja the soil was a rich red colour. This deep tilth produces one of the most wonderful wines in all Spain. Even Dominique had been impressed by the bottle we had shared at Leyre. The landscape of the Rioja is also notable for its market gardens. The towns were different also from the stout stone and slate of Navarre. In the Rioja the predominant building materials were brick with or without a stucco covering and red pantiles on the roofs.

The Ebro was once one of the fairest and mightiest rivers in Europe. Modern irrigation diminishes its volume, but its beauty suffers from careless pollution by industry and agriculture. A grimy froth sullied its surface as we crossed the Ebro on a new bypass which avoided the centre of town. As we sped along two tough looking policemen waved us down. We approached them with guilty apprehension. (Why do policemen make us instinctively feel guilty? Its rather like being summoned to the head-teacher when a child at school. What is it that I have done that they have found out about?) Our fears were unfounded because when they discovered that we were foreign pilgrims on our way to Compostela they could not have been more genial.

Logrono is a busy, commercial town, but it was not the historical centre of the Rioja. That honour belongs to the ancient town of Najera further to the west which had been the centre of the short-lived kingdom of the Rioja before it was absorbed by the growing might of Castile, but Najera is also reputed to have been the focus of stirring events which influenced the subsequent history of all of Spain.

A few miles to the south of the city lies the small town and castle of Clavijo. Ancient stories claim that an outnumbered Christian army had been cornered by the might of Islam there in 844AD. The invaders were routed in a story that was embellished over the centuries. Legends spread that the Christian host had beaten their enemies because of divine intervention. St. James himself had been seen riding on a great war horse as he scattered the soldiers of the Moors with a flailing scimitar. The precise facts surrounding the actual events of Clavijo are obscured by the mists of time, but the cult of St. James began its rise to national prominence from the mid 9th century and the power of the Moors was rarely to threaten the north after the reputed events of Clavijo.

In the centre of Najero there is a huge equestrian statue of the apostle wielding his scimitar and his prancing steed reveals in the words of Edwin Mullen *"a stallion equipped with the most heroic genitals in all Spain, a sight to make any surviving Moor feel inadequate and run for cover".*

This representation of St. James "Matamoros", the Moor

Slayer, was to be a recurring motif along the route to Compostela. It was one which I found profoundly unsettling. St. James had been the first of the apostles to be martyred. He had been bishop or leader of the earliest Christian community in Jerusalem and in 44 AD. he met the grisly end awarded to a heretic and a vexation to public order. He is often represented as a gentle pilgrim with scallop shell and staff. Doubtless the warrior aristocrats who themselves had bathed in Moorish blood appreciated the transformation of the pacifist bishop into a blood thirsty cavalryman, and for centuries Spanish armies plunged into battle with the cry of Santiago, St. James, on their lips in an encouraging memory of Clavijo.

This Spanish story of divine help in a national crisis is not so very different from that which established St. Andrew as the patron saint of Scotland. A Scottish army had been confronted by the apparently overwhelming numbers of an English army at much the same time as Clavijo. Appealing for the intervention of God against the invaders, the Scots, according to the story, were mightily encouraged when the clouds formed into the configuration of a white saltire cross against the blue background of a summer sky. The Scots then hacked their enemies into pieces apparently with divine approval. National pride seems to need the apparent sanction of Heaven for its excesses.

One of the clues which perhaps points to a core of truth concerning the overblown mediaeval romances of Clavijo and Athelstaneford can be found in the well documented record of the much later Battle of Bannockburn. Robert Bruce and his army were blessed and encouraged on the morning of the battle by the presence of the Monymusk Reliquary in which was contained the relics of Columba of Iona. The simple presence of relics of James and Andrew at the earlier battles could have spawned the stories which followed.

A better documented battle than Clavijo took place near

Najera at the little town of Navarette in the mid 14th century. An Anglo-Gascon army under the Black Prince had crossed the Pyrenees with the avowed aim of including the Kingdom of Castile in their sphere of influence. At Navarette the deadly archers of the invaders destroyed the cavalry of Spain in the same manner as they had annihilated the chivalry of France at Crecy and Poitiers.

Many of the Spanish warriors were fighting in the style which they had learned against the swift, light cavalry of the Moors and the Arabs. They rode small and nimble horses, but unlike the knights of northern Europe they did not attempt to press home their charge with lance and mace. Instead they wheeled around their enemies and hurled javelins. This method of warfare had been hugely successful in its day, but it was suicide when confronted by the archers of England and Wales and the steady soldiers of Gascony.

Although they won their battle the army of the Black Prince failed in its attempt to control northern Spain, even though other English adventurers rose to positions of great influence in neighbouring Portugal. Simple geography made Najera a cockpit for war. Its situation near the headwaters of the Ebro was the key which unlocked the invasion routes into northern Spain. The armies of Rome and of Charlemagne had campaigned here and given rise to the heroic fable of how the Frankish general Roland, later to be killed by the Basques in the Pyrenees, had challenged the Moorish champion Farragut and killed him. Farragut was reputed to have been a Syrian giant and a descendant of Goliath with the strength of 40 men. Farragut was also called Feracute, or Sharp Iron, and at the base of the legend there is a memory of the skirmishes and battles which the Franks of Charlemagne had fought with the Moors.

The wind grew in strength and the temperature dropped, but visibility was clear. We could see far to the north the

Cantabrian mountains which are a continuation of the Pyrenees. The small, rounded hills of the Rioja created a more intimate landscape and in the well-watered valleys market gardens were models of small scale fertility. We often saw figures toiling with bent backs among their productive allotments. The road descended to the Rio Oca which gave its name to the Rioja. On the banks of the River Oca has developed the town of Santo Domingo de la Calzada.

We had not travelled a great distance since Leyre, but against a strong headwind it had seemed much more that a mere 150 miles. I wondered how our Bavarian friends of the morning were coping with their push bikes. On the outskirts of the town we noticed a camping and caravan site. It was surrounded by a high wire fence and savage guard dogs were chained beside the entrance. The proprietor charged us a not inconsiderable sum, but we thought our gear would be safe from pilfering and there were shower rooms with hot water that we could enjoy. It was a more prosaic setting for our camp than on the two previous nights in the depths of the countryside. We found a quiet spot enclosed by hedges where our only neighbours were a Dutch couple in a caravanette.

A heavy rucksack had limited our sightseeing throughout the journey, but we could leave our belongings with safety in these surroundings. I felt as though I was walking on air without the weight of my baggage as we set off to explore the narrow streets of the old town. It did not seem to be nearly as prosperous as the Basque towns of the morning. Jobs and money were apparently not easy to find and many of the elderly buildings were scruffy and run down, but I liked the place and its inhabitants for their sheer human exuberance and noisiness. Multiple conversations were being shouted between buildings above our heads.

The old town had begun its development in the 11th

century as a refuge for pilgrims. It had been founded by a hermit called Santo Domingo de la Calzada, or St. Dominic of the Roads. Throughout the busy years of his long and unconventional life he organised the building of a bridge across the wide Rio Oca and many miles of good roads on either side to help pilgrims on their way. He provided travellers with places to rest and with food in great, steaming communal bowls into which the hungry could dip the scallop shell of their pilgrimage as their spoon. Other Spanish countrymen and women devoted their lives to building and improving the Pilgrim Way, but Dominic of the Roads is one of the best remembered.

We went to visit the immense church that had been built above his mausoleum. Like Breton churches it had developed continuously in a melange of styles that spanned the Romanesque of the 12th century through Gothic intervals into the epoch of the Counter-Reformation. However, Breton ecclesiastical architecture of the 16th century and the 17th century was in a relatively restrained neo-classical style. It was not so in Spain. Hugely exuberant and overpowering swirls of decoration illustrated the Spanish origins of the Baroque.

Underneath tall towers were quiet cloisters adjoining the church. In them the treasures of the centuries were displayed. Euromoney has not only been channelled into waymarking the Pilgrim Way to Compostela, but it is also being used in large quantities to restore the historical churches along the route.

The 19th century had been a difficult time for the Roman Catholic church in Spain. Its wealth had sharply declined when anti-clerical governments in Madrid confiscated many of the estates of the church. As a consequence many great church buildings had declined into dereliction. Timeous Euromoney is restoring this heritage of architecture and art. These stone ships have sailed through time in their glory and have contained in their day the echoing cadences of choirs and vast arpeggios on pipe organs which accompanied sonorous Latin liturgies.

The 16th and the 17th centuries were the epoch of Spanish greatness. Galleons from the New World brought Aztec and Inca gold to finance the armies of Spain which controlled Belgium, Holland, and much of Italy and Germany and threatened the Protestant north. Much of the gold of the Americas found its way to the coffers of the church and financed its grandiloquent architecture.

Dominic of the Roads seems to have been a gentle soul innocent of the temporal power which a later church was to wield. One of the stories associated with him was the intervention of the saint to restore to life a young French pilgrim who had been hung on the public gibbet at the order of the local warlord. Santo Domingo found the baron preparing to eat his evening meal. Two roast chickens lay on the table in front of him. At the saints command the two birds grew feathers and fluttered away very much alive. The Frenchman was cut down from the gallows and he too was returned to life. As a memorial to these events a hen and cockerel are kept in a gilded cage within the church.

We went down the stairs into the crypt to pay our respects to the man whose life had created so many memories.

In mediaeval times people lived in feudal societies. A friend at the court of a local aristocrat or ruler was a great advantage when advancement or success in a lawsuit depended on patronage and who knew whom. In much the same way a saint was thought to have access to the ear of the High King of Heaven. Entreaties, prayers and petitions for help have poured from the lips of supplicants in this ancient, subterranean shrine. Martin Luther disapproved of prayers to saints arguing that God can hear the prayers of every human being without the pestering of saintly intermediaries. If we had been travelling on foot like pilgrims of a previous age the journey through Spain would have been a continual sequence of visits to saintly shrines and the pilgrim would have felt he was introducing himself to a wide circle of friends at the court of Heaven, courtiers whose favours would bring blessings in much the same manner as aristocratic patronage brought more mundane benefits to earthly lives.

In the shrine of Santo Domingo there was a marvellous air of sanctity and even a fragrance that was not incense. I uttered a prayer as had so many before me in that place invoking the protection of the saint until I returned safely home to Galloway and my friend to the arms of his family in Lavour.

Dominique had fallen into a rapt contemplation and I left him in the crypt. He had been particularly moved by the story of his namesake and he had finally managed to purchase a candle to give to his Buddhist friends. He was making his private communion and I was staring at the huge timbers and the ornate carvings which created the stalls of the choir when the peace of the church was shattered by the raucous crowing of the cockerel in the gilded cage. Dominique appeared beaming from ear to ear. He took the sound as a sign of the saints blessing on him. The crowing of the cock has been identified over the centuries with the irrepressible nature of the French people.

When we emerged from the church we strolled through streets that were alive with human activity. The Spanish generally retire to their houses for the afternoon siesta and emerge for sociable evenings. This was one such evening!

We returned to our campsite and braved the dogs at the entrance. I hated to see the plight of these imprisoned beings. I was to see chained dogs everywhere in Spain. The Spanish even more than the French seem indifferent to the sufferings of animals, whether it is overburdened donkeys in country villages or bulls in city bullrings.

On our return we found that the tents had been ransacked, not by a human but by a feline. I was just in time to see a scrawny cat slither through the hedge with the sausage from Lavour that was to have been our supper. The cheese too had been gnawed, but the thief hadn't fancied our fruit from Pamplona and so we were thankful for small mercies.

The whistling winds of Spain soughed through the branches of poplars and the rattle of their leathery leaves mantled every sound of night, even the distant purring, I thought, of a cat more contented than most.

THE RIOJA

CHAPTER THIRTEEN
"The puddle of pleasures and the swill of swine"
Cranmer

Santo Domingo de la Calzada, San Millan de la Cogolla, Yuso and Susa.

I woke to the same rustle of poplars that had brought sleep the night before. The same cold wind drove from the west and we huddled in the lee of the hedge as we stowed our gear. We bought "coffee" from a machine that dispensed an odourless, brown liquid in plastic cups, but at least it was warming as we spread our maps and puzzled over where we would go. This was to be our last day together. Dominique needed to return to his family on the next morning and so we resolved not to travel any further west. Santo Domingo de la Calzada was as close to Compostela as Dominique would reach.

To the south of us lay the Sierra de la Demanda. These mountains rise to over 6,000 feet and they are covered with thick oak forest. Bears, wolves, and the wild boar still survive in the fastnesses of the trees. High in this unspoilt wilderness is one of the most ancient churches in Spain. It is dedicated to the memory of San Millan. This pioneer of the church lived some 500 years before Santo Domingo. He was a contemporary of Gildas and Columba. Millan is also remembered in the St. Emilion district of France near Bordeaux which is famous for its wines. He had once been active along the coasts of Gascony as far as the Gironde and his teacher had been San Felices, the "happy saint" of Bilbao on the coast of the Bay of Biscay. With his maritime connections it is inconceivable that this hermit of the Sierra de la Demanda had had no connection with the widespread influence of the Celtic church.

An hour on the bikes brought us out of the Riojan farmland and into the mountains where mist wrapped the moist musk of the forests. A huge Romanesque monastery greater even than Leyre towered over the lower reaches of the valley. Santo Domingo had asked to join the Benedictine community that once lived there, but they haughtily rejected him as being unsuitable for regular ecclesiastical life. The more I learned of Santo Domingo the more I liked him.

We decided not to visit the huge monastery until after we had been to the more ancient Visigothic monastery which Millan had founded in the 6th century. He had chosen a remote place high in the mountains for his hermitage. A small road spiralled up into the heights under the eaves of the oaks. It led to a sheltered clearing which enfolded the ancient walls of the monastery of Suso, meaning "above". The architecture of this ancient building was most unusual. A squat tower not unlike an oriental pagoda rose in tiers above a small church with a balcony overlooking the valley. The arches were Moorish in style and the masonry was of huge blocks of red volcanic stone which had been quarried from the nearby bluffs that rose up out of the forest.

We decided to spend the day in peacefulness and ease. We would travel no further than Suso, and we would pitch our tents for the night in the woods beside the ancient Visigothic building. Later in the day we planned to visit the great monastery of Yuso, meaning "below", in the valley where we hoped to purchase provisions.

We climbed into the forest above Suso where I was determined to experience the Spanish custom of siesta in the dappled sunshine. Protected from the wind the sun began to grow warm. The diurnal range of temperature I had experienced in recent days was impressive, from the near zero of night to the searing heat of noon. It was good to have a day when we did not have to wrestle with the bikes in a cloud of dust.

The little monastery of Suso has no permanently resident monks these days, and even in Yuso the hundreds of Benedictines who lived there in previous centuries have gone. Only a thin scattering of Augustinians rattle around the empty corridors, though I was to discover later that much Eurocash has gone to create a school for the study of the Spanish language and its literature. This has recently been housed in a wing of the monastery.

Yuso was established in 1054 when the threat of Islam was on the retreat and the influence of the French church was growing along the Camino Frances. Isolated Suso had endured and survived the centuries of vulnerability to the Moors, but when the body of San Millan was removed from its eyrie to the new Roman Catholic monastery it was symbolic of a profound change that was to overwhelm the distinctive expression of Christianity in Spain that had survived from the Visigoths.

San Millan had withdrawn into these mountains to live the life of a hermit. Gradually companions had been attracted to the company of the wise man who denied his simple hospitality to none. A collection of woodland huts grew to surround the cave in which the saint lived. The fame of Millan eventually reached the ears of the royal Visigothic city of Toledo. Yuso was endowed with lands and privileges, and stone buildings rose in the forest clearing above the burial place of the saintly hermit. Iona became the burial place of the Kings of Scots for centuries because of its associations with Columba. It was the same at the grave of Millan and Visigothic princes were interred alongside the simple saint of the mountains.

Few written records of the church in Spain have survived from the centuries of Visigothic influence. We know that San Isidore when bishop of Toledo in the 7th century presided over a culture which still preserved the learning and the libraries of the ancient civilisations of Rome and Greece.

The Visigoths, or the Western Goths, had been a most unusual people. They had crossed the Danube into western Europe in the 4th century and loyally served as federated allies of the Roman legions in their efforts to defend the frontiers of the Empire against the seething mass of German tribes which threatened invasion. The Visigoths were a Germanic people themselves, but they had been profoundly influenced by their long contact as allies of Rome. They adopted a form of the Christian religion even though they did not at first accept an orthodox understanding of the Christian doctrine of the Trinity. They could not accept that the human Jesus had been of the same substance as the Creator or the Holy Spirit. Bishop Isodore and San Millan had been instrumental in bringing them close to the mainstream of theological thought.

The Visigoths had crossed the Pyrenees in the 5th century when the power of Rome had collapsed in western Europe. They presided over post-Roman Spain with relatively little disruption to the continuity of culture when compared to the more cataclysmic changes further north where the more barbarous Franks and Anglo-Saxons made their conquests. The civilised Visigoths saw themselves as the inheritors of the traditions of Rome and they chased out or subdued the more barbarous German invaders of the Vandal and Suevi tribal confederations who had crossed the Pyrenees, though the Vandals bequeathed their name to the southern kingdom of Andalusia.

Under the Visigoths the church in Spain developed an organisation and an architectural and liturgical tradition that was as distinct from that of Rome as was the Celtic church of the north. However, the Golden Age of Celtic Christianity was to be eroded by the incessant attacks of the Vikings in the 9th and 10th centuries, and the Golden Age of the 7th century Visigothic Church of San Isidore and San Millan was brought to an abrupt end in 711. The Visigoths had provided a warrior aristocracy for Spain, but when their King Roderic and the flower of his followers were destroyed in Andalusia by an Arab and Moorish army from Morocco the collapse of their hold over Spain was swift. His successors were unable to resist the power of Islam as it flooded in from Africa.

It has been estimated that over a million people took part in this invasion of Spain when the indigenous population of the Iberian Peninsular was only five million. Only a fraction of that total were fighting men, for they brought their wives and families with them, and of the fighting men only a fraction were Arabs or followers of Islam. The vast majority of the invaders were Berber tribes from Morocco and Algeria. These Berbers (Barbarians) of north Africa had never been conquered by Rome and they had given the Arabs of Islam a difficult half century of resistance until Arab and Berber found a common cause in the conquest of Spain and the loot that was available.

The impact of these pagan Berbers brought a horrific cataclysm on the Visigothic kingdom. The more sophisticated Arabs made the city of Cordoba their base, but the Berbers were primarily out for loot and lands to make their own by killing and driving out the indigenous settlements. Arab and Berber were to fall out within 30 years of the invasion and their internal conflict enabled the surviving Christian areas of northern Spain to regroup their defences and build the foundations of the future kingdoms of Aragon, Navarre, the Rioja and Castile through which I was travelling.

The sight of the Berber clans and tribes on the move must have been awesome. They were a pastoralist people who travelled with their herds and flocks and pitched temporary cities of tents. Their progress would have been marked by towering columns of dust.

In many ways they were not so very different from the German tribes which had surged over Europe after the collapse of Roman power, or from the earlier waves of the Celts which had stalked the continent before the rise of Rome.

Vivid descriptions of the Celtic and German migrations were written in Latin describing how they travelled with great ox-drawn wagons surrounded by thousands of cattle and horses. Such migrations by Berber, German and Celt were powerful in the plains, but mountains and forests were much more inaccessible to them. Life was harsh for these warrior nomads, and the old and the sick were abandoned if they could not keep up with the march of their clan.

Somehow the monastery of Suso survived the centuries.

We sat in the oak trees and pondered that this was just the kind of place Celtic Druids would have chosen. The earlier waves of Celtic migrations had influenced the history of Spain as much as those of the later Germans and Berbers. The Celiberians who had resisted both Rome and the Visigoths were descended from migrations that had forced their way through the Pyrenees in the 5th century BC. Their descendants in the Cantabrian coastlands and in the far west of Galicia provided safe havens in which the fightback against the Arabs and the Moors could be based.

In many ways the work of Millan had mirrored the achievements of Ninian, Columba, Samson and Gildas among the Celts of the north. Bishop Isidore of Visigothic Toledo was working with a sophisticated urban population which lived a Roman style of life. Millan was working among country people whose legends and myths shared a common heritage with the northern Druids. Did Millan relate the Druid Trinity of Past Present and Future to the Christian Trinity and did he compare Yesu with Jesus ?

When the Benedictine's began the building of their huge monastery at Yuso it was at a time when the Roman papacy was extending its influence. This involved a deliberate campaign to iron out the surviving idiosyncrasies of the Visigothic and Celtic traditions in the western fringes of the continent. Very little of the literature of the Spanish church from before the 11th century survives. The suspicion remains that the expanding power of centralised Roman Catholicism expunged the record of Visigothic Christianity from the shelves of monastic libraries. It was the same in southern Scotland. Much of the library of the Celtic traditions of Govan and Glasgow survived into the 12th century, but not thereafter. The rising force in mediaeval Christianity was centred on the ecclesiastical influence of Italy and France backed up by the might of the Norman and Frankish war machine.

Dominique started to paint with water-colours whilst I luxuriated in doing as little as possible. Occasionally buses full of tourists arrived to disturb the peace. Tour guides spoke to the passengers through loudspeakers about the history of Yuso. The passengers then spilled out to mill around the old walls but no-one ventured into the forests where we lay hidden in the greenery. From time to time bursts of song and the sound of clapping rose up through the trees and then with a revving of diesel engines the buses would disappear and tranquillity returned. The sun began to dip into a long afternoon and we decided to visit Yuso down below.

The ancient monastery in the mountains was dwarfed by the Romanesque masonry of the French Benedictines who had extended the influence of the Pope into the Rioja.

We set off to explore the cloisters and I was fascinated by a series of paintings from the 16th century when hundreds of monks had lived at Yuso. From the evidence of the subject matter these monks lived in the perpetual fear of hell-fire. Many were the awful representations of demons in an obsessive fascination with the eternal tortures of damned souls. The theological emphasis of this later Spanish Christianity was very much on the depravity of human nature and the doctrine of Original Sin. Little enough emphasis was placed on the original blessings of life. Dominique was repelled and we did not linger even though beautiful vaulting spanned a Romanesque nave that was the equal of Durham cathedral for size, majesty and beauty.

We left for the streets of the small town that clustered outside the ecclesiastical walls of the monastery. The town of Yuso was handsome and built with the same golden stone as the monastery. Many of the buildings were hundreds of years old. Iron balconies and balustrades overhung the streets and we went in search of a shop and provender. A student from the language school gave us directions and we entered a low dark room that was full of savoury smells. It was presided over by a tiny and ancient lady. With smiles and sign language we chose what we needed. The village baker produced large round loaves of a greyish coloured bread with a thick crust. We chose two loaves and local fruit, wine, olives, tomatoes and onions. The old lady had nothing to replace what the cat had stolen the night before, but she gave us directions for the butcher in the village. He proved to be a mountain of a man who was very affable and helpful to the two dusty strangers. We bought from him a length of his home made sausage and a piece of smoked and dried beef. Dominique was much taken by the man and his produce.

Spanish and French are not dissimilar languages and the two of them were soon involved in an enthusiastic conversation, though how much of what was said was understood is uncertain. Both the old lady and the large man were visibly pleased to be of service to foreign pilgrims. Our thanks to them both had been heartfelt.

We were thirsty after the long, hot afternoon in the forest and it had been days since I had tasted beer. The butcher gave us directions for a local meson or bar. It was in an upstairs room at the top of a flight of stone steps that had been worn down by generations of booted feet. A dozen or so men were scattered about the cool, high-ceilinged room. Their attention was fixed on a television that was blaring out sound at a very high volume. Our entrance merited only the occasional distracted nod for a bullfight was in progress.

Ornamental, short jackets stiff with brocade, tight knee breeches and a lacquered hat made up the livery of the matadors as they taunted and teased the enraged animal that had been driven into the ring with blows. Before him the matador flourished a cloak behind which he held a blade of sharp Spanish steel. The bull was tiring and its hide was already streaked with blood from many wounds.

We sat by the balcony and tried to ignore the slow torture of a brave beast in an unequal contest. As a form of public entertainment it was vile. If an animal must be killed for food in a hungry world then let it be done with the speed of the mighty butcher of the village. He killed animals with one swing of his great hammer to the forehead, but the matador's sword only played with the bull in a slow and sustained bloodletting.

The pre-Christian world of Rome enjoyed the spectacle of animals and humans forced to fight to the death in the public arenas of the city coliseums. The Spanish bullring of the 20th century seemed to be a continuation of the social customs of ancient Rome. It had once been fashionable to throw the earliest Christians to ravening lions that had been deliberately starved and baited into a fury. These hideous happenings gave rise to the story of Androcles and the Lion. Androcles had once come upon an injured lion in the wilderness. Compassion made him take the time to heal the animal of its hurts. They parted company as firm friends, the lion and the man, only to meet each other in the coliseum before the blood lust of the crowds. The lion refused to harm his benefactor. This ancient story reveals that the early church set its face against the torture of animals. Gautama of India preached a gentle creed which insisted that animals as well as humans were deserving of gentle compassion. Francis of Assisi preached to the birds which flocked around him in their thousands in a response to the tangible aura of his gentleness, and stories associated with Celtic saints abound with incidents recording their love and respect for the animals of the natural world. One of the hermit friends of Columba wrote a letter to the great Abbot of Iona bemoaning the death of a pet fly which evidently used to walk along the lines of manuscript to give the recluse his place when reading. Other clerics in the Celtic church showed a similar relationship with the animals of nature. Serf of Fife is said to have harnessed a deer and a wolf side by side to pull his plough in a practical exposition of the biblical text that *"the lion would lie down with the lamb"*.

Meat was only rarely eaten in Celtic monasteries and was usually reserved for building up the strength of invalids. The animals on the monastic farms often responded to the human love of the monks with a devotion of their own. On the day of his death Columba took a short walk to feed his eyes for a last time on the beauty of the Hebrides. The exhausted old man sat resting by the side of the road. One of the faithful friends of the monks was passing by. This was a horse which worked on the monastic farmlands. According to the story the wise animal knew that the Abbot was at death's door. The horse stopped and laid its great head on the old man's lap and wept great sobs of grief and love.

All of these stories speak of the fact that Celtic Christianity had a sensitivity and a respect for our fellow creatures. After all, Jesus was born in a manger, in a byre.

A sudden pandemonium in the meson was equivalent in volume to the noise in the pub in Cashel when the Republic of Ireland had scored a goal in the World Cup. Then, the ball hitting the net was repeated in slow motion on the television screen so that viewers could relish the moment again and again, but this was no goal.

Spanish bulls are bred for their aggression and stamina, and this bull had turned the tables on his persecutor. A charging horn had lodged in a fold of the matador's cloak and had ripped it to shreds. The cloak was vital to mask the movements of the man's legs as he side-stepped the onslaught of two tons of beef, horn and hooves. With only shreds of his cloak left to him the matador was suddenly in deadly danger. At such moments picadors emerge from behind stout wooden screens to divert the attention of the bull from the matador. Picadors are mounted on horses that wear protective armour. Picadors are so called because of the long spears they carry which they leave sticking into the bull's flesh, but this time they were too slow off the mark. The shredding of the matador's cloak had taken only an instant. The television showed the terror in the matador's face and the fierce triumph of the bull. Blood, human blood this time, stained the matadors clothing as he was gored and tossed and trampled before the picadors could drive off the powerful animal. Time after time in slow motion the television repeated these images. The injuries to the man were not fatal, but the bull would die in rage and agony. We did not wish to see the end and so we drained our glasses and left.

Shadows were darkening in the forests and the moon rose over the shoulder of the hills as we climbed up to Yuso. It was good to return to the Visigothic monastery and cleanse the memories of the meson in the clear welling spring that had been Millan's original water supply. Over the centuries it had been thought to have healing and recuperative powers. It tasted of the cool, green depths of the forest and it banished the memory of the cruelty of the bullfight.

There was a picnic place beside Millan's spring with a table and benches set in the overgrown remains of the monastic garden. Soon candle light flickered on the table and Dominique busied himself with preparing the meal. The bread from the village was delicious and quite different from plastic wrapped, sliced pap to pop in a toaster. This was bread which exercised teeth and jaws. We soon had a salad of mild, raw onion, olives and tomatoes to accompany the sausage and smoked meat we had bought from the butcher. This was Spanish mountain food and not the mass-produced imitations which are sold in supermarkets. As we dined we could see the lights of the town grow in the valley below.

We uncorked the first bottle of wine and drank to friendship. We wallowed in *"the puddle of pleasures and the swill of swine"* in the memorable phrase of the first Protestant Archbishop of Canterbury who had been critical of the luxury of the lives of many of the Roman Catholic senior clergy, but there were moments when we broke and shared the bread and poured the wine that were echoes of an earlier last supper between friends.

Stars and galaxies wheeled across the sky, the water from the spring splashed in its trough, and the night air grew cold. Shadows flickered in the branches as we reminisced over our adventures during our few days together.

In the morning we would part company and we shared cups of kindness. Dominique hoped to return the 400 miles to

Toulouse in one day if he stuck to motorways and had the wind at his heels. Ahead of me lay the wide and dry plains of Castile which stretched for 300 miles westwards to the granite mountains of Galicia. I hoped to be there before the next nightfall.

A cold dew settled over everything as we clinked our glasses and retired to our tents.

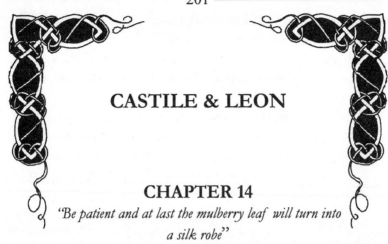

CASTILE & LEON

CHAPTER 14

*"Be patient and at last the mulberry leaf will turn into
a silk robe"*

Confucius

San Millan de la Cogola, Burgos, Leon, Astorga, O Cebreiro

We heard the noise of several large animals during the night. They snuffled and tramped around the camp site. Neither of us felt like investigating. I was convinced we were surrounded by wild pigs. The safest policy was to lie quiet. Of course the noise could have been caused by overactive rabbits or blundering badgers, but we did not think so at the time.

We lay quiet in our tents until our nocturnal visitors went on their way. Long before I had been kept awake by the noises of wild animals. In the wilderness of northern Minnesota I had listened to wolves howling at the moon. Wolves, bears and lynx still prowl the Sierra de la Demanda, but in pitifully diminished numbers. It had not been always so, and pilgrims in earlier centuries were in great danger from wolves. When continual warfare diminished human populations and left unburied corpses by the thousand as carrion the number of wolves in Europe often reached plague proportions. In the bitter civil wars which followed the burning of Joan of Arc in the 15th century packs of wolves entered a Paris whose inhabitants were enfeebled by famine and bubonic plague, and also diminished in numbers by the other associated hardships of war. These wolf packs killed and ate several dozen Parisians before they could be driven out of the city.

My sleeping bag was insufficient protection from the chill night air. At first light we emerged to a world that was dripping in dew and our legs quickly became soaked as we brushed through long grasses. Silken spiders' webs were decked in liquid diamonds of light. We waited in quietness for the rising sun to flood into the clearing which had once heard the singing of Millan and his earliest friends. They had chosen the site of their little monastery with great care. Not only did it enjoy the sweet waters of the abundant spring, but it lay in a fold of the hills that captured the early morning sun. Tendrils of steam rose from the dew until it was dry enough for the dust to begin its dance in eddies of wind. The wind was rising in rather an ominous fashion as we stowed our gear and prepared for departure.

We said our farewells. It had been a joyful week in Dominique's company. We knew that we would meet again and share other adventures in the future. Our friendship would span the years. "Au revoir"................I waved to him when we came to the parting of our ways at the foot of the mountains, and I was utterly alone.

Dominique had the wind at his heels for his eastwards run to the French frontier. I had to contend with it in my teeth. Nevertheless I intended to ride for the west, following the sun until dusk. Ahead of me lay the long plains of Castile and Leon, but first I had to cross the Montes de Oca. These rolling ridges are higher than the Grampians and they are heavily forested with pines and heathland rising out of the oaks which cover the lower slopes.

The descent from the Montes de Oca was swift on a new

ribbon of smooth tarmac. Traffic was light until I neared the great city of Burgos. This had been the ancient capital of the Kings of Castile. The name Castile has the same origin as Cashel in Ireland. Castile is the "Land of Castles". The initial invasions of the Arabs and the Moors which destroyed Visigothic power in the 8th century soon conquered and overran the plains of Spain. It had been in the inaccessible mountains of Galicia and the northern coastlands that Christian resistance had held out against the marauding Saracens, but it was on the plains of Castile that this resistance first gathered its strength to drive back the southern invaders.

Modern Burgos is a prosperous city of much the same size as Dundee. Euromoney has recently developed a new network of high-speed roads in Spain, but this construction work has yet to provide many urban by passes and it was necessary to go through the centre of Burgos. Cork had been the last city that I had needed to negotiate. I was soon entangled in heavy traffic and congested lines of slow moving vehicles. The fug of fumes tasted vile after the pine scented air of the mountains.

The outskirts of Burgos are an uninspiring rash of modern tenements and poured concrete. There was little garden ground and fewer public parks, but the centre of the city was delightful with the shade from avenues of trees beside a clear river decorated with iris and water lilies. Long tendrils of green weed waved in the gentle current. The colossal silhouette of the largest Gothic cathedral in Spain loomed above the secular city. A spiky, octagonal central tower dominated everything.

Burgos is a city rich in history, and I could have spent a memorable day in her streets, but I was impatient to head for the west. The borderlands of Galicia were within 250 miles of Burgos. There had been a surfeit of ecclesiastical architecture in previous days and so I headed out of the city on the road for Leon as fast as the traffic allowed with the interior of Burgos cathedral unseen.

The armies of Napoleonic France captured Burgos and looted most of the cultural inheritance of the city that was portable. They even desecrated the tombs of the Kings and Queens of Castile in their greed for jewels, gold and costly fabrics. In the outskirts I passed the ornate Hospital del Rey, the "King's Hostel" which once provided shelter for pilgrims. French cavalry regiments had used it as a stables for their horses. The main doors of this stately edifice have survived. They were constructed out of huge mahogany timbers that had been brought from the Americas in the 16th century. These doors mark the high tide of the popularity of the Compostela pilgrimage as clearly as the strange minaret north of the Gironde marks the limit of the high tide of Islam. In the years after these great portals were hung from their massive iron hinges the religious interest of northern Europe ebbed away from the mediaeval tradition of pilgrimage. It was not until the 19th century and the development of new cults at places like Lourdes that pilgrimage was rejuvenated.

Burgos was home for a time to the legendary figure of El Cid who in the late 11th century crushed a powerful Saracen lunge against the Christian enclaves of the north.

The main power in Islamic Spain had been centred on the city of Cordoba in Grenada. This cosmopolitan city was more populous and prosperous than any other in all of western Europe. It was part of a flourishing civilisation that spanned the Sahara to the gold centre of Timbuktu and from there to Egypt, Syria, Persia and the Silk Road to China. In comparison with Cordoba, Burgos had been an uncouth village in the time of El Cid.

Cordoba had been the centre of a powerful Caliphate that was independent from the Abasssid Caliphs of Baghdad. The Abassids had overthrown the Umayyad dynasty which claimed descent from Mohammed himself. A lone survivor from the massacre which the Abassids perpetrated on the Umayyads escaped to Cordoba. This Abd al Rahman in 756 established the Umayyads as rulers of Islamic Spain for the next 250 years.

Richard Fletcher of York University is a distinguished scholar of Islamic Spain. He states that *"in Spain only about 8% of the population were Muslim by 800, that the proportion had crept to 12 ½% by 850; that it had then leapt to about 50% by 950 before peaking at about 75% by the year 1000. The period of the most intense transfer of confessional allegiance was therefore between circa 850 and 950".*

This rapid Islamicisation of society was not without its consequences. Many Mozarabic Christians who had lived under the Cordoban regime began to migrate to live in areas under Christian control. They brought with them to the warrior societies of the north the sophisticated traditions of Cordoba and also the memories of Visigothic glory. These Mozarab Christians brought with them the Arab alphabet. As late as the 11th century Kings of Castile signed official documents in that flowing script and not in angular Latin lettering.

As the popularity of the Compostela pilgrimage grew it brought a flood of northern Europeans to Castile, many of whom settled in the new "villa francas". The cultural expression of the Mozarabs was alien to them. As a matter of state policy to integrate themselves more closely into the European mainstream the Kings of Castile decided to foster Roman Catholic institutions in their territory in the same way as in Scotland Queen Margaret persuaded her husband Malcolm Canmore, the slayer of MacBeth, to turn his back on Celtic customs and lavish patronage on new Roman Catholic foundations.

The great abbey of Cluny in France was the centre from which this process was master-minded. The influence of Cluny would bring armies of French, Norman and German knights to fight alongside the Castilians against the Saracens. In effect Cluny would create a western Crusade to attack Islam at the same time as the eastern Crusades to Palestine were carving out French speaking dominions in the Levant and even capturing Jerusalem itself for a time. In return the Kings of Castile undertook to send huge annual payments of gold to Cluny.

This bullion originated in Africa to the south of the Sahara. Salt, textiles, ivory, metal and beads from the north were bartered for this precious gold dust. Long lines of camels took the merchandise across the desert sands between Timbuktu and Morocco. African gold underpinned the power of the Caliphs of Cordoba, but in the early 11th century the institutions of the Caliphate fractured in what became known as *"the breaking of the necklace of pearls"*. Small kingdoms and city states asserted their independence from Cordoba. These now "taifa" kingdoms did not combine their forces against the Christian north. On the contrary, in pursuit of their own internal wars they often employed Christian mercenaries to harry and plunder their fellow Muslims.

The "taifa" Kingdom of Toledo found itself vulnerable to the growing power of Castile. In the same manner as the Kings of England had been forced to pay "Danegeld" as protection money to Viking warlords, Castile demanded increasing amounts of African gold from the rich manufacturing city of Toledo which had once been the Visigothic capital. It yielded tribute to Castile, and much of this went to empower Cluny in its drive to reform the native traditions of Spanish Christianity.

The Mozarabs wore different vestments and recited different prayers and lexicons; the laity took communion in both kinds and when they recited the Creed they said "natum non factum" rather than "genitum non factum", born not made instead of begotten not made; and when the Lord's Prayer was recited Spanish custom said Amen after every clause instead of just once at the end. These deviations from the Roman Catholic rite were looked upon with disfavour by the Cluniac reformers who were determined that the ancient and much loved Spanish liturgy should be replaced by Roman usage.

It was all very reminiscent of the process which had begun at the Synod of Whitby in 664 to force the idiosyncrasies of Celtic spirituality to conform more closely to the continental mainstream.

The huge Romanesque basilicas which Cluny caused to be built were visible manifestations for the new ecclesiastical focus in Spain, but these developments were imperilled when there was a sudden rejuvenation in the Islamic world and a mighty army gathered in Morocco to surge into Spain. The Almoravids were an ascetic movement which originated south of the Sahara in Senegal. These Muslim fundamentalists greatly disapproved of the "taifa" kingdoms which paid tribute to Christian warlords. In 1089 the Almoravids crossed the Straits of Gibraltar and filled the vacuum of power that had been left by the collapse of the Umayyads. In the years which followed the Almoravids brought ruin and defeat to the Christian north. Cluny lost its annual supply of gold. In this dark time of defeat it was El Cid who broke the power of these African invaders and gained his place as the hero of Spanish legend.

There was a second African invasion in the 12th century when the Almohades matched the Almoravids in puritanical religious fervour and ferocity. The Muslim religion preached "Jihad", the doctrine of holy war by which their faith was spread at the edge of the sword. Jihad fell heavily upon Castile.

To every action there is an equal and opposite reaction. The defeat of the Visigoths had been swift and the early Caliphs had been relatively tolerant towards the Christian and Jewish communities they encountered, but as Islam rose to a more complete dominance in the 10th century the result was a stiffening of Christian resistance and an increase in Muslim intolerance. The Jihad of the Almoravids and the Almohades was met with the response of Crusade. This was the cultural context which transformed St. James from the gentle apostle to the mounted warrior wielding a scimitar, and this was the historical context which made Burgos the cockpit of the north. By the 13th century the Saracens were in retreat and the power of Castile stretched south. As power moved south so did the royal court. First Toledo became the royal capital and then Madrid grew to become the centre, weaving webs of dominion over the whole Iberian peninsula before the dynasty which originated in Castile united with the Hapsburg heirs of Charlemagne to add Austria, Hungary, southern Germany, northern Italy, Burgundy and the Low Countries to the responsibilities of those who governed from the Escurial palace of Madrid.

It was from the Escurial that the orders were issued which subjugated the Aztecs and the Incas of the Americas and sent Spanish mariners to span the globe in their galleons and secure an Asian Empire in the Philippines .... and this accumulation of world-wide power began in Burgos.

The Roman Catholic establishment which the Kings of Castile had endowed with the gold of Africa was also to grow to world-wide prominence alongside their royal patrons. This church had been moulded in the style of the Norman and French culture of Cluny. It had been shaped in its attitudes by Jihad and Crusade until in the years of its victory it had become inflexible. Visigothic and Mozarabic achievements were to be erased from the record. The civilisation of Jewish and Muslim Granada was likewise destroyed and its influence banished from Spain; and when faced with the intellectual challenge of the Protestant Reformation the response of the Spanish church had been the Inquisition which burned "heretics" and "witches" wherever Spanish armies were in control.

Beyond Burgos the road entered the plains of Castile which occupy the centre of the country and which stretch east and west from Portugal to the mountains above Valencia, and from the Ebo to the Andalusian valleys. Sir Victor Pritchett was an Englishman who travelled widely in this immense region, having survived the slaughter of the First World War. He described the landscape in these terms: *"Nine months of winter, three of hell, is the proverbial description of Castilian weather, the weather of half of Spain: a dry climate of fine air under a brassy sun, where the cold wind is wicked and penetrating, a continual snake-fang flicker against the nostrils. Castile is a steppe. Its landscape is the pocked and cratered surface of the moon.*

Dust and yellow earth have begun; the grass, if there are patches of it, is wire, the trees only mark the roads, there are no others, and the roads, too, are rare. It is steppe, not desert, a steppe variegated only by wilderness. And there appear those strange flat-topped hills of the country. A half-mile long, perhaps, and anything from 400 to 450 feet high, they have been planed off at the summit and are water-hollowed in their flanks. They are as pale as china clay. Half a dozen of these dry hills would be a curiosity like the Wiltshire barrows, but these mesetas stretch in their hundreds, miles deep like some geometry written on the land by wind and drought, an immense, wearying encampment. Some are pocked with tufts of grass: here and there some peasant has tried to cultivate a lower slope, but the water clearly drains off them and most of them are bare. No house or village is on them; they are the ghosts of nature and they pass in pointless fantasy.

These hills bleach the country and, in the heat, the air trembles over them."

The night air at our campsite in Suso had been frigid, but as the day approached noon a brassy sun had climbed high into the sky and the air trembled in the beginning of a heat haze. Soon I was drenched in perspiration to which the dust from the road stuck in a grimy mask across my face. The countryside of Castile was not densely populated with only the occasional small town and village. Beside the new Euroroute there was an air of modernity and prosperity, and indeed the new supermarket lifestyle which has recently invaded Spain was everywhere in evidence with carelessly dumped plastic bags containing disposable plastic items, glass bottles, old tin cans, and wide assortments of other cast offs, but away from the main road it was quite different. The old pilgrim roads led through villages from an earlier Castile and I followed the new signposts of the Compostela Pilgrim Way to escape from the high speeds of the Euroroute for a more gentle hour or so.

I came to a decaying sequence of villages which were inhabited mainly by the elderly. The young have gone to new lives in the cities and emptied the countryside as thoroughly as in Donegal. Scotland has suffered in recent years from desperately high levels of unemployment that have affected as many as 1 in 10 of the working population. In many parts of Spain long term unemployment is twice as bad as in Scotland. The new wealth of the Republic of Ireland is spread patchily enough, but in Spain abject poverty co-exists with the most garish expressions of personal wealth. Many of the older houses in these little Castilian villages of the plains are built out of adobe. Their earth walls crumble and children, dogs and chickens play in the dust, but I liked these rural Castilians. They held themselves with a natural dignity and grace and I often heard the cry "hola, peregrino" as they wished me a safe journey.

I stopped at a meson for lunch and asked for an omelette. I was given a small earthenware jug of the local wine with my meal. It was the most marvellous liquid, and I wished Dominique had been there to taste it. Even he would have been impressed. This country wine had been made in the locality. I had often seen strange air vents and small doors rising out of low mounds in the fields. These are "bodegas" or wine cellars in which the raw, new wine is left to age and mature. The glorious wine I had tasted came from the bodega of the proprietor of the meson.

I was tempted to find another jug and then take a siesta in the shade, but I was impatient for Galicia and so was soon back on the bike. The strong wind of the morning had fallen away, but the air was clear and visibility was as good as it had been in the Pyrenees. Far in the north beyond the endless plain rose the Cantabrian Mountains against the horizon.

The Castilian plain is an ordeal for the pilgrim on foot. It is dry, thirsty country with very little shade, but new stretches of the Compostela Pilgrim Way have been planted with young saplings for mile after mile. In time these will mark a green and shaded ribbon through the countryside.

Gradually the landscape softened until it was one huge, continual wheat-field. The old peasants of the adobe villages had worked this soil with hand tools and only mules and donkeys to aid them, but agriculture has become a hi-tec business where machinery has replaced the traditional workforce so that the young have had to leave for the cities.

I returned to the Euroroute feeling that I had tasted the flavour of rural Castile on the back roads of the Pilgrim Way that meandered alongside the new high-speed road.

The next significant settlement was the town of Sahagun. It had once been a major ecclesiastical centre. In 904 a group of monks fled from an increasingly Islamicised Cordoba. They established themselves at Sahagun where they continued to develop their rich Mozarab and Visigothic inheritance. This earlier Christian witness was obliterated in the 12th century when Sahagun was given into the control of Cluny. Latin plainsong began to echo in the new stone basilicas. Sahagun was endowed with wide estates and it grew in wealth. It also maintained several pilgrim hospices and its libraries made it a place of great learning.

In the 16th century the monastery produced two men of great stature. Fray Pedro Ponce de Leon was the first man to teach the deaf to speak, read and write. Before his time it had been believed that the deaf were incapable of education. His achievement speaks volumes about his selfless commitment to the charges in his care. His methodology was the foundation on which all subsequent work with the deaf has been based. Fray Pedro remained quietly in the cloisters of Sahagun, but Fray Bernardo de Sahagun crossed the Atlantic. With mounting horror and compassion he watched the devastating impact of Spanish colonisation on Mexico. In a monumental work entitled "A General History of the Things of New Spain" he recorded in Aztec, Spanish and Latin all that he could about the native American civilisations he encountered. In the words of the explorer Robin Hanbury Tenison who has written a fascinating record of his own pilgrimage to Compostela on horseback *"he was one of the first Europeans to describe rubber. Even more was the information he gleaned from the Indians whom he troubled to question about their world and their gods at a time when most of his contemporaries still regarded them as animals without souls who could be slaughtered freely and who knew nothing. He has been called the father of modern ethnology"*.

It was men and women of the calibre of Fray Pedro and Fray Bernardo who were the continual inspiration of Spanish Christianity in every century. The tolerance and kindness of Pedro, Bernardo, Domingo and Millan stand in sharp contrast to the cruel certainties of the Inquisition. Presbyterian Scotland was disfigured enough by its own thought police who brought the blight of the witch hunt in the 17th century, but the temporal power of the mighty Spanish church was underpinned by the everyday human compassion of countless individuals whose inspiration was the life of a Jewish carpenter; as it was in Scotland.

The road beyond Sahagun is surrounded by fields trimmed with poplars in the thin ribbon of lush green that runs beside the Rio Cea. Legend has it that Charlemagne once fought the African chieftain Agiolando at the river crossing. After the battle the victorious Franks buried their dead and placed spears to mark the graves. These spears sprouted leaves and grew into mighty poplars according to the old story as a sign that these Christian martyrs had safely entered paradise.

There had been another battle in these same fields during the Peninsular War when British troops gained a short lived victory over the vanguard of Napoleon's army. The Scottish general Sir John Moore commanded an army that was a fraction of the size of the French forces which threatened encirclement and destruction, and so began a terrible retreat in the depths of winter over snow bound ground where frostbite, hunger and wounds brought death to many. There was little else to eat but their horses. For 250 miles discipline held and they fought off and outmarched their pursuers. Eventually at Coruna in Galicia the survivors were rescued by the Royal Navy in a forerunner of Dunkirk. Sir John Moore was killed in the final battle whilst his troops were being evacuated. Less than five years later the French were thrown out of Spain by Wellington, and Napoleon had learnt to his cost the consequences of a long retreat in winter on the road from Moscow. From Sahagun I would be following in the footsteps of the last journey made by Sir John Moore.

The endless landscape of wheat-fields was only interrupted where the rivers flowed south from the Cantabrian mountains. Trees grew beside them and marked their meandering flow, but as I drew closer to the city of Leon irrigation channels became more frequent and market gardens and vineyards marched beside the road.

Leon had once been the centre of a powerful kingdom which grew to prominence when Castile was a hard pressed frontier settlement ruled only by lowly Counts. The name Leon is derived from the word legion. The Romans had built a major military base by the banks of the Rio Bernesga and around the old legionary walls grew the city of the future. The Roman military machine left its stamp on the place names of Spain to mark the inexorable pressure that penned the Celtiberians into the coastal highlands in the 1st century BC. Pamplona evokes the memory of Pompey and Zaragusa derives its pronunciation from its ancient title as the city of Caesar Augustus.

Leon defied the Saracens before being absorbed by Castile and it remained a great and influential city whose cathedral is said to be the loveliest in Spain. It is dedicated to San Isidore, the patriarch of Visigothic Toledo in the 7th century. I did not visit the historic centre of the city because of my impatience to eat up the miles to Galicia, but I did stop on the outskirts of town to stretch my legs and smoke a lazy cigarette. I parked my bike beside the bullring of Leon, but it was a small church with a belfry that attracted my attention. The bell tower was crowned by a mass of twigs like an oversized rook's nest. Perched on it was a great white bird which stretched its wings and inspected the outspread plumage with a long pointed beak. I still had not heard a nightingale, but I had seen my first stork. The Spanish think that storks bring them good luck when they return every year after their long migration from Africa. These beautiful birds are under no more threat from humans than swans in Scotland.

I was encouraged in my own journey by the sight of these intercontinental travellers. I realised that my impatience to reach Galicia meant that I would have to miss the treasures of Leon. The Royal Pantheon of San Isidore is the burial place of Kings and Queens and it houses the largest surviving collection of Romanesque paintings in Europe. These illuminate the life of 12th century Leon. Most poignant in the huge and varied collection are scenes from the yearly calendar of tasks which record the mediaeval life of a farmer: *"Pruning the vines in March and gathering the grapes in September; shaking acorns off the oak tree in October for the pigs and killing them for winter meat in November; sowing in April, reaping wheat in July, threshing it in August; and finally sitting in front of a blazing fire with a glass of wine on the table, a loaf of bread in one hand and the other raised in benediction for all the good things in life. When there was peace there would have been an ample surplus".* The land gave bountifully having not yet been abused, deforested and polluted, in the opinion of Robin Tenison who visited the Pantheon.

There are those who argue that the model of a sustainable agriculture for the future can be found in the 12th century paintings of the Pantheon of San Isidore, rather than hi-tech machinery and chemicals but the gravitational pull of Galicia won the struggle and I left Leon for the lure of the west with the Pantheon unseen.

Breasting the rise beyond the old city revealed a new range of mountains hemming the western horizon. These were still far distant, but my eyes could see the first slopes of Galicia.

The landscape grew more hilly with every mile. Bare limestone ridges nurtured only a thin scattering of scrubland and the afternoon sun burned in the sky. Sweeping round a bend with the Yamaha purring beneath me brought into view the small city of Astorga clustered around the towers of a 15th century cathedral. Guilt at having turned my back on the cathedrals of Burgos and Leon persuaded me to spend a quiet hour in Astorga. The old city had been a Roman settlement (Astorga = Augustus) and in ancient times it had been the axis of 9 roads which joined there. It is built out of a warm pinkish coloured stone and it exudes an atmosphere of being at ease with itself. I parked the bike in the main square behind the cathedral and went in search of someone to sign my pilgrim passport.

The Bishop's Palace houses an exhibition of the Compostela Pilgrim Way but much more interesting is the building itself which was designed by Gaudi, the brilliant architect of 19th century Catalonia whose inspiration created Barcelona cathedral.

Astorga cathedral boasts exuberant baroque flourishes, but

lovely though it was my attention was drawn to the much earlier church dedicated to San Juan. It was built with the simple style of the Mozarabs, but several elderly ladies were arranging flowers for a wedding. I felt like an intruder and so I returned to the cathedral to sit for a while in the cool shadows which were pierced by dusty arrows of light from high celestory windows.

As the sun began to slant into evening I left the old city and climbed through rising country towards the wilderness of Galicia. These hills behind Astorga were home for many centuries to a most unusual people. They called themselves the Muragatos and they were described by a Victorian traveller as *"perhaps the most singular cast to be found amongst the chequered population of Spain. They have their own peculiar customs and dress, and never intermarry with the Spaniards. Their name is a clue to their origin as it signifies "Moorish Goths" and at the present day their garb differs but little from that of the Moors of Barbary as it consisted of a long tight jacket secured at the waist by a broad girdle, loose short trousers which terminate at the knee and boots and gaiters. Their heads are shaven, a slight fringe of hair being left only at the lower part".*

I saw no Maragatos in their traditional finery but the geology of the countryside was fundamentally different from the plains of Castile and eastern Leon. I was drawing close to the borderlands of Galicia and the mountainous bastion of the Celts in the Iberian peninsula.

In the valleys below the Euroroute I began to see sights that were reminiscent of Glamorgan in Wales. I had not seen a countryside disfigured by heavy industry since the huge cement works in Pamplona, but these last valleys of Leon showed the scars of large scale coal mining and iron ore extraction. The little towns were either grimy with coal dust or powdered with the red dust from iron ore. The long roads since Suso had mostly been free of traffic and a pleasure to travel, but after Astorga my route lay along the main corridor for traffic to the large Galician cities of Lugo, Vigo, and La Coruna. In a growling cavalcade of lorries I plunged though the gloom of tunnels and soared on concrete spans across chasms while I ate the stench of diesel.

During my earliest childhood I had lived in Northumberland before my family moved to East Lothian. My parents were from Edinburgh and at every opportunity we drove north for the Scottish border. When we reached Berwick on Tweed there were gleeful shouts of homecoming. I was approaching Galicia with the same childlike fever of anticipation.

The coalfields of Leon extended beyond the rather scruffy industrial city of Ponferrada where the reek of coalsmoke competed with the fumes of the internal combustion engine. I continued to joust with the growing traffic of a sunny Friday evening in early summer, though I did stop once to buy some cherries from a roadside vendor.

The mountains began to hem the road into an increasingly narrow valley down which a torrent of water as well as vehicles wound their ways side by side. Leafy foliage and clouds of insects were proof that the rains are more copious in these parts than in the dry mesetas of Castile. The Castilians have an unkind name for Galicia. It rains so much there that they call it the "urinal" because it is always dripping. The valley was soon engulfed in shadow as the sun sank lower in the sky.

The new Euroroute began to climb up a side of the mountains in a sequence of tunnels, bridges, and massive embankments. The old road which was in use until a few years ago follows a much more tortuous course in a switch-back of hair-pin bends and narrow, pitted tarmac. The new road has cut the journey time through the mountain barrier that divides Spain from Galicia by several hours, but it was with great relief that I turned off the Euroroute onto a small country road. I had rejoined the Camino Frances, the Pilgrim Way to Compostela, and I would follow its signposts to the first village in Galicia.

This mountain top settlement is called O Cebreiro.

It had been a long week in the saddle from Lavour. I decided that my aching limbs needed more comfort than the tent could offer. I thought longingly of hot water, hot food, and a warm bed.

The road climbed up and up as though the ascent was never ending. My ears popped in the higher altitude as had happened in the Pyrenees. The valley below was fading into blue shadows when I emerged into the last rays of sunshine from a setting sun that brimmed the horizon with fire. Ridge after ridge of mountains flickered in the orange light which bathed my arrival in O Cebreiro.

When the ignition key had stilled the noise of the engine and with the helmet removed I began to take in the peace of my surroundings.

The village is a small clutter of a few dozen dwellings that have been built with rough walls of local stone and granite cobbles for the roadways between grey slate roofs. The houses clustered together for cosiness. At 3500ft. above sea level O Cebreiro is often assaulted by mountain storms and blizzards. Small windows peeped out of thick stone walls. I could have been in Ireland, Wales or Brittany.

The "meson" of the village was in the largest house. A bright fire flickered in the main room which had stone walls and stone flagging on the floor. Large timbers supported a low ceiling. Bottles glinted in the firelight.

The proprietor was a burly red-faced gentleman who would not have looked out of place at a cattle mart in Galloway. He called for his daughter who spoke a little English. She was perfectly charming as she showed me to a neat, tiled room with a bathroom annexe. Outside my window chickens scrabbled through the dust and the next building housed some brown and white milk cows. Evidence of their daily journey to and from the fields could be seen in the streets of O Cebreiro.

Exhaustion was only held at bay by hunger. After a rejuvenating bath a few locals came in for the equivalent of a pint and a gossip, though they seemed to favour generous measures of brandy. Realising that I could not speak Spanish they smiled and nodded and left me to myself. I found a quiet corner while waiting for supper. I ordered a bottle of wine and watched the television in rather a vacant state of mind as I struggled to keep awake. The sun had set and a long gloaming still bathed the Galician mountains in a dusky crimson half-light that shimmered like silk before my eyes.

Supper arrived, hunks of thick crusted bread were served alongside an immense, steaming bowl of stewed beef and vegetables. A variety programme came onto the television with a group of songsters in full voice, but as I cleared my plate of the last of the gravy a troop of Galician dancers took their turn on stage before the television cameras.

The dancers formed sets of eight as they do in Scottish country dancing and the accompaniment of bagpipes, fiddles, flutes and accordions was not unlike an outlandish version of Scottish or Irish jigs and reels. The traditional costume of the dancers seemed to involve a great deal of lace, petticoat and shawls for the women and the men wore white breeches that flapped over their boots and brought to mind the description of the old Maragotos of western Leon.

The village of O Cebreiros is home to many wonders. They could wait till morning.

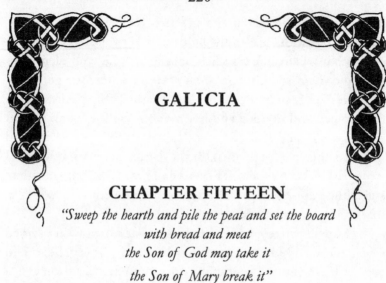

GALICIA

CHAPTER FIFTEEN

"Sweep the hearth and pile the peat and set the board
with bread and meat
the Son of God may take it
the Son of Mary break it"

Traditional Isle of Barra

Galicia, O Cebreiro, Samos, Partomarin, Mouzoi

My bovine neighbours grew restless in the early morning as they awaited milking. Small herds of dairy cattle where the farmer know the names of his animals are mostly a thing of the past in Galloway. Large operators have squeezed out the small farmer and milking time in modern Scotland is a dreary business among the splattering excretions of many dozens of nameless animals wearing plastic number tags. Morning milking in O Cebreiro was a much more gentle and leisurely process, and the mild eyed animals emerged to wander through the streets and be greeted with their names until it was time to take them to the fields.

Breakfast was a substantial omelette washed down with draughts of coffee. I had enjoyed my stay in the meson and I paid the modest bill and thanked the proprietor. He asked, through his daughter, where I was from. When I said I had travelled through Ireland and Brittany from Scotland and that I would be returning via Cornwall, Wales and the Isle of Man a gleam of appreciation shone in his eyes. With great formality he bade me welcome to Galicia and signed my pilgrim passport with relish. *"Galicia and Scotland are one"* said his daughter and I was made aware by these kind country people that they considered Galicia to be part of the Celtic family.

The Galicians differ from the Spanish in many respects. There is not a single bull ring in all of Galicia, but they do have a tradition of playing very loud bagpipes which some people consider to be just as much of an affront to civilised sensibilities as the cruel baiting of animals.

On the previous evening I had been too tired, dirty, hungry and thirsty to have had much energy for exploring the village before it was dark, but I was in no rush to leave O Cebreiro. Compostela was little over 75 miles distant and I had promised myself an easy day.

In the gloaming of the previous evening I had noticed that while most of the roofs in the village were made with thick, irregular rough-cut slabs of slate that looked like shimmering fish scales there was also a cluster of thatched buildings near the low church. I negotiated friendly cows and preoccupied chickens to reach the older heart of the village where thick thatch rose above granite walls. Galician granite is white like that of Aberdeen, but it was the shape of the old houses of O Cebreiro which attracted my attention. These single story dwellings were round and oval in shape. They looked like illustrations in an Asterix and Obelix cartoon. Their pre-historic design has survived little changed from the dwellings of the first Neolithic farmers some 7000 years ago. The earliest round houses of Europe had their doorways facing west to catch the evening sun, but in the Iron Age of the first millennium BC. when the Celts rose to prominence the customary site of the door was moved to the eastern side so that on leaving the house for the days work in field and forest and returning in the evening the inhabitants would face the rising and the setting of the sun. Sunrise and sunset were thought to be holy moments of great significance to Druid understanding. It was an astonishment to see these "palloza" dwellings still surviving in O Cebreiro and in daily use.

Beyond the thatched houses rose a low church of great antiquity. Elias Valena had been priest of O Cebreiro for many years until his recent death. Father Elias provided the inspirational force which did so much to arouse new interest in the Compostela Pilgrim Way. He pestered officials and beurocrats and lobbied politicians until in 1987 the Council of Europe gave its support to the recreation, repair and sign posting of the old pilgrim routes through France and Spain. This public statement of support galvanised the bureaucrats in Brussels to invest considerable funds in the project and it culminated in the papal visit to Compostela in 1989.

I went into the church to contemplate the achievements of this Galician priest and to say a prayer for help in the recreation of the Whithorn Pilgrim Way. I felt Father Elias might have some sympathy for the trials and tribulations I had encountered in dealing with the Galloway variant of the bureaucratic mind-set, both ecclesiastical and secular. It lent a certain fervency to my prayers that morning!

The shelter of O Cebreiro at the summit of the high pass at the entrance to Galicia had been much appreciated by the pilgrims of every century. This is wild and rugged country where blizzards are frequent in winter, but this remote village became famous for other reasons than topography and climate.

Pilgrims knew that they were nearing their destination of

Compostela, often after months of arduous travelling, and they had entered the mysterious and misty land of Celtic legend.

One of the most spectacular of these stories had its origins in an incident which is reputed to have taken place in the church at O Cebreiro when Robert the Bruce had been King of Scots in the early 14th century. The fame of this story spread throughout Europe and in the sentimental romanticism of the 19th century the German composer Wagner used the Holy Miracle of O Cebreiro as the basis for his opera "Parsifal".

According to the old story a peasant from the village of Barxamayor down in the valley below had struggled up through snow drifts in a raging gale to attend the daily Eucharist in the old church. He was the only member of the congregation and his attendance shamed the priest who would not otherwise have said the divine office on that tempestuous day but for the presence of the persistent peasant. When the priest raised the chalice and blessed the bread the wine visibly turned into blood and the bread into a portion of human flesh. I found the story moving in its simple piety and disgusting in its imagery. As a Scots Presbyterian I believe in the real presence of God in the evocative symbols of bread and wine, but I deny the mechanistic literalism of the doctrine of transubstantiation and cleave instead to the understanding that the Last Supper is a parable of great profundity which speaks to the universal human predicament. *"Hear us, O merciful Father, we beseech thee; and grant that we receiving these thy creatures of bread and wine according to thy Son our Saviour Jesus Christ's holy institution, in remembrance of his death and passion, may be partakers of his most blessed Body and Blood: who in the same night that he was betrayed took Bread and when he had given thanks he brake it and gave to his disciples saying, take, eat; this is my Body which is given for you: Do this in remembrance of me".*

I could not help but think that the legend of the Holy Miracle was a convenient vehicle for the emerging mediaeval doctrine of transubstantiation. Even so, the fame of O Cebreiro became widespread. As the story became embellished with frequent telling it was also claimed that the chalice in which the miracle took place was the Holy Grail, the cup which Jesus had shared with his friends before his arrest and torture, the Cup of the New Covenant between God and humanity. The chalice of the Holy Miracle is still preserved in the church where Father Elias worked and dreamed of his great venture.

The architecture of the granite building was very similar in scale and style to the early churches of Ireland and Scotland. The ancient sanctuary dedicated to Mary of Nazareth in O Cebreiro was not in the grand scale of the towering naves of Castile or the convoluted and costly carvings of Astorga. A few narrow windows allowed daylight to percolate into the interior. There was a greenish quality to this light from the leaves on the trees outside. It was cool, tranquil, and refreshing. At the west end there was a huge stone font carved out of a single lump of rock. It had been used when the rite of baptism involved total immersion as had been done in the rite of the Visigothic church at Riojan Suso.

I wondered if the tale of the Holy Grail in a remote mountain village had reached the ears of Robert the Bruce and had triggered the adventure of his embalmed heart in the casket carried to Spain by loyal Sir James Douglas.

The tradition of the miraculous chalice in O Cebreiro may have had other origins than 14th century credulity. Many tales would have been told to travellers in the flickering firelight of the hospice in the village, and many of these stories would have been survivals from the legends of the pre-Christian Celtic tribes of Galicia. In Brittany, Ireland and Scotland stories abound about magical cauldrons that were an inexhaustible source of plenty rather similar to the biblical story of the never empty jar of flour and cruise of oil which had sustained Elijah when he was in hiding at a poor widows house from a vengeful King of Israel. Greek myth too described the overflowing horn of the cornucopia of plenty.

Other aspects of the traditional story associated with the cult of St. James at Compostela may also have had their origin in pre-Christian myth. The body of St. James was reputed to have travelled from Palestine to Galicia on a stone boat which floated above the waves and was propelled forwards as though by unseen and miraculous hands. This echoes Celtic legends about the levitation and flight of great stones under the control of the wizards whom they thought had built the stone circles and raised the henge stones of Atlantic Europe in the forgotten past. The half legendary figure of Merlin is reported to have flown between Britain and Ireland on a great stone as though it was a magic carpet in a story from Arabia.

The apostle James had absolutely no connection with Spain whatsoever during his lifetime. He was kept busy as the leader of the first Christian community in Jerusalem. Unlike Peter and Paul he did not travel to distant lands. When eventually he fell foul of the secular and the Jewish religious authorities his body was recovered from his executioners and buried with great reverence. Helen, the mother of the Emperor Constantine, visited Jerusalem in the 4th century and noted the grave.

The great city which the first Christian Emperor founded at Constantinople grew to eclipse Rome. When the western Empire fell to barbarian invasions in the 5th century the eastern Empire of the Balkans, Greece and the lands which are now Turkey, Syria, Palestine and Egypt remained safe under the protection of mighty Constantinople until the early 7th century when Persian invaders crossed the desert from Iraq and captured Jerusalem.

These Persians had little love for the official religion of their enemies and many precious relics from the churches of

Jerusalem were removed from the city to protect them from the hands of impious looters. When I thought of what the Napoleonic French had done in Burgos I could quite understand the rationale behind the decision.

The casket containing the remains of James was taken for safekeeping into the wilds of the Sinai desert where Moses had roamed for 40 years and the Israelites had lived on manna and quails. In the depths of Sinai below the mountain on which Moses is reputed to have received the 10 Commandments stood a monastery dedicated to St. Catherine, an early martyr of the church who died the horrific death of being broken on a wheel, a grisly end the memory of which gave rise to the name of the well known spinning firework.

Further wars and rumours of wars made even a remote oasis in the middle of a mountainous desert an unsafe resting place.

A few decades after the capture of Jerusalem by the Persians events in Arabia were to change the history of the world. The Arabian peninsula exploded with the new-found vitality and strength brought by the message which Mahomed had preached at Mecca and Medina. The victorious armies of Islam swiftly defeated the Persians and drove back the armies of Constantinople. As a consequence of these developments the casket containing the relics of James left Sinai for a new refuge in the marshes and reeds of the Nile delta. There the trail goes cold in the late 7th century.

The Christian community of Egypt shrank under the withering blast of Islam in the same manner as the Visigothic church in Spain was subsequently to do. We know that the bodily remains of the apostle Mark had been revered in Egypt for many centuries until bold Venetian adventurers smuggled the relics out in a barrel of pork to deter Muslim searchers. The Venetians then built their exquisite cathedral in honour of Mark in their

Adriatic swamps.

Did something similar happen to the casket of James? To the 20th century observer such a prosaic method of travel seems more plausible than levitating stone boats.

According to the mediaeval traditions of Compostela the bodily remains of the first bishop of Jerusalem were taken to Galicia by two loyal henchmen on a miraculous stone boat shortly after his execution. The burial place of the apostle was then "forgotten" until its miraculous finding in 814 when the power of Islamic Cordoba was pressing heavily against the threatened Christian enclave of Galicia. Such a miraculous discovery would certainly have been a boost to the morale of those who faced the might of Islam in the field.

Miraculous discoveries were a mainstay in the development of the mediaeval cult of saints throughout Europe. Some were more blatant than others. The monks of Glastonbury in England "discovered" the burial place of King Arthur and also his famous round table in the precincts of their abbey. It was to prove a lucrative find for the monks and it brought great benefit to the Somerset tourist industry of the time.

A closer parallel to the wanderings of the casket of James from Jerusalem to Sinai and Egypt can be found in the record of the Northumbrian church which was founded by Celtic missionaries in the same decades of the 7th century that saw the spectacular rise of Islam. Bishop Cuthbert had been the abbot of the Celtic monastery on Lindisfarne. The calamity of invasion and war came upon Northumbria not from the world of Islam, but from the Vikings of Scandinavia. The Isle of Lindisfarne was horribly vulnerable to Viking attack. In the 9th century the monastery was abandoned and the monks took to the road with their two most precious possessions. These were a casket containing Cuthbert's remains and a wonderfully beautiful manuscript copy of the Gospels. For two centuries until the power of the Vikings was broken neither book nor casket had a permanent resting place until Cuthbert's remains were interred at Durham where a great cathedral to rival anything in France or Spain was raised on a hill above the River Wear.

The 9th century was a turbulent time in the history of Christian Europe. Barbaric and cruel Vikings savaged the northern coastlands. Corsairs from Muslim northern Africa captured Sicily and plundered Italy and southern France whilst the Saracens of Spain dominated most of that peninsula. In this maelstrom of instability it is possible that the wanderings of a devoted company of Egyptian monks with the precious casket of the apostolic remains could have brought them among the Celts of Galicia. Links between Egypt and the Celtic world had not been without consequences. Many of the pigments used in the illuminated manuscripts of the Celtic church had originated in Egypt as had the communal life of monasticism itself.

At the same time as the cult of the first bishop of Jerusalem began to develop in Galicia another apostle became the focus of much devotion in western Europe. Andrew, the fisherman who introduced his brother Peter to the strange young rabbi from Nazareth came to be the patron saint of Scotland when according to the old traditions some of his bodily remains were brought to the old Celtic monastery of Kilrymont in Fife which came to be called St. Andrews. The prestige of apostolic remains made St. Andrews the ecclesiastical centre of the Scottish church throughout the mediaeval centuries after the defeat of the Vikings.

There is another St. Andrews on the Atlantic coast of Europe. Santander on the Cantabrian coast of Spain also came to be linked to traditions associated to the Galilean fisherman. Santander has developed into a major port in the modern world and it was my plan to take a ferry from there to Plymouth at the end of the Spanish journey.

I had sat in contemplation and speculation in the wonderful, mysterious atmosphere of the old church in O Cebreiro for longer than I intended until out of my reverie I became aware of the sound of birdsong. It was time to return to the motorbike and complete the last miles to Compostela.

It was a glorious, sparkling morning and I gazed out over the Galician borderlands. This most westerly mountain range in Europe is much older in geological terms than the Pyrenees. Like Scottish and Irish uplands the Galician peaks had been ground into smooth flowing lines by ice and age. Stands of bright yellow broom stood in contrast against the lush green of summer growth that had not been burned the dull dun of the landscape of Castile.

The engine of the Yamaha spun into action at the first kick. Yamaha make musical instruments as well as motorbikes. The steady pulse of the reliable little two-stroke was music in my ears as I adjusted helmet, goggles and baggage and set off into the blue yonder in the direction of Compostela. The scale of the Galician mountains was daunting, dwarfing even the majesty of the Scottish Highlands. In Scotland though, at 3,500 ft above sea level the prevailing conditions are Arctic in their severity, but the fields around O Cebreiro at that same altitude were productive pastureland. Higher up beyond the last conifer plantations the mountains were bare moorlands sweeping up to rugged ridges of rock. The valley in which the devout peasant from Barxamayor had once lived lay at least 2000 ft below the road.

A mile or so beyond O Cebreiro stands a handsome statue of a Compostela pilgrim with a wide brimmed hat on which a scallop shell was prominently displayed. In his hand he carried a stout stick also bedecked with scallop shells. Pilgrims carried staves not only to support themselves whilst walking but also as a protection against roaming dogs. I carried a stick in my baggage because I had heard nightmare stories about rabid dogs in Spain. Limited funds had dictated that I slept in a tent for much of the journey. My stick was as much a necessary part of my equipment as it had been for generations of earlier pilgrims.

Most of the dogs I had seen in Spain were poor tethered animals whose movements clinked the chains of their imprisonment in a pitiable manner. I was to discover that in Galicia many dogs are left to run loose in areas away from busy main roads and sometimes a yapping mongrel would snarl at my heels as I manoeuvred my bike through narrow village lanes.

Yellow painted arrows and Pilgrim Way signs pointed away from the tarmac along gravel tracks. I followed these arrows to get the flavour of the depths of the Galician countryside. Hedges accompanied these meandering lanes that wound along the sides of the mountains.

Unlike the unfenced landscapes of France and Spain the Galacian landscape is subdivided into many small enclosures and I began to see the lamentable sight of barbed wire as well as more pleasing stone dykes. In some parts of Galicia enclosures are made with huge slabs of slate as they do in Caithness and Orkney. The size of the small fields in Galicia is visible testimony to the fundamentally Celtic nature of the rural society which shaped this landscape. In cultures which were dominated by Germanic and Latin influences like those of the early Franks and Normans primo-geniture was the norm. The eldest son took the bulk of the inheritance at the death of his father. This had resulted throughout most of Spain in the "latifundia", the great estates which had dominated the landscape of Castile. The Celtic tradition of the Galicians where the inheritance was shared out among the siblings has resulted in the "multifundia" of sub-divided holdings. It had been the same among the Irish whose fields echo the pattern of Galicia.

Many of the houses in the remote villages and little

clachans that I passed through had no electricity. Little cash was in evidence. People seemed largely to live a subsistence lifestyle. They had wood for fuel and the harvest of their fields and gardens for their larder. Life would be hard in wintertime, but on that bright summer morning bees bumbled and hummed among buttercups.

Bullock carts sometimes blocked the lanes and patient donkeys stood dozing at field entries. The tarmac of the new Euroroads skirts the life of these tiny mountain settlements on the ancient, rutted tracks which had once been the most famous road in western Europe. Occasional stretches of concrete had been laid close to houses in an attempt to ameliorate the worst of the winter mud, but I became increasingly concerned in case the rough road surface punctured a tyre. Before returning to the tarmac I came across a tiny stone church under a heavy slate roof. A small extension above the gable contained a bell which had pealed out over the valley for centuries.

The countryside of Greece contains a plethora of small churches and I was to discover Galicia was no different. In Brittany I had seen many tiny, ancient churches and I knew that in the centuries of the Celtic church much worship had been in the open air and stone enclosed sanctuaries were usually small. The clachan with the tiny church was called Fonfria, meaning Cold Fountain. It would have been a welcome halt for pilgrims. I also discovered that there had been an ancient pilgrim hostel in the neighbourhood dedicated to Santa Catalina, St. Catherine. Had a wondering group from Sinai and Egypt trudged this way under the weight of a precious casket?

I eventually regained the tarmac with the bike and my legs covered in mud and worse .... bullock carts!

Gradually the road descended from the flanks and into the depths of the valley. Huge chestnut and walnut trees overhung the road and I travelled through moist shadows. In cold winter months these deep valleys would be dank and sunless. I could appreciate why Galicians preferred to build their dwellings in these parts higher up the sides of the valleys. The mountains on either side grew smaller and the valley widened while the river became less turbulent and flowed through water meadows. I passed a little village called San Martin before arriving at the much grander settlement of Samos where a monastery to rival Leyre or Cogola towered above the houses.

I stopped to explore. It was quite late in the morning and the monastery was open to the public. At the reception desk I asked a jovial monk to sign and stamp my pilgrim passport. We spoke in French. Father Augustine loved his monastery even though few monks now lived there. He invited me to join a guided tour that was already in the cloisters. There I joined a group of pilgrims who had walked from the Pyrenees. They had stayed for the night at the hostel in the village that was reserved for walking and cycling pilgrims. These hostels provide a gregarious aspect to the pilgrimage, but I was a lone wolf who had travelled with his own thoughts in a cocoon of rushing wind. It was good to be included in the multilingual banter of Germans, English and French. There was a friendly murmur of welcome for a fellow traveller on his mechanical steed. A voluble guide in monkish garb conducted us through an architectural treasure house.

Wide, cloistered courtyards enclosed green gardens. Glazed balconies three stories high led to the living quarters of the monks. Eventually we came to a sequence of murals depicting the same horrors of hell-fire that had disgusted Dominique at la Cogola. I detached myself from the group and went to sit in the quietness of the monastic church.

The external flavour of the monastery was 17th and 18th century and gave much the same expression of gracious living as the chateau near Lavour. The French chateau had been built with the wealth extracted in heavy rents from the peasants who subsisted on the estates of the blue blooded aristocrat. The opulence of the living quarters at Samos had a similar source. In the 18th century two thirds of Galicia had been in thrall to monastic landlords.

In France the eventual reaction to this rural injustice had been the revolutionary guillotine. Similar disruptions eventually tore Spanish society apart in the 19th century and resulted in the dreadful cruelties of the Spanish Civil War in this century. The monastic estates that had sprawled over the country for a millennium contracted.

However, the great church at Samos enclosed a mediaeval splendour whose acoustics had rung with the sounds of choirs and musical instruments in a blaze of colour and incense,

According to local traditions there had been a monastery at Samos since the 7th century and the influence of this community on the surrounding countryside had been much more than that of rapacious landlords. Monasteries prospered because they were long term corporations that spanned the generations. They developed horticulture and farming, but they were also master water engineers constructing mills, fish ponds and advanced systems of drainage. They also pioneered many industrial ventures including mining, smelting, tanning and textiles.

Samos had been a Benedictine establishment affiliated to Cluny, but in the 12th century there had been a reaction against ecclesiastical grandeur. A new order of monks rose to prominence. These Cistercians followed the inspiration of a Frenchman called Bernard. He taught that monks should not rely on a feudal peasantry. Instead they should labour themselves in field and workshop. Early Cistercian communities were established in Galloway at Dundrennan and Glenluce. Their architecture was simple and austere in comparison with the grandeur of Benedictine Samos.

Bernard wrote in his criticism of the Cluniac approach *"the church is resplendent in her walls, beggarly in her poor; she clothes her stones in gold and leaves her soul naked; the rich man's eye is fed at the expense of the indigent"*. These are powerful words that mirror the militant vigour with which Martin of Tours had argued for social justice at the birth of western monasticism.

Samos had once housed an important library. Much of this was destroyed in an explosion. An entrepreneurial abbot had hoarded petrol for sale in the thin years at the end of the Second World War until an accidental spark brought catastrophe. The monastery still sells petrol and I filled my tank to the brim.

The country beyond Samos became more populated than the wild highlands, and the road dipped down to the wide valley of the Rio Mino. The stretch of river I encountered has been flooded by a great dam downstream. A new concrete bridge crossed the reservoir to the small town of Portomarin which huddles around a handsome church with a rose window. It had originally been built as a Galician base for the Crusading order of the Knights of St. John who had once defended Malta against the Turks.

The original situation of the church and village had been below the waters of the reservoir. The buildings had been dismantled and rebuilt on higher ground.

It was lunchtime and I stopped at an ordinary looking meson. Rolling farmlands soothed my spirits as I shook the dust of Portomarin from my shoes. I began to see a most unusual kind of woodland which I had never encountered before, but the scent of the resin that perfumed the air was familiar. My nostrils recognised the trees as eucalyptus.

In Scotland huge tracts of countryside have been planted with confers. I had seen plantations of spruce and pine in the Galician highlands, but eucalyptus has been planted in the lower country for the past half century. These trees produce good timber and they grow quickly, but they have a major drawback which is proving a terrible blight.

The eucalyptus evolved to fill an ecological niche in the dry climate of Australia where drought is frequent. The wood is impregnated with fiercely combustible tar and oils and the bark flakes off to litter the ground with dry husks that can flare like tinder in the slightest spark. In short, the eucalyptus is natures pyromaniac. It has evolved to survive forest fires which wipe out competitor species and indeed it has evolved to create the conditions which favour fire. After the inferno the roots of the eucalyptus remain alive and send shoots to surge skywards in new growth.

Forest fires are frequent in Galicia and often they are not accidental. Many of these plantations were created in the time of the fascist dictatorship of Franco. This regime ignored the traditional rights of local farmers to pasture cattle and sheep on what had been common grazings administered by village elders and ancient custom. Many fires are the result of arson and long nurtured grievance.

There are other signs of Galician discontent with Madrid. Road signs use the Castilian spelling of place names and not the Galician version. The Celtic speech of Galicia did not survive the Middle Ages any better than in Lowland Scotland, but the Galicians have a unique dialect which is as different from Castilian Spanish as Lowland Scots from London English. For example, Junta is Castilian for not only a clutch of fascist generals organising a putsch, but also for the administrative council of a local authority. In Galician the word is Xunta. Galician activists go out at night with paintbrushes to correct the offending Castilian.

In Brittany, French and Breton spellings are given side by side on road signs. In the Scottish Highlands road signs give

Gaelic and Lowland Scots versions, but Madrid does not bother to acknowledge Galician sensibilities. I remembered the road signs in the Basque countryside damaged by gunfire.

I knew that Galicia abounded in fortifications built by the Celts in their long resistance against the Romans. These forts were called "castros". I also knew that there were stone circles like the one at Torhousemuir near Wigtown. In search of ancient monuments I followed a small road that I thought would lead to a castro. Instead I became lost in eucalyptus.

The heat of the afternoon was intense and I stopped for a brief siesta in the scented woods before the final 20 miles to Compostela.

As I neared the city the Pilgrim Way leaves the main road past a busy airport and follows a portion of mediaeval road to Lavacolla. Here pilgrims traditionally washed and prepared themselves for the entry into the holy city. Beyond Lavacolla rises the hill of Monxoi (Galician) or Monte de Gozo (Castilian) which means the joyous hill. From its vantage point weary pilgrims gained their first glimpse of Compostela and the spires of the cathedral.

In the Protestant journey of the imagination written by John Bunyan in the confines of his prison cell the final ridge in the Pilgrims Progress was called the delectable mountains. Joy and delight. I arrived at Monxoi and parked the bike before climbing towards a flashy metal monument that marks the spot where the Pope had preached to 500,000 people in 1989.

I gazed out over a lush valley of vineyards and trees. Compostela is the administrative centre of Galicia. It is a prosperous city of much the same size of Perth and much modern concrete and plate glass sprawls over the outskirts in oblong slabs, but at the centre of the city towers, spires and cupolas gave a lovelier skyline.

I was not alone on Monxoi. Many visitors to Compostela

arrive by plane, car and bus, but many remember the old custom of pausing on the delectable hill before entering the city. Some of these were singing a canticle to St James

> "*Primus ex apostolis*
> *Martyr Jersosolimis*
> *Jacobus Egregio*
> *Sacer est Martyrio*".

Without realising what I was doing I raised my voice in the 24th Psalm when they had finished.

> "*But who is he that is the King,*
> *The King of Glory? Who is this?*
> *The Lord of hosts and none but he*
> *The King of glory is.*
> *The Lord of hosts and none but he,*
> *The King of glory is*" *Alleluia.* *Amen.*

This ancient Hebrew song had been written to celebrate the entrance of the Ark of the Covenant into Jerusalem when King David danced before it. In Scotland it is sung on Communion Sundays and the words sprang unbidden from my lips as I gave thanks for safe arrival.

SANTIAGO DE COMPOSTELLA

CHAPTER SIXTEEN
"Nephelococcygia - Cloud Cuckoo Land:
"Cuckoo city in the clouds"

Aristophenes

Compostela to Punta Roncuda

Compostela is a beautiful city built out of granite. Many churches and monastic houses compete with the cathedral of St James for attention. Everywhere I looked there was carved stone work.

The Breton roadside calvaries had told biblical stories in stone for a rural population that had never learnt to read. The great churches in Spain were also built inside and out as parables in stone for an illiterate populace. Old Testament patriarchs and prophets sat beside the later apostles and saints of the Christian epoch.

Compostela is also a university town. The dreaded season of exams had just passed and there was an air of genial celebration among the young people who crowded the pavement cafés. Some of these students swaggered around in harlequin costumes of cloaks and knee breeches like 17th century gentlemen. The university is an old institution and like Oxbridge it is a riddle with quaint traditions that co-exist with its computer terminals.

The ancient heart of the town is closed to motor traffic. I had been about to go the wrong way down a one way street when I had been stopped by a policeman energetically blowing his whistle. He gestured for me to leave my bike where it was, giving the reassurance that he would keep an eye on it. He looked at the dusty, muddy, dung encrusted machine and noted the Scottish number plate. "Hola peregrino....."

It was a busy Saturday afternoon and crowds thronged the elegant square in front of the cathedral. One week earlier I had been listening to the clock ticking in the living room of Father Raphael in St. Agnan. Two weeks earlier I had been making my way to Gartan Lough by Lough Neagh. I had arrived at my destination.

A long flight of steps mounted up to the great portals of the western facade of the cathedral. Entering the huge church I stood where so many others had stood before. In the words of Walter Starkie who spent much of his life in Spain *"in the distance the main altar was a blaze of lights and an apotheosis of baroque ornamentation with its twisted lamps, Salomonic columns, chubby angels, scrolls, escutcheons and riding high above the extravaganza the Moor-slayer in full panoply. Even the venerable 13th century stone statue of the apostle was so bedizend with shells and scrolls and precious stones that he looked like a heathen idol".*

The plan of the cathedral was the same as in the other pilgrim churches I had visited at St. Bertrand de Commingues and Santo Domingo de la Calzada. The main altar was built above an underground crypt in which the holy relics are kept. Dozens of people were wandering around gazing at the architecture. Others rested in silent contemplation and from the direction of the crypt came the cadences of solemn song.

The underground sanctuary was absolutely packed. In among the throng I noted those dusky and radiant pilgrims who had walked or cycled under the burning Spanish sun. This for them was the fruition of months and weeks of toil. I also felt a sense of achievement at having fulfilled a dream that had begun on a cold December day in Edinburgh under the saltire banners of St. Andrew, the Galilean friend of St. James.

Around me soared on every side a riot of shape and colour beneath the tallest Romanesque vaulting. Generations of Europeans had thought this spot to be holy and I struggled to respond but found my response wanting.

I had been a student at the ancient university of St. Andrews. That old town beside the grey North Sea was dominated by the ruins of a huge cathedral that had been no smaller than Santiago de Compostela. The tall tower of St. Regulus had been preserved from decay. We used to climb this tower with our red gowns wrapped round us against the chill to gain a view which stretched northwards over the sea to the Grampians. Below us lay the ruined remains of one of the great pilgrim centres of northern Europe. I had raised my children in the rural peninsula of the Machars of Wigtownshire at whose tip lay the ruins of Whithorn Priory and the cathedral of Galloway. Both these ancient Scottish cathedrals had been great pilgrim centres in their day, but .... In 1560 there had been a revolution in Scotland which established a Protestant regime in the country. The power and wealth of the Roman Catholic establishment was ended after five centuries of a royal patronage that had been continual since the time of Malcolm Canmore and Queen Margaret. At St. Andrews and Whithorn in wind blown ruins we had used our imaginations to recreate the cultural glory of music, vestments, candles, incense, poetry, sculpture, painting, textiles, stained glass, metal work and carved wood which had once embellished these places. The cathedral of

Santiago surpassed my imaginings. It was overwhelming.

Martin Luther attacked the traditions of pilgrimage as superstitious which divert attention away from the true interior journey of spirituality throughout the years of life. Protestant theologians and philosophers questioned the validity of sacred relics and ridiculed bogus claims which deluded the credulous.

Biblical religion had taught that the souls of those who had lived good and kindly lives would be rewarded with the eternal delights of paradise by the same divine generosity which Jesus had shown to the thief crucified beside him at Golgotha. This doctrine was developed in the Christian centuries until it was thought that the sacraments of the church administered by celibate priests were thought to control the flow of divine grace. Paradise is derived from the Persian word for garden. The promise of entry to the new Eden was the lure which ultimately impelled pilgrims towards the physical destination of their pilgrimages. The cathedral of Santiago had been seen as a power house of grace bringing the salvation of heaven to sinners. Sadly, throughout the centuries there seems to have been little satisfaction in the contemplation of heaven for oneself if one could not similarly contemplate the horrors of hell for others.

The other side of the doctrine of an eternal Eden was the alternative fate of hellfire and damnation for all eternity; a teaching to chill the bones. The souls of Saracens, heretics and pagans lived beyond the saving sacraments of the church as did those of unrepentant sinners.

Perhaps in an attempt to ameliorate the harshness of a doctrine that divided humanity into sheep and goats, into wheat and weeds as though they were new arrivals at Auschwitz being selected or not for immediate despatch to the gas chamber .... perhaps because of this there developed the doctrine of purgatory. This was portrayed as a condition between heaven and hell. Purgatory was thought to be like a rather unpleasant celestial reformatory where souls were cleansed of sin after death and prepared for an ultimate and long delayed entry into the bliss of heaven.

Another idea developed in parallel with the mediaeval doctrine of purgatory. This was the notion that a man or woman could make acts of contrition which would be rewarded by a significant remission of the time that would otherwise be required in the celestial reformatory. In effect these acts of contrition involved paying cash to ecclesiastical authorities in return for a document called an "indulgence". Gradually the license to issue indulgences and pardons became concentrated in papal hands. It became big business and a lucrative source of papal revenue.

Martin Luther savaged these notions. He argued that nothing controls the free flowing of the divine grace which brings eternal salvation but the love of the Creator.

Another aspect of mediaeval religion which Protestants dispensed with was reverence before the mortal remains of saints. The cult of holy relics had reached the proportions of a major industry with salesmen duping customers with enough pieces of the "true" cross to build a navy and equip a deceased saint with as many arms and legs as a Hindu goddess.

At Whithorn and St. Andrews the holy relics of the pilgrim shrines were destroyed, but Compostela had survived as a mediaeval pilgrim centre into the modern world.

Reverence for the bodies of cherished people is a universal of the human experience. Archaeologists know that Neanderthal often buried their dead in cascades of flower petals. Ancestor worship was and still is widespread throughout the Orient and it was a large part of the domestic aspect of the religion of pagan Rome. Egyptians built pyramids above the embalmed corpses of their rulers and the people of Carnac built the hollow hills of their communal burial mounds, but few monuments from the centuries can rival Santiago de Compostela for magnificence.

Scholars disagree about the origin of the word Compostela. Some think it signifies *"field of stars"*. A less poetic and more prosaic school of thought considers that the name is derived from the Latin *"compostum"*. This gives us our modern word compost, as in compost heap, but its original meaning was burial place.

I liked the notion of the *"field of stars"*. Most major centres of the early church developed out of places which had been centres of the pre-Christian religion of the area. Had Celtic sages from the iron age and farmers from the Neolithic and the bronze ages gazed out at the celestial firmament from a place which was later claimed to be the burial place of James? Stone circles like the one at Torhousemuir near Wigtown dotted the Galician countryside. These had been used as astronomical observatories whose circumference and alignments recorded the movements of the heavens and predicted eclipses and comets. The name "field of stars" was suggestive of an older continuity.

I left the cathedral in search of the pilgrim hospice so that I could get my pilgrim passport completed and in return receive a certificate which no doubt I could wave at the high heid yin of purgatory and gain early release. At the culmination of their pilgrimage devout Roman Catholics seek to make their confessions to a priest and gain absolution for their sin. I would enter into my own soliloquy with my Creator in an attempt at self awareness with smug conceit stripped away, but first I needed to gain my pilgrim certificate so that my family did not think I had spent the time in Blackpool.

I went into an imposing building to ask for directions. It was a government office and a crop-haired young soldier was on duty behind the desk in the foyer. He was friendly and helpful and showed me the direction with a stubby finger on my street map. I noticed that above his immaculate uniform he sported a magnificent black eye. I winked. He laughed.

At the hostel a steaming throng of French cyclists were registering their passports and claiming free accommodation for the night before attending mass in the cathedral on the Sunday. I had thought about booking into a hotel and remaining for the night in Compostela, but I ached for the sea. I lived my life in Galloway in sight of salt tides and the memory of the great waves on the Gascon shore was in my nostrils. I yearned for billowing breakers and the sound of shingle as waves withdraw to hurl again against the thousands of tinkling pebbles. I decided to return to the bike and race for the coast to find a quiet cove and camp in the elements where I could search for the still quiet voice within to which I had been deaf in the bustle of the cathedral.

I was mindful that during the previous year the 5th World Congress on Faith and Order had gathered in Compostela for an ecumenical dialogue between Orthodox, Roman Catholic, Copt, Armenian, Ethiopian and every wild variety of the Protestant traditions. I considered myself a Catholic Christian, in the sense that catholic means universal. I knew that the accretions of history and cultural variety inevitably cause divisions, but there was much in the Spanish expression of the faith to which I could not warm.

I remembered the poverty stricken villages of the mountains that had been bled dry by centuries of ecclesiastical rents and I contrasted them with the opulent grandeur of Compostela. The words of St Bernard of the Cistercians returned to haunt me. *"The church is resplendent in her walls and beggarly in her poor: she clothes her stones in gold and leaves her soul naked; the rich man's eye is fed at the expense of the indigent."*

Suddenly the chaos of the French cyclists subsided and I was standing before the desk of the young man who issued the pilgrim certificates and checked the pilgrims passports. I explained that I had come by motorbike and that I wasn't expecting a bed in the hostel which I knew was reserved for walkers and cyclists. He replied in excellent English. I gave him a sheaf of leaflets about the Whithorn Pilgrim Way. I had cheekily distributed these throughout my journey. I also gave him two books for the hostel library from the Iona Community and the Whithorn Pilgrimage Trust. I thought guiltily about the Iona Cross which I had broken at Corrymeela. In a way the broken symbol of an ancient tradition had been prophetic of my experience at Compostela where I had been a detached observer and not an involved participant.

I had seen in the great churches of the journey the legacy which 16th century Scotland had spurned and in that loss there was much to lament for the withering of an impossible beauty, but whatever else it had achieved the Presbyterian tradition in the north had established literacy and democratic ideals that broke with the feudal grip of mediaeval institutions. A literate populace and the foundations of democracy are not inconsiderable achievements.

Santiago was not without its own lasting achievements. Above all the cult of St. James had encouraged resistance to the encroaching power of militant Islam, but I had wearied of stallions, scimitars and the bombastic self regard of nationalism.

However, the Scots can claim an honour which outshines even those given by grateful French Kings for help in wars against England. In November 1917 the 52nd Division of the British Army drove strong Turkish, Austrian and German forces out of the Judean Hills and thereby opened the road to Jerusalem. That victory ended 13 centuries of Muslim rule over Palestine and for better and for worse ushered in the immigration which founded the modern State of Israel. The 52nd Division was recruited in southern Scotland. These Lowland regiments sang psalms before battle like their Covenanter forefathers and their quality was further illustrated by the lack of cruelty they showed to their defeated foes. An army of Calvinists had capped the achievements of Roman Catholic Crusaders.

I regained my bike and my luggage from under the eye of the watchful policeman. After thanking him for his kindness I turned my back on Compostela. I half intended to return on the next day to attend worship in the cathedral, but I felt guilty that the philistine in me had not warmed to the cultural experience of the city that is the historical focus of Spanish Christianity. I preferred the Susa of Millan and the mystery of O Cebreiro. I had seen enough imposing ecclesiastical architecture and enough domestic squalor in tumble-down, poverty stricken villages.

I needed the cleanliness of the sea in solitude with the elements of nature to soothe my soul.

Finisterre, or the Galician Fisterra, means lands end. I intended to find a place to camp at that ultimate projection. However, I became lost in the bewildering plantations of conifers and eucalyptus and when I eventually reached the coast at the little town of Punta Roncuda I discovered that I was well to the north of my intended destination. Sheer luck had brought me to a secluded bay of white sand enclosed by granite bluffs. Trees grew down to the strand over which a stream swirled to the sea.

The wind was rising in force and the boom of waves on the headlands was a counterpoint to the rustle and rumble of the swaying trees. Barefoot I walked to the tideline and stood watching the sun sink into the west. I struggled to find meaning in the experience of the cathedral of Santiago. In the immensity of sky and sea I considered my own bewildered insignificance of little more worth and stature before the cosmos than a grain of sand below my feet. Questions grew in my mind. Whether there is a God? How do you explain evil? What happens when we die? Why are we here? How ought we to live our lives?

And then I remembered the comfort I had tried to bring to the bereaved at countless grave sides during my work as a parish minister. *"Lord, thou hast been our refuge: from one generation to another. Before the mountains were brought forth, or ever the earth and the world were made: thou art God from everlasting and world without end........ a thousand years in thy sight are but as yesterday, seeing what is past as a watch in the night".*

I considered the essential Christian doctrine that the creator of all this physical immensity and complexity of size and time had friendship and love for each human being in their blinks of lives. The compassion of God guides the events of human history and had even guided me to this lonely Galician beach where I watched the waves dance against the land and the sky.

"Let the sea roar and the fullness thereof; the world and they that dwell within. Let the floods clap their hands. Let the hills sing for joy together"

Psalm 98.

A cuckoo replied to my singing. The cuckoo mocked all my certainties.

THE COSTA VERDE

CHAPTER SEVENTEEN
"Humanity's stumbling rush since the Neolithic"
Levi Strauss

Punta Roncuda, La Coruna, Aviles, Gijon, Santander and Santillana.

I did not return to Compostela on the Sunday morning, but I woke to the knowledge that every day I had travelled until then had taken me further away from Wigtown. With every mile that followed I would be returning home.

Santander was 400 miles to the east along a green and mountainous coast. Ferries for Plymouth sailed on the Tuesday and Thursday. With luck I could get to the Spanish St Andrews in two days. My cushion of money had become much depleted, but once back in the UK I could get further funds. Also I had wearied of being in a country where I could not speak the language; and Cornwall, England and Wales have their own exotic attractions for a man of the north.

Other motor cyclists were up and about on that Sunday morning and I noted with great interest a Galacian adaptation that was well suited to local weather conditions. It consisted of a heavy apron of waterproof material attached to the handle bars. A rider placed the apron against the chest and it gave excellent protection. I could have used one myself that day because a cold northerly wind was snatching at my breath. It was uncomfortably chilly but not without its compensations. Strong winds often bring clear visibility and I could see wide stretches of the Galician coast with wild hills rising behind. It was early on the Sunday morning when I arrived at La Coruna where Sir John Moore had been killed as he supervised the embarkation of his troops from under the French guns.

Modern Coruna is a large industrial town. Steel mills a mile long belch out noise and smoke over the cranes and slipways of ship repair yards. The harbour was a wide silver ria that could have enclosed the anchorage at Cork several times over. General Franco spent his childhood in a house overlooking the shipping of La Coruna. The town prospered under the fascist regime.

The two main Galician ports of Vigo and La Coruna claim to be among the busiest fishing harbours on the planet. The tonnage of ships engaged in fishing under the Spanish flag is the third largest in the world after Japan and Russia. The Spanish have a passion for sea-food and the Galician fleet has earned in recent years an ugly reputation for a piratical disregard of conservation regulations. Steel hulled predators of several thousand tons go to sea for months on end until they have filled their vast holds with refrigerated fillets. They use radar to target shoals. Some purse seiners have nets bigger than a football field. Other techniques of maritime plunder involve nylon drift nets that are several miles in length. The mesh on these nets is frequently of an illegally small size so that immature fish and the breed stock of entire species are destroyed. The Spanish consumer has a predilection for immature fish in the same way as the French consumer relishes baby veal.

I looked out over the throng of shipping in La Coruna and I thought of Wigtown harbour empty of vessels. When the fish have gone from the sea la Coruna will be a graveyard. In my childhood there were dozens of little wooden fishing boats in every harbour round the Scottish coast. Their crews used small drift nets of tarred hemp and long lines of baited hooks. If modern methods of industrial fishing were banned and only traditional techniques on small boats working off their own coasts were encouraged then the oceans could be preserved as a sustainable resource.

Modern Galicia has also gained a less than savoury reputation in another area of maritime concern. It has become a major entry point for the contraband of South American drug barons. The attempt at the Prohibition of alcohol in the USA before the Second World War only put millions of dollars into the hands of men like Al Capone and created the international power of the Mafia. Ever since the behaviour of American conscripts in Vietnam alarmed the Pentagon there has been a war on drugs. Drugs have been the modern witch hunt conducted with the same vindictive self righteousness of any other in history and with as much ultimate success. Billions of dollars are put into the hands of a new generation of Al Capones. Worse though is the hopelessness of young people in the cities of Europe who face the blight of unemployment or who toil for a meagre wage in circumstances of repetitious boredom far from the sun and wind. Another generation of desperate youngsters in the trenches of the First World War were sent comfort boxes by parents and sweethearts which were purchased in the local pharmacy and delivered by the Royal Mail. I cannot believe that the criminalisation of drugs does more than enrich racketeers. The problem is a social and medical one and the moral ethics of the situation are not unrelated to the wider context of economic justice in a European society that seems to tolerate intolerable levels of unemployment.

In the open country beyond La Coruna eucalyptus

plantations stretched to the horizon until rising granite hills brought swelling moorlands. Larks were singing high above as they do in Galloway. At the small town of Xermade in the depths of the moors the road was blocked by a milling crown of people. Fireworks were exploding to the accompaniment of gunfire. Men and women were dressed in traditional finery and there had been dancing in the main square. Unfortunately the bagpipers had retired to the meson for necessary refreshments by the time I arrived. Xermade was indulging in a "fiesta".

Much of inland Galicia is thinly populated and towns and villages are infrequent. Many families have left the countryside in search of an easier life in the cities. Like their Celtic cousins to the north many Galicians have also left for new lives in the Americas. Some of these exiles have returned wealthy with the savings from relatively prosperous years in Chicago or Houston. They build brash, flashy concrete status symbols not unlike those which disfigure much of Ireland. Doubtless some of these large ostentatious houses will have been bought with the profits of illegal fishing and the smuggling of contraband.

Galician granite had enfolded me for hours of green inland miles when far to the east I saw ranges of very different mountains whose jagged precipices were reminiscent of the Pyrenees. I was nearing the end of Galacia. The mountains of the Asturias were in sight. Glinting in the distance was the Bay of Biscay, but the brisk breeze of the morning had become a howling gale out of the north east. The Rio de Ribadeo is a narrow inlet of deep water rimmed with golden sands. A new concrete bridge spans the mouth of the ria and as I crossed it gusts of wind played the same unkind tricks as they had on the great estuary bridges of France.

The geology of the Asturias is markedly different from Galicia. Much of the countryside is composed of convoluted bands of limestone that have been crumpled into mountains by the same forces that built the Pyrenees. A thin band along the coast is quite heavily populated, but the inaccessible mountain valleys were the strongholds of the earliest successful resistance to the Saracens in Spain. The narrow table land between the mountains and the sea provides green and fertile fields. This is the Costa Verde, the Green Coast, but wherever a river descends from the mountains it has cut a deep ravine into which the motorbike plunged before a grinding ascent through hairpin bends. It was an exhausting sequence and Sunday afternoon traffic made the road busy. At least in the depths of the ravines there was respite from the shrieking of the wind through my helmet.

The topography of the Asturian countryside does not welcome invaders. Roman and Visigothic influences were slight over the centuries, but the initial invasion of the armies of Islam in Spain had met with such startling success that by 718 there was a Saracen governor and garrison lording it at the main Asturian town of Oviedo. At Cavadonga in that same year a band of insurgents under the command of a chieftain called Pelayo fell upon the Saracen interlopers and utterly destroyed them. The heart of the Asturias lies between inland Oviedo and the Gojon peninsula which is straddled on either side by the twin industrial towns of Aviles and Gijon. This is the most densely populated part of the entire Costa Verde between Galicia and the Cantabrian port of Santander.

In 1075 King Alfonso VI with El Cid in attendance spent the season of Lent in the Asturian heartland and the legends which followed this royal visitation are of relevance to the development of the cult of St. James at Compostela. According to the ecclesiastical records of Oviedo cathedral Alfonso after lengthy fasting and spiritual preparation was present when an ancient casket was opened. Inside the chest was an unbelievable treasure of relics. *"There were fragments of the true cross and of the*

*bread from the Last Supper, phials of the blood of Jesus and of the Virgin
Mary's milk, relics of St. John the Baptist and several apostles and St.
Steven the protomartyr and of at least 60 other saints".*

The 11th century was a time of credulous superstition that
demanded signs and wonders, but behind the hyperbole of these
claims may lurk an earlier memory of a treasured casket which
arrived from the east bearing the bones of St. Andrew and St.
James which had been rescued from the expansion of Islam and
taken to the uttermost western coasts of the continent.

The towns and villages of Asturia were whitewashed and
trim. Glazed balconies overlooked the sweep of the sea. A
narrow gauge railway that was a triumph of engineering
accompanied the road along the coast. However, grass grew
between the tracks and the iron rails were speckled with rust.
The railway is little used these days when passengers and goods
take to the ever spreading tarmac. A new Euroroute is being
built alongside and massive new bridges span the ravines to bypass
the loops of the old road as visible testament of the huge influx
of Euromoney into Spain in recent years.

At the little town of Cudillero I booked into a small hotel
with a view over a turquoise bay into which great rolling waves
smashed with flurries of spume. The public rooms of the meson
were crowded with locals celebrating a holiday weekend and I
sat in my room watching television and the occasional train which
rattled past outside my window. I hadn't seen a newspaper in
nearly three weeks and a news programme came on the screen.
I tried to decipher the Spanish of the newsreaders. Images of
the Rwandan massacres came onto the screen. In the 1970's
Elizabeth, my wife, had worked in Rwanda as a volunteer teacher.
She was forced to flee for her life when her pupils began to
butcher each other according to their tribal predilections. Rwanda
was followed by images from Bosnia. There was also great
excitement in the news room over the impending results of the

Euroelections in Spain. The Asturians have a traditional sympathy for the left of centre Socialists who have been in power in Madrid since the fall of fascism. During the Civil War the Asturians fought against Franco. At first they had few weapons and miners and quarrymen attacked fascist columns with dynamite. One of the most tragic aspects of this conflict was the treatment of prisoners by both sides. More people were killed in the cold blood of the execution yards than in the hot blood of combat.

Civil wars whether in Rwanda or Spain tend to be ugly conflicts. Indeed the bloodiest war of all time was probably the Chinese Civil War of the mid 19th century when the Taiping Rebellion attempted to topple the imperial Manchu administration and failed.

In the morning I continued my anonymous journey eastwards. The hours from Punta Roncudo to Cudillero on the previous day had been the most arduous of the entire journey. The Galician mountains and the ravines of the Asturian cost in the tempestuous winds of the previous day had pushed the Yamaha to the limits of its performance. I examined the chain and tightened it and smeared the worn links with liberal amounts of grease. There was no further space for adjustment. The chain was worn out. I would replace it once back in the United Kingdom.. The spark plugs too were pretty chewed up and also needed replacing, but Santander was little more than 175 miles distant. This was my last full day in Spain. The wind had stilled and the heat from the sun was warm upon my skin.

Beyond Cudillero the old road through the ravines had been replaced by the broad ribbon of Euroroute which soared on bridges over deep valleys. Despite sensations of vertigo I made good time until the cities of Aviles and Gijon obstructed progress eastwards. Both cities have large steel mills that date from the Franco era. The air tasted burnt and bitter and lay like a brown blight over the Asturian heartland. I wondered how the Spanish had managed to maintain the steel industry of the north coast. In recent years the Scottish steel industry had seen plants far more modern than those of Aviles and Gijon being forced by Brussels into closure despite their proximity to the biggest market for steel in Europe - the Scottish oil and gas fields of the Atlantic and the North Sea. Madrid has defended the interests of the Asturias more successfully than Westminster has defended Scotland's interests.

The steel industry of northern Spain were built by the fascist command economy and their ramshackle technology is not much in advance of the Communist inspired factories of eastern Europe. The Ravenscraig steel mill near Glasgow now is only a memory despite the fact that it used the most modern methods to control pollution and "wash" poisonous emissions. These precautions do not seem to have been given any priority in Aviles and Gijon. Rivers steamed and stank in poisoned sterility and urban apartment dwellers had to endure vile air. People on the streets looked undersized and worn out and my heart went out to them. Spanish working people have traditionally had to toil for measly wages, but it seemed to me that there is one law in Brussels for Scotland and another more liberal interpretation which has allowed massive subsidies to prop up the obsolete Spanish steel industry.

Finally I was free from the densely populated urban areas and the road climbed into the hills beyond Gijon and left behind lowlands wreathed in brown murk. Towns with names like Lastres and Llanes seemed to suggest an ancient contact with Brittany and Wales, but the settlement of Villaviciosa sounded less welcoming.

After San Vicente de la Burquera, a handsome town on a promontory between two rias, I entered the old province of Cantabria, the land of the Celt-Iberians. The coastline became lower and less precipitous with wide bays of golden sand. The hills inland became rounder and greener. The open fields of the Asturias were replaced by hedged enclosures and turf dykes. Orchards and vineyards thrived in sheltered valleys until the wide estuary of the Rio Besaya forced me inland to the industrial town of Torrelavega where the scent of green pastures became the stink of an industrial sewer. The clear mountain waters of the wide river became black and lifeless before reaching the Bay of Biscay.

I wanted to find somewhere on the shore to camp for the night, but this was a very different coastline from the westernmost extremities of Galicia. Santander was less than ten miles away and as I drew closer to the city traffic became heavier. A sprawl of prosperous suburbs accompanied the coast in a rash of new concrete developments. I hesitated at a junction, not knowing which way to turn, and I nearly jumped out of my skin at the shock of a blaring car horn behind me. A large new car contained a flashy, gesticulating female in heavy makeup. I smiled sweetly at her which only resulted in more horn blaring. It was enough to make me turn tail for the countryside. I would negotiate the urban labyrinth of Santander early the next morning and find the ferry terminal, but for my last night in Spain I wanted to be away from urban frenzy. I turned the bike for the west in hope of finding a quiet spot for the tent further back down the coast.

By great good fortune I stumbled upon the magical little town of Santillana. The golden stone of this ancient town nestled behind a low ridge of hills a mile inland from the sea.

The air in the heat haze of the Cantabrian hills was cleaner than in the suburbs of Santander, but everything, my brains included, were broiling under the sun as I swung round a bend to follow the tarmac into Santillana. In cool shade beside splashing fountains I found an old inn where I would rest for the night. The bike clicked as it cooled in the courtyard, as did my larynx to the first swallow of cold beer. What a journey it had been!

For three weeks I had been living in the saddle and dossing in hedgerows. I had decided to use the last of my pesetas for food and wine for my stomach and a bed for my back. My conscience told me that I needed copious amounts of hot water before mingling with my fellow passengers on the ferry.

After beer, hot water and clean clothes it was time to stroll around the narrow lanes that protected the old town from invasion by cars. I had arrived in the full heat of the afternoon when sensible Spaniards take their siesta. The town came alive in the cool twilight as alabaster windows glowed in the last rays of the sun, but Santillana had secrets other than its glorious Romanesque basilica which was old before the Normans landed at Hastings.

On the edge of town there is a network of deep limestone caves. 15,000 years ago when Britain and Ireland were mantled in glaciers by the last Ice Age the caves of Santillana had sheltered clans of Mesolithic hunters. Paintings of bison, deer and elk were daubed by these people in red ochre and cunning dyes with astonishing beauty on the walls of these caves. With fire, flint and bone the inhabitants of these caves had become the most deadly predators on the face of the planet. When the Ice Age ended the descendants of these hunters ventured north beyond the Gironde and the Loire in skin boats. Their journeyings brought them to Carnac where in time they would blend their bloodline with the farmers who had come from the east. They ventured from Armorica to Britain and Ireland where their hybrid descendants built the stone circles of the north until the arrival of the Celtic men of iron in the last millennium before the birth of Jesus. In Santillana my pilgrimage had brought me to the homeland of the ancestors whose bloodline still flows with mine.

They would stay in the caves during winter, but every summer they followed the seasonal movements of their prey.

They were nomads who in the days before the wheel and domesticated draught animals had had to travel light of necessity.

A mediaeval pilgrim was perhaps following some primeval subconscious memory of a nomadic existence that still lives in us. The people of the Mesolithic lived in the same manner, in balance with nature for thousands of years until the discovery of agriculture taught us to rend at the earth on the long journey to the Tower of Babel that is the modern megalopolis; but the ancient Hebrew story of Eden tells us that our earliest ancestors knew a way of living in harmony with the created world.

To make a special journey to the halls of Lhasa, the sacred waters of the Ganges or the minarets of Mecca seems to be one of the universals of the human condition, common to every religion. Our nomadic background has left us with itchy feet. It is in our nature to want to see over the horizon. A pilgrimage is the perfect excuse, if excuse is needed, for wandering.

I ended my last evening in a low ceilinged bar with mediaeval beams. Spanish brandy was very good indeed and as I drained my last glass I reflected on a journey that had taken me south of Biscay and over the Pyrenees to unfold the sierras and plains of Spain before my eyes.

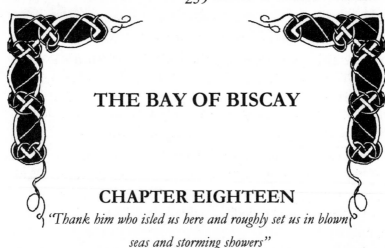

THE BAY OF BISCAY

CHAPTER EIGHTEEN

*"Thank him who isled us here and roughly set us in blown
seas and storming showers"*

Tennyson

Santander, Plymouth.

I sat on the top deck of the Val de Loire with a knotted
handkerchief upon my head. She was a sister ship to the
Duchesse Anne in which I had sailed from Cork. The sun beat
down with a brassy heat on the huge white ship as the rumble of
the propellers churned through the water of the deep ria around
which the industrial city of Santander has developed.

Long spits of yellow sand at the mouth of the harbour
were crowded with deck-chairs, parasols and gambolling bathers.
Rows and clumps of apartments, tenements and commercial
buildings rose up the steep hillsides on which the Cantabrian
capital had grown over the centuries around the cathedral
dedicated to the fisherman from Galilee called Andrew, but the
less than savoury industrial developments of Santander and the
seething rush of cars and lorries had turned the air over the city
into a brown reek of chemicals that caught at the throat and

stung the eyes.

The last day that the heat had been as oppressive had been on the afternoon Dominique and I had crossed the Pyrenees into Spain. The water of the harbour and the open sea alike were glassy smooth with only a gentle swell to remind of the week of wind which had accompanied the journey through Spain. The great bonus of that blustery weather had been the days of crystal clear visibility which had unrolled the stunning panorama of the sierras of the 1000 miles of Aragon, Navarre, Castile, Leon, Galicia, the Asturias and Cantabria, but the murk of Santander reduced visibility on this airless day to little more than a mile or three.

I had cursed the wind when it screamed in my teeth and chilled my bones, but I began to think that my Spanish pilgrimage would have been more arduous without the fierce winds. As a man acclimatised to the north, great heat left me lethargic, damp and exhausted. At least on the Val de Loire I needed to do absolutely nothing. I subsided into my chair and watched the French Tricoleur at the stern begin to rise from doldrum folds and flutter in the breeze of the ships movement.

I had left Santillana at first light and gained the ferry terminal while the citizens of Santander were still in slumber. I watched the city waken and the maelstrom of motor vehicles begin to clog the streets as people hurried to their places of employment. I had spent much of my working life teaching in schools, but as a younger man I had worked in the fresh air on building sites and as a farm labourer, forestry worker and green-keeper. There had been grimmer and more lucrative episodes in a foundry and on an oil rig, but I had never worked in an office. With a mounting pity I gazed on the wage slaves of modern Santander as they hurried to the bureaucratic hierarchies of the office blocks they inhabit for five days a week. We all wear chains of necessity and obligation, some more heavy than others, but the circumstances of repetitive boredom and sycophantic prudence which hem so many lives into a commuter snarl-up on the way to the computer screen seemed to me at that moment to be a terrible imprisonment.

"Fine white seagulls all sea singing" twitched their wing-tips to keep pace with my deck chair as the great Spanish city disappeared into its blanket of pollution.

After the weeks of French and Spanish it was strange to hear English voices all around, though I did meet the familiar northern accents of a Dundonian who had also been on a motorbike adventure through Spain. He had blatted down to the Costa del Sol. He expected to be back in Scotland on the afternoon of the day the ship docked at Plymouth. My own journey would take somewhat longer. His bike was an enormous new Triumph with over 100 horse power under the tank and an aerodynamic fairing to deflect the slipstream of great speeds away from the rider so that he travelled in a cocoon of still air.

My own little machine was much more basic; just an engine in a frame with a wheel on either end, but it was going to take me west from Plymouth into Cornwall before returning into Devon for the run through Somerset to the Severn Bridge and Wales. Once into the Principality I would head for St. Davids at the western tip of Dyfed before following Cardigan Bay to Snowdonia.

From there only Lancashire and Cumbria spanned the distance to the familiar miles of Dumfries and Galloway after which I would rest my hand on the latch of my own door in Wigtown. However, the planned route of the pilgrimage also demanded a final detour to the Isle of Man so that the circuit of the Celtic nations of Western Europe would be complete.

The ship ploughed out into the Bay of Biscay and the air grew cleaner and the temperature more comfortable.

The last few days of having been an anonymous stranger

without the language of the land and without a companion since Dominique's departure had left me reluctant to engage in conversation with my fellow passengers. It had been different on the gregarious and music fuelled voyage to Roscoff. I was content to watch the wake of the ship and the occasional sight of other vessels.

We must have been at the latitude of the Loire when we passed the enormous, rusty hull of a supertanker that floated high out of the water after having discharged her cargo of crude oil. Such leviathans bring to the shores of Europe the petrocarbon muscle that powers the commuter rush and the office air conditioning of modern city life. Crude oil also provides the raw material out of which the plethora of disposable plastic is manufactured.

The coasts of Europe are horribly vulnerable to the shipwreck of these enormous tankers which are often larger than 100,000 tons. Galicia, Cornwall, Brittany and Shetland have all had to endure the slime and the lingering after effects of these toxic shipwrecks that have brought ecological disaster to entire coastlines in recent years. Perhaps the oil that had been brought by the supertanker whose course crossed that of the Val de Loire had brought a cargo from the Scottish oilfields to the refineries of Nantes on the river of that name?

In the still of evening I watched gannets dive into the sea. They too would probably have had a Scottish origin in the great gannetries of St. Kilda, Ailsa Craig and the Bass Rock. I yearned for the north as I watched them plummet in a flash of yellow and white. Few chicks reach maturity, but an adult bird that has mastered the technique of diving into a darting shoal of fish can live for many years on broad wings that can span half the Atlantic.

The long hours in the broiling sun had generated a thirst that needed quenching. I went in search of beer. The voyage to Plymouth took a day and a night. A professional band of musicians were employed by the ferry operators to help shorten the hours. The bar was loud with the sound of amplified music.

I ended up in conversation with some English holidaymakers from Surrey. They were keen fishermen who had spent a week together in pursuit of the giant catfish of the River Ebro. They had been shocked by the filthy state of the Spanish river and contrasted it with their beloved Thames which they claimed had been sufficiently redeemed from pollution for salmon and sea trout to return, but they gleefully recounted the triumph of their watery safari. They had found the ideal place for cunningly baited hooks and lures close to where a huge industrial complex raised poultry in sheds. The organic waste and the dead from 100,000 birds were simply bulldozed into the river where appreciative catfish dined and grew to great size. The mediaeval legends of the Compostela pilgrimage had grown fanciful elaborations, I thought, in much the same way as these exuberant fishermen exaggerated the size of the monsters they had captured. These genial enthusiasts were good company.

When I told them about my journey to Spain which had begun with the ferry to Northern Ireland I was amazed at the response and the sudden change of mood of my companions. Their faces darkened as they spat out the sound that "I.R.A." makes through closed teeth when the larynx is a low growl.. Their hometown was Guildford. Twenty years earlier Irish terrorists had detonated bombs in two crowded pubs in the town. No warning had been given. Dozens had been maimed and killed. There was a passion in their speech that matched any of the historical resentment I had heard voiced in Ireland concerning the tensions and contradictions in the relationship between Irish and English identities and interests down the centuries.

I shared with them my conversation in the little village pub near Cashel and that I thought there should be a Re-partition in Northern Ireland. The men from Guildford simply wanted an end to the terror bombing which had caused the multiple murders of innocent people in English towns and cities. I could only feel sympathy for them. The I.R.A. has never targeted Scotland or Wales, though enough Scottish and Welsh soldiers have fallen victim to stealthy ambush when on duty in Northern Ireland.

The conversation returned to catfish, but they wanted to hunt the I.R.A. godfathers as they had the great carnivores of the Ebro. I shared with them the teaching of Mao Tse Tung who had likened the terrorist to fish. The support of the populace was like water in which the terrorist could swim to escape pursuit. Drain the water away and the fish is left flapping helplessly. A Re-partition of Northern Ireland could achieve the same purpose and reduce the size of the pond in which the I.R.A. have lurked like pike snapping at unwary ducklings and with as much savagery. The conversation turned to lighter topics as more empty glasses accumulated on the table.

I went outside to watch the sunset and to regain the silence that had accompanied my solitary wanderings.

I slept under the stars as I had done on the Duchesse until I was woken by French crewmen at first light. They wanted to hose down the deck before other passengers were awake.

Tennyson had written of Britain isled in *"blown seas and storming showers"* but I had awoken to a windless morning in which the sun was climbing into a cloudless sky. Soon the long line of the English coast grew into focus. It was possible to distinguish field patterns in a patchwork of greens on rounded hills.

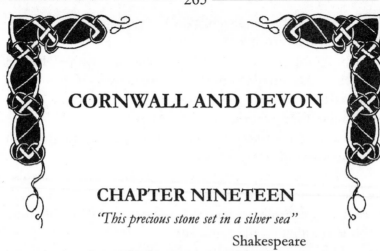

CORNWALL AND DEVON

CHAPTER NINETEEN
"This precious stone set in a silver sea"
Shakespeare

Plymouth, St. Cleer, Bodmin Moor, Launceston, Dartmoor and Buckfast Abbey.

Before the Val de Loire approached her berth in Plymouth she had first to negotiate the moles and fortifications with which the Royal Navy had made an impregnable bastion.

Plymouth has been battered about by the centuries. In the Second World War the Luftwaffe tore the heart out of the old city in their unsuccessful attempts to cripple the base which controlled the western approaches to the Channel. The loss of the facilities at Cork had placed a near insupportable burden on Plymouth, but it survived to provide the spring board for American forces when they lunged at the D.Day beaches.

In the years after the war much of the bomb damaged districts were rebuilt in the whitewashed stucco architecture and curved windows of the Fifties, but an irregular jumble of Victorian and Georgian buildings remind of the antiquity of the old town and the busy trades of the skilled inhabitants who had once lived there. Shipwrights, rope makers, sail makers, foundrymen, tailors and victuallers had thronged these narrow streets to make possible the exploits of the Plymouth men o' war which broke the power of Napoleonic and Bourbon France as well as the immense fleet of galleons which Spain sent northwards on the ill fated venture of the Armada in 1588. It was on the Plymouth foreshore that Drake continued his game of bowls as the enormous enemy fleet darkened the horizon with the forest of its masts.

Plymouth knew many victories, but there were defeats also for the corsairs of Brittany, particularly crews from St. Malo, were the most deadly enemies to English seafarers on the entire Atlantic coastline of the continent.

This ancestral enmity between the Bretons and the southern English of Wessex dated back to the time of King Arthur.

The long defence of the Celts against the encroaching Anglo-Saxons enabled the Christian church to put down deep roots and grow luxuriant foliage in the south-west of the island of Britain. In Cornwall and Wales I hoped to encounter the legacy of those days.

Disembarking from the great vessel that had brought me from Spain I had to pinch myself to remember to drive on the left.

Beyond the busy environs of the city green fields of deep soil were enclosed in hedges growing out of heaped earth dykes. I headed for the small ferry that shuttles across the broad ria that gave Plymouth an expansive anchorage able to contain entire fleets. The tidal waters of the River Tamar stretched northwards to divide English Devon from Cornwall. An elderly vessel clunked its way along chains to the other side. I looked back at the roof tops of Plymouth and the country which Shakespeare described as *"this precious stone set in a silver sea...........this blessed plot, this earth, this realm, this England.........this land of such dear souls, this dear, dear land". "England, their England"* as a Scotsman once replied.

Cornwall is a land set apart as is Brittany from France and Galicia from Spain. The influence of the larger neighbouring cultures have not obliterated the distinctive character of the communities descended from the Celts whose languages survived in these westerly projections for two millennia.

Cornwall has a history that was quite distinct from England until recent times. Cornish people spoke their own distinctive language until the 17th century. Despite local variations of accent Cornish speech was perfectly understandable by their Breton and Welsh neighbours. The growing use of the King James version of the Bible and the spread of the Protestant idiom gradually eroded the native speech of Cornish fishermen and miners until like the Lowland Scots the Celtic tongue of their ancestors was replaced by their own vibrantly different and distinctive version of the language of Shakespeare.

I noted the Cornish flag and coat of arms which were prominently displayed by the slipway for the old chain ferry. The Cornish white cross on black was reminiscent of the Breton flag. The names of the villages on the roadsigns were also reminiscent of Brittany.

Had every day of the journey to Compostela been spent in exploring Cornwall I would still only have skimmed the surface of an intimate, hidden landscape enfolded in secret valleys that can only be approached along narrow lanes between huge hedges. The soft climate still allows fig trees to flourish in cottage gardens and wide sandy beaches welcome Atlantic waves to tempt the surfer. The rugged coast of headlands and coves has many holiday developments, but inland the pace is less hectic.

It was my intention later that day to swing east and cross Dartmoor before descending to the Devon coast at Exmouth where I would spend the night with friends I had known a quarter of a century earlier at St. Andrews. Before then I had a few hours in which to absorb the atmosphere of Cornwall and so through Menheniot and Liskeard I headed north for Bodmin Moor.

This upland area is a swelling of granite that butts a thousand feet above the ocean to give the backbone to the peninsula of Cornwall.

The heat and pressures which formed this intrusion of molten igneous rock shaped the topography of the landscape, but when the new rocks cooled they left a geological legacy which would shape the future of the people who would come to live there. The granite of Bodmin is shot through with veins of tin.

In the ancient world tin was the most valued metal after gold and silver. Copper was worked in Egypt before 4000 B.C. Copper is plentiful and smelts at relatively low temperatures, but though the metal can be burnished to shine like gold it is soft and does not provide durable implements or weapons. However, if tin is added to copper and smelted together the resulting alloy is hard and can be honed to a sharp blade. This alloy, called bronze, was in widespread demand, but tin was in short supply in the prosperous Mediterranean world. Cornwall contained the largest reserves of tin in all Europe. Long before Moses guided the captive Hebrews out of Egypt questing ships from Lebanon reached Cornwall. Every summer they returned to trade for precious ingots of tin.

At the little village of St. Cleer I reached the skirts of the uplands. I stopped to wander streets between cottages with lupins and hollyhocks in their gardens and fragrant roses around their doors. A small granite church stood at the heart of the village. In the churchyard an ancient carved cross dated back to the time of the Celtic "sancti" who had travelled between Iona and Noirmoutier and perhaps as far as the shores of Cantabria and Galicia.

Up on the heights of the moor the single track road wound

between stands of broom and gorse which filled the air with the scent of coconuts. Tall, unfurling clumps of bracken and wide spreads of heather reminded me of the moors of Galloway as much as the sweet smelling highlands of Galicia that I had encountered after O Cebreiro.

Stark granite buildings scattered over the landscape were unique to Cornwall. These were the abandoned pump houses in which steam engines had consumed coal to drain encroaching water from the subterranean mine workings which yielded the precious tin.

The moorland behind one of the most dramatic of these engine houses was punctuated by the perimeter of concentric stone circles known as the Hurlers. It was built by the same culture which had raised Carnac and the more modest circle at Torhousemuir near Wigtown. Near this monumental legacy from the Neolithic rose another carved cross from the epoch of the Celtic Church.

I followed the ribbon of tarmac down the flank of Bodmin to Launceston which was once the administrative centre of Cornwall. The title of the Duke of Cornwall eventually became the prerogative of the eldest sons of the Kings of England in the centuries after the Norman Conquest, but in the centuries before 1066 the Anglo-Saxons had rarely been able to subdue the Cornish to their authority and the Vikings had never managed to subjugate the irrepressible native princes who led warbands which traced their lineage back to Romano-British notables from the time of Arthur.

The Cornish could retire with their families to the vastnesses of the undergound mines and sally forth to take the invaders by surprise. Even so, they were not a numerous people and accommodation usually had to be reached with those who ruled the more populous lands to the east of the Tamar.

Launceston was the traditional place of parley between

the Cornish and the English. In 1067 an army marched there through a Devon which had sent its warriors to form the shieldwall that had stood for so long against the Norman cavalry. They were only broken when their King Harold was killed by an arrow to his eye.

Many of the archers who disembarked from the Norman fleet at Hastings were not Normans. They were Bretons who like their cousins in Wales had grown to excel with bows of yew and deadly, yard long arrows.

The cavalcade which dismounted at Launceston in 1067 were not Normans barking out the alien French language. This army was the retinue of Prince Brian of Brittany. They spoke the same language as the Cornish and these incomers were welcomed as liberators from the overbearing English. A great castle was built at Launceston and I climbed to the top of the highest turret to gaze out over the green landscape of neat and hedged pasture

Tin ensured that Cornwall prospered and this economic muscle resulted in a remote peninsula with a scattered population sending more than its due proportion of M.P's. to the parliament which evolved throughout the centuries at Westminster.

From Launceston the road descended to the wooded banks of the Tamar. This river flows from a spring only a few miles from the north coast. It nearly severs Cornwall from England with a watery moat that gives a distinct border.

The countryside of Devon beyond the Tamar was more spacious than Cornwall and the swelling ridges of Dartmoor overtopped those of Bodmin. The sun shone in a sky that was a paler blue than the southern sky of Spain. Paler people than Spaniards lay sunning themselves beside pools in the rivers that tumble off Dartmoor and delighted children ran bare foot on the sheep cropped turf.

As the road climbed into Dartmoor I began to encounter

the wild ponies that are born free in the uplands. Mares nuzzled and gentled their foals. I then came on a sight which caused me to stop the motorbike and reach for my camera. An enormous grizzled sow was surrounded by a mob of piglets as happy as the human children I had encountered further down in the valley. It was marvellous to see these intelligent and playful young animals basking in the sunshine. Too often pigs are encased in concrete in conditions little different from the poultry horror on the Ebro so that low cost bacon can be provided for the supermarkets.

A mother's love for her offspring is one of the most poignant sights in nature. Only the cuckoo dupes others to care for its own. A ewe with her lambs or a vixen with her cubs are both following the maternal instinct with which that enormous sow provided the warm and comforting centre of the universe for her piglets. The plaster cast statues of a Madonna and child that I had seen in the roadside shrines of Ireland were telling the same parable. The sow was telling me to leave. I did, hurriedly.

Nestled into the valley of the River Dart as it flows into the lowlands to the east of Dartmoor is Buckfast Abbey. In much of Scotland it is known as Fastbuck Abbey because of the strong wine which is manufactured there from imported grape juice. This wine is much favoured by the inhabitants of the poorest urban areas of Strathclyde where unemployment and aimlessness have eroded morale and abuse of alcohol is prevalent, but the monks of Buckfast are notable for other achievements than those of a purveyor of alcoholic beverages.

Spain and France stayed loyal to the Roman Catholic church at the time of the Reformation. However, the secular ideals of the French Revolution resulted in a great hostility towards an ecclesiastical institution that had identified itself too closely with the feudal aristocracies of the "ancien regime" in both France and Spain. Throughout the 19th century whenever left of centre administrations were formed in Paris and Madrid legislation was enacted to curb the power of the ecclesiastical institution and to confiscate church lands.

In 1907 after one such legal expropriation a small group of Benedictines left France for England in the attempt to establish a community away from the hostility of the Paris government. Shipwreck did not deter them and they eventually settled at Buckfast. None of the French monks had any building skills, but they immediately set out the design for a great cruciform church that was to be built with the rounded arches and precise symmetry of the Romanesque style of the 11th and 12th centuries when the Benedictines of Cluny were at the peak of their power and influence. By 1937 the abbey church of Buckfast was completed.

I parked my motorbike beside rows of buses and hundreds of cars. The abbey is a major employer in the district. Fine cloth, wine, condiments and food are sold at a complex of shops and restaurants, but as well as commercial acumen the monks continue the wise tradition which Benedict began in the mountains of Italy. The destruction and murder of the barbarian invasions of the rich heartlands of Rome in the 5th century had the same effect on Benedict as it had on others when the old certainties and stabilities of the "Pax Romana" were ended. In uncertain and violent times men and women turned to the church with new fervour. Italian Benedict was the architect of a style of monasticism in which the rule of communal living eschewed the hard denial of asceticism and enjoyed the simple pleasures of frugal comforts. Above all Benedict taught that *"God is everywhere present, but no more so than when we are at prayer together"*.

Mindful of this teaching I entered the church of Buckfast Abbey and was entranced. At Quiberon cathedral organ music had filled the nave, but only in the pilgrim crypt at Compostela had I encountered worship in the sequence of great abbeys I had visited. At Buckfast children from schools throughout Devon had come together for a service and the singing of hundreds of children was a complete delight. Kind and simple words of benediction from clergy in white albs and embroidered chasubles ended the proceedings. I waited until the excited and happy chatter of departure had subsided into echoes. As I explored the church I came across a notice board on which petitions for prayer had been affixed. Children with terminal illness and adults wounded by woes asked for the compassion and supporting outreach which is the prayer of healing. I too was mindful of a sickness which blights lives and so I wrote my prayer on a scrap of paper and pinned it to the board. It read *"as a pilgrim returning from Compostela and as a minister of the Scots Kirk and the Iona Community I pray that there may be peace between Protestants and Roman Catholics, especially in Northern Ireland".*

In the grounds of the Abbey the families of the children were standing around and chatting. How pale and languid they were after the voluble and exhibitionist Spaniards! Calm and unhurried they strolled on the green lawns of Devon.

During the terrible Civil War of the 17th century there had been savage fighting between Cavalier and Roundhead when Englishmen killed Englishmen until famine came to kill thousands more. Since those hard times this has been a landscape of peace and prosperity.

The Yamaha spun into life and I headed for Exmouth and a reunion with old friends.

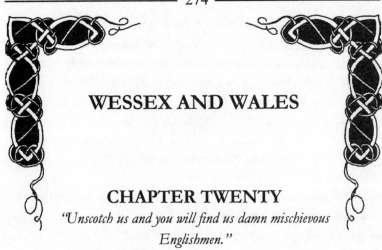

WESSEX AND WALES

CHAPTER TWENTY

"Unscotch us and you will find us damn mischievous
Englishmen."

Sir Walter Scott

"Should auld acquaintance be forgot and never brought to mind?"

Robert Burns

Exmouth, Glastonbury, Wells, Llantrisant and St. David's

Cumberland, and Northumberland I had known since infancy and Yorkshire and Lancashire with their great and exotic cities had often given family holidays among friends. North-country English beer is excellent, though the stronger tang of hops makes their brews quite different from the softer flavours of Scotch ale, but a good traditional Bradford Vindaloo or a Manchester Bengali confectioner can knock spots off the cuisine from anywhere else on the planet, better than tripe and mushy peas, anyhow.

However, great swathes of England were unknown to me and Devon was a delight. The towns of the English north country often bear the grim and sooty stamp of architectural uniformity. Rows of drab brick from Victorian times can make Liverpudlian drizzle in November seem depressing indeed, but the English south-country in June was as lovely as any I had ever seen.

Softer and more gentle even than the sweet lowlands of Lothian and Angus, the meadows and fields of Devon were fringed by mighty trees. Hay making was in progress and pollens filled the air.

I had arrived in Exmouth to find the little terraced house in which my friends lived. They were still out at work and so I took the Yamaha to the local motorbike shop to get a new chain and plugs. Beside the bike shop was an old fashioned cobblers. My leather satchel needed running repairs also. I'd collect both bike and satchel in the morning. It was strange being separated from these companions of the last few weeks together.

In the interests of necessary research into a favourite subject I entered an inviting looking pub to sample south-country beer while I waited for my friends to return home.

This Exmouth pub was spacious. The basic structure of the building was workmanlike Georgian and many of the structural timbers were exposed. Horse brasses and harness were festooned on the walls between nautical prints and maritime themes. It was ersatz, but pretty enough. Comfortable chairs clustered around battered, old oak tables. The only visible reading material in many Scottish pubs is the racing page in the sports section of a tabloid, but in this Exmouth establishment there were shelves of books. I was dumbfounded when a book seemed to leap out of the shelf at me in one of those episodes of uncanny coincidence that had accompanied each day of the journey.

The proprietors of the pub had probably bought a job lot of old books after a house clearance to acquire objects that would give a more genteel ambience to the place.

I wiped the froth from a pint that was no match for Yorkshire bitter and opened the book that had jumped down from the shelf. It turned out to be a scholarly tome by a 19th century cleric from Edinburgh. He was examining the origins of the Anglican liturgy in the prayer book of which Archbishop Cranmer of Canterbury had been the chief architect at the time of the Reformation. The influence of St Chrysostom and the Greek Orthodox traditions were contrasted with the contributions of Erasmus. Reference was made to the Scottish Prayer Book of 1637 which had led to the rebellion of Presbyterian Scotland in an act of defiance which triggered the English Civil War. The compiler of the problematical Scottish liturgy was Archbishop Maxwell of Tuam. He had been a child of my old parish in Galloway and so loyal was he to Charles I that he died of a broken heart when told of the execution of his king by the regime of Oliver Cromwell. The phrase from one of his prayers was this plea for deliverance from his enemies *"abate their pride, assuage their malice....."*

One of the great contributors to the development of the Anglican liturgy and the translation of the Authorised Version of the King James bible was Myles Coverdale who had briefly been Bishop of Exeter. Devon had been in his pastoral care. He had been driven from his diocese by the Roman Catholic reaction of Mary Tudor, which brought for a time the terror of the Inquisition to England. Cranmer himself was burned as a heretic and the persecution of the leaders of the English Protestants only ended when Elizabeth Tudor became Queen on the death of her elder sister.

However, Myles Coverdale was not restored to his episcopal state. He had become too much of a radical in the mould of the Sicilian Briton who castigated the self-seeking wealth of the late Roman Empire when the church was young.

Coverdale was a gentle mystic who had studied and taught for many years at Cambridge, but the poetry and power of his language still echoes down the centuries: *"in life we are in the midst of death"*.

Elizabethan England was racked by poverty. That was the reason so many emigrants were willing to face the dangers of the Protestant colony in Ulster and later the American frontier beyond the Atlantic. Seeing the destitution of his countrymen the erstwhile bishop of Exeter made this public declaration *'I beseech thee, thou that hast the riches of this world and lovest God with thy heart, to lift up thine eyes and see how great a multitude of poor people run through every town, have pity on thine own flesh, help them with a good heart and do with thy counsel all that ever thou canst, that this unshamefast begging may be put down, that these idle folk may be put to labour and that such as are not able to get their living may be provided for. At the least thou that are of counsel with such as are of authority, give them some occasion to cast their heads together and to make a provision for the poor."*

Perhaps the foundations of the Welfare State are deeper than 19th century socialism? *"Give them some occasion to cast their heads together and to make provision for the poor."*

That prayer would not have gone amiss in the Edinburgh of December 1992.

The horror of the Clearances from Donegal and the Scottish Highlands had not been without precedent in the British Isles. Elizabethan England witnessed the dispossession of much of the rural peasantry when the spread of the cash economy severed the old feudal ties of the Middle Ages. These dispossessed provided England with the crews of their warships and the regiments which were to so disconcert the continental powers of the 17th and 18th centuries.

Myles Coverdale was excluded from positions of influence and power, but when he died impoverished in London, tens of thousands jammed the streets and brought the city to a halt for his funeral, so greatly loved was he by the poor. Of course the origins of Christianity were among the poor and the despised.

The "Age of Hypocrisy" began when ecclesiastical hierarchies walked hand in glove with the dominant segments of secular society after the conversion of the Emperor Constantine.

I returned to the house of my friends.

Years ago we had been students together at St. Andrews. When we had finished our studies we did not leave for the cities, but found wages and cottages as farm labourers in the depths of Fife. Adam had become the gardener looking after an 18th century walled enclosure with an acre of rich soil and mature fruit trees.

He and Jo had been founder members of Friends of the Earth. He still worked as a gardener and their lifestyle was simple and frugal, though abundant in those pleasures which do not cost the earth.

After supper we strolled along the sea front and they introduced me to Devon cider. It was the most dangerous liquid I had encountered in the whole journey. I dropped a copper penny into the glass and watched the dull oxidisation vanish to swiftly reveal the bright metal. I knew what it was doing to my head. I just didn't like to think about what it was doing to my digestive tract.

We shared with each other the frustration of having lived our lives with ideas that were dismissed as stupid by orthodox evaluations. We had believed since our youth that organic horticulture, agriculture and forestry could redeem the countryside from ecological ruination and that renewable sources of energy should replace fossil fuels and nuclear power. Above all we believed that there was the right kind of economic growth in environmentalism that could create millions of jobs for the urban unemployed.

To a certain extent our youthful enthusiasms had been vindicated by subsequent events. Acid rain and ozone depletion had become everyday phrases of cocktail conversation, but few had taken the next step of logic to conclude that personal frugality and simplicity must replace consumerist waste.

As I listened to the conversation of our fellow customers I became aware of something astonishing. In England, Europe is somewhere else! Scots see the context of their identity as European, but not the English patrons of this sea-side pub who had drawn us into their chat. There were other idiosyncacies in their attitudes. When they heard that I had been travelling abroad they welcomed me "home". It was endearing as well as irritating to be treated as an honorary Englishman. In a way it was a great compliment to the Welsh and Scots with whom they share the island and a testament to the alliance which was forged to protect men like Myles Coverdale and the more abrasive John Knox from the Inquisition ..... an alliance which was to conquer half the world and ultimately having outfaced Hitler, to withdraw from a world-wide Empire that had been more tolerant of diversity and less brutal than most expansionist imperialism in world history. Perhaps that was part of Myles Coverdale's legacy to the future?

It occurred to me that there are worse neighbours than the English. It is just that their identity has given little elbow room to the individuality of their Celtic neighbours in these islands.

I headed north the next morning for Wales ruing my encounter with Devon cider. In the depths of Somerset I took a detour along the foot of the Mendip Hills to visit one of the most fabled locations in Europe.

Glastonbury has been called "the Place of Dreams". Like O Cebriero in distant Galicia this ecclesiastical centre once claimed to be the resting place of the Holy Grail. These legends told the story of Joseph of Arimathea, the uncle of Jesus, travelling to Britain as a trader in tin from the eastern Mediterranean. In some versions Joseph brought his nephew with him.

As William Blake questioned *"and did those feet in ancient times walk upon England's mountains green? And was the Holy Lamb of God on England's pleasant pastures seen?"* And did a Hebrew princess in earlier centuries bring Jacob's Pillow to the shores of Lough Neagh?

Glastonbury is built on a low rise of hills clustered below the steep slopes of the Tor which is a landmark for miles around. This higher ground was once islanded in the meres and marshes of a great inlet from the Bristol Channel. Orchards and fields of asparagus surrounded the trim and prosperous town.

Glastonbury was once called Avalon, the Isle of Apples and it was the reputed burial place of King Arthur, but its significance to European history is older than that. The same ancient civilisation which revered Carnac also revered Avalon. Some scholars can detect in the field patterns of the surrounding countryside the signs of the zodiac of the heavenly constellations. Modern Glastonbury is situated in a field of stars, by their computation a veritable Compostela.

I did not linger in the town. There was too much chewing gum on the pavements and too many tourist buses. The road led me to the city of Wells and I stopped to marvel at the cathedral.

English Gothic is more graceful than the heavier Spanish version. The Protestant element in Anglicanism had emptied the cathedral from much of the clutter of mediaeval side altars and saintly shrines, but Wells cathedral is dedicated to Galilean Andrew. Had a party of questing Egyptian monks come to Glastonbury with a precious burden and left a reliquary in the district as a monument of their passing?

The great city of Bristol loomed on the horizon and I had no option but to take to the motorway for the Severn Bridge and the journey into the Principality of Wales.

Gwent of the South Wales borderlands looks out over the

swift tides of the wide Severn estuary. A suspension bridge almost the equal of the Forth road bridge spans the gap. Advocates for renewable energy have advised the government in London to build a tidal barrage that could generate huge quantities of electricity with a road link on top of it. These ideas have been spurned. The present bridge is only three decades old but is becoming structurally unsound with the continual pounding of modern traffic. A new bridge is being built parallel to the old one and electricity is generated by the squat shape of a nuclear power station on the English shore.

Turning my back on it I entered Wales. Heavy traffic rushed along the motorway as I headed into Glamorgan towards the small, hilltop town of Llantrisant where I would spend the night.

The countryside of South Wales was blitzed by the Industrial Revolution. The Steam Age was powered by coal and wide seams of Welsh anthracite were worked by armies of miners who lived in drab brick rows that line the valleys and clustered at the pit heads. In the last two decades the Welsh coal industry has withered away and unemployment has grown inexorably. I'm sure many enough of the unemployed of South Wales would welcome work on a Severn Barrage and the creation of a cleaner form of energy than coal.

My friends in Llantrisant were of a similar mould to Adam and Jo in Exmouth. They had been gardeners for many years who grew most of their own food. We had shared a small-holding together in Dumfriesshire when we had been young teachers at Annan Academy. After the parsnips and goats milk of Annandale they had gone to live and work in Mexico before returning to Wales. In swift succession three sons had been born to them and the house would be a mayhem of nappies and rumbustousness until the boys were packed off to bed.

Nick and Lizzie were surviving the years, but they longed

to escape the busy environs of Cardiff. Their house is built into a steep hill above which rise the towers of an ancient castle. Llantrisant was one of the most important centres of South Wales. Llantrisant means the place of Three Saints.

The hidden valleys of Wales and the best archers in Europe saved this countryside from the worst ravages of the Anglo-Saxons after the fall of the Roman Empire. In Wales the church flourished behind this staunch defence.

Monastic enclosures were called Llanes in Wales, like the Llanes I had passed in Cantabria. Hundreds of Llanes dot the Welsh countryside in the place names of today as a memory of the "sancti" from the time of Arthur.

Of all the Celtic peoples of the west it is the Welsh who have best kept their language in everyday use. The three wee boys who rushed around the house were bilingual in their incomprehensible excitement.

Early forms of the Welsh language were spoken in a great arc from Scotland, through Cumbria, in Wales itself and south through Cornwall and Brittany. This Cymric Celtic language differs from its kindred Gaelic Celtic of Ireland mainly in its use of consonants; Gaelic speakers converting P sounds from the lips into Q sounds from the back of the tongue and the palate. 19th century scholarship explained these differences by insisting that Gaelic speech was the more archaic version which had developed among the earliest waves of Celtic colonisation into the islands and that Cymric was a later interloper from the continent.

Another theory seeks to explain this divergence of the Celts. Waves of migrating Celtic tribes surged over Europe from the 6th century BC. Those who settled earliest in Britain came from France. According to this theory it was the Gaels who were the later arrivals. Marauding Celts had crossed the Pyrenees into Iberia. Spanish and Portuguese speech to this day has a most idiosyncratic use of consonants when compared to other western European languages. The influence of Iberia shaped the speech of the incomers in the centuries before the Celt-Iberians had to face the expanding might of Rome.

As the legions pressed further into their fastnesses, refugees took to ships and fled northwards to settle on the west coast of Ireland where in time these warlike incomers who had faced the might of Rome gradually grew to a dominance over the native Cymric speakers of Ireland.

After the noisy and joyful hospitality of Llantrisant the road for the spiritual centre of Wales at St David's led far west to the ultimate extremity of Dyfed.

The landscape of Gwent and Glamorgan in my youth had been that of the desecration and ugliness of the coal bing and pit villages. The intervening years have gentled and changed South Wales. Trees have grown to cover the wounded countryside and landscaping has restored the verdure to poisoned hillsides. Beyond Swansea industrial Wales was left behind and Carmarthan Bay twinkled to the south. The sun had not been obscured by a single cloud since I had landed at Plymouth and the day was warm and clear.

St. David's cathedral is built in a low valley a few miles inland from the last ria I would see before the glaciated landscape of northern coasts reappeared. The Anglican ethos which has dominated this ancient building since the Reformation still keeps the casket containing the relics of St. David behind the high altar which had drawn pilgrims to this sacred place from all over Wales and beyond for a millennium. I touched it with my hand and uttered the prayer "speed me home".

Outside the wind was rising in force and with delight I noticed it had veered to the south-west. Had David answered my prayer as had Columba at Gartan when I had chuckled at the story of the cross stuck in the doorway of the visitor centre?

The new spark plugs had greatly improved the performance of the bike and with the wind behind me I flew along the winding roads beside Cardigan Bay until I neared the mountains of Snowdonia.

It was a dance through midsummer delight as Dyfed became Gwynned. The outliers of Snowdonia reminded me so much of Galloway that I felt pangs of longing for the north, but before I ended my pilgrim journey there was one particular destination that I could not miss when in this part of the world.

In a disused quarry above the town of Machynlleth is the Centre for Alternative Technology. Two decades ago it had been an inspiration to those of us who thought like my friends in Llantrisant and Exmouth.

Perhaps at Machynlleth I would find a message to take home to Wigtown that I had not found at Compostela.

It had been a dozen years since I had last visited the Centre. I swung the bike into the carpark and was overwhelmed by the changes that had taken place in the interval.

THE PLACE OF DREAMS

CHAPTER TWENTY-ONE

*"As my body continues on its journey my thoughts keep
turning back and burying themselves in days past"*
Flaubert.

Machynlleth, Snowdonia and the Clwydian Range.

Previous visits to the Centre for Alternative Technology had been in the early years of the project. The aim had been to develop a practical exposition of the simple technologies that are required to wean our modern civilisation away from its dependency on petrochemicals and nuclear fission.

The establishment of productive orchards, gardens, greenhouses and fish ponds had been a priority from the beginning, but windmills and a small hydro generator had been built to provide the human community that settled in the dereliction of the old slate quarry with electric light and power. Houses and the library, shop, restaurant and visitor centre were designed so that they blended in with the new verdure of the organic gardens and poultry and goat enclosures. Pigs were used to clear new ground on the side of the mountain above the old quarry and a network of paths connected the buildings of the new, growing village. Turf roofs were covered with daisies.

In the early years of the Centre visitors had to climb a steep path from the car park, but a most marvellous contraption lowered itself down the hillside to haul me in comfort up the steep side of the valley. It was a water powered funicular train. Two carriages on parallel tracks were linked by a cable. The carriage at the top of the incline contained a tank which was gradually filled with water from the outflow of the small hydro-electric generator. The carriage at the foot of the slope emptied the water from its tank until the weight of the higher carriage was sufficient to haul its twin up to the top with the weight of its descent. This simple system could provide the basis for the transport network of hillside towns and it is used on the canal system of the continent as an alternative to ladders of locks.

Twenty years earlier and there had been virtually no soil in the dereliction of the abandoned slate workings. As the funicular railway hauled me to the top in a clanking of iron and a gurgling of water I saw everywhere the fecund growth of the new trees and gardens. In two decades the Centre has clothed the quarry in soil made from compost heaps and the organic waste which elsewhere is flushed down the loo and forgotten. A new Eden has been recreated. Birds and insects thrived in an environment that has been spared the biocides of modern agribusiness.

It was late afternoon and only days before midsummer. It had been my intention to head for Heysham on the Lancashire coast and catch the ferry to the Isle of Man. There was a sailing in the small hours of the next morning.

Man is a lovely place. From the Machars of Galloway it crowns the southern horizon, dipping as it does in and out of the mists of the Irish Sea.

In its own way it is the centre of a particular cult of pilgrimage. Every summer enthusiasts gather from all over the world for the Manx T.T. motorbike races. It had been a conceit of mine that the last episode of my Spanish pilgrimage should include a self-congratulatory circuit of the route of the T.T., but as I sat in the gardens on the hillside above Machynlleth I decided to change my plans.

The sweet anticyclone that had followed my from Spain was being pushed away by a vicious area of low pressure that was already drenching Ireland. The brisk wind that had pushed me from St. David's was a precursor of this Atlantic storm and I could read the warning signs in the high clouds that were gathering over the mountains of Snowdonia. The Isle of Man would not be much fun in vile weather and I decided to race for Wigtown and home. The lure of my family was stronger than Manx delights.

With the decision made I rested for a few long moments before what would be at least six hours in the saddle. With luck I would cover 350 miles before midnight.

Machynlleth had played a notable role in Welsh history. The last independent, native Prince of Wales, Owen Glendower, convened parliaments here and received ambassadors from Ireland, Scotland and France at the beginning of the 15th century. This last flowering of Welsh power was to be extinguished, but before the century was out a dynasty that traced its roots to Welsh origins had made the throne of England their own. These Tudors intermarried with the Stuarts of Scotland and ultimately created the conditions for the enactment of the United Kingdom in 1603.

The evening traffic on the winding roads of Snowdonia was sparse and the motorbike danced round the curvaceous tarmac. Beyond the mountains lay the open heathland of the Clwydian Range after which the road descended to the English Border and industrial Merseyside.

I stopped for a necessary break with one foot in Wales and the other in England as I thought back to the Centre for

Alternative Technology. In its practical loveliness and in the co-operation and frugal sufficiency of the life-style of the residents I knew it to be a lineal descendant of the same tradition which had inspired the Celtic sancti and the continental innovators like Benedict and Martin. David had been the great inspiration of Wales and Ninian had come to Galloway like the first pebble which starts an avalanche of change. This had been at a time when the old civilisation of Europe was in terminable decline. The early Christian church among the Celts pioneered a new and better pattern of communal living for the benefit of the future.

The dedicated inspiration of the modern centre at Machynlleth was doing the same. It was a manifestation that all of Wales could become a productive garden bringing the dignity and prosperity of good livelihoods to generations blighted by urban unemployment. No less than Glastonbury this was a "Place of Dreams".

On the lonely Galician beach I had listened to a cuckoo mock my visit to Compostela, and in the great Cathedral of Spain the ecclesiastical accretions of the centuries had left me unmoved. The breaking of the cross at Corrymeela was symbolic of the snapping of the chords that had bound me for long years to the embrace of the Calvinist institutions of Scotland, but on the edge of England I gave thanks for my ultimate pilgrim destination before my return to my family.

'I pray to the Three
The Author, the Word Incarnate and the Wandering Story-Teller;
To the Three,
The Creator, Created Creator, and Creating Creator;
To the Three,
Lover, Beloved and Loving,
That the Church might learn to
sing the Lord's Song anew.

Yet I know
That the Three in One
Will always speak, live and move
Across our world and beyond,
And I know
That if the Church cannot sing the Lord's Song,
Then the Spirit of the Three will seek others
Through whom the Three can speak, move,
And manifest their love".

    Amen.

The words of the prayer are those of my friend Martin Palmer who has worked for many years with the World Wide Fund for nature, but the sentiments with which I recalled them utterly filled the moment.

And then I went home.

HOME AND MAN

CHAPTER TWENTY TWO

"Scotland will never be free until the last minister is strangled with the last copy of the Sunday Post".

Tom Nairn.

The M6, Gretna Green, Wigtown, the Isle of Man and Wigtown.

I lost my race with the storm, but the southerly wind hurled me northwards along the M6.

The familiar hills of Lancashire were obscured by the first dampening drizzle and the slate roofs of the terraced houses were black in the developing down-pour. These north-country towns had suffered hardships no less than those of Ireland and Scotland. The rural peasants of England had been driven from their ancestral fields and herded into mills and mines to sweat from infancy for measly wages in the disease ridden squalor of the Industrial Revolution.

Michael Davitt, the great 19th century campaigner for Irish freedom had worked in a Lancastrian textile mill whilst only a child. An arm had been torn from him in an industrial accident. Despite this agonising experience he spoke ever afterwards with love and compassion for the ordinary people of England who had had to endure the misery of their own economic subjugation by the power and greed of the mill owners, the proprietors of mines and the iron masters. Davitt always insisted that Ireland's quarrel was not with the labouring poor of England.

In the last 150 years the English dispossessed have risen to claim their democratic rights through the long struggle of the Trade Unions and the Co-operative Societies which gave birth to the eventual Welfare State.

With a whoop of triumph I crossed the Border at Gretna Green and swung west for Wigtown. My heart rose within me.

"Huh, Dad's back" .... and I was home, but not for long. When the storm had passed we all went to the Isle of Man. I conducted my triumphal circuit of the Manx T.T. at the wheel of a battered van belonging to a builder friend who lives in the old capital of the island at Castletown.

Scotland and England tussled for dominance over the island for centuries. Towns like Ramsey and Douglas speak of the close links with Galloway, but the symbol of the Manx identity is three, armoured, running legs. A local saying explains that there is "a boot for England, a boot for Scotland and a boot for Ireland".

The islanders are a blend of Celt and Viking, and Manx Gaelic was the language of the farms until recent generations. They are proud of their ancient parliament, the Tynwald, and of their autonomy from the interference of Brussels and Westminster. They have what most Scots want.

At the southernmost extremity of the Isle of Man is the little village of Cregnesh. It has been restored by the Manx Government as a monument to the tough self sufficiency of the islanders. Thatched and whitewashed cottages like the one in Cashel dotted the hillsides around an old church. Inside the churchyard is a tall wooden cross. On it are inscribed three words, *'Love one another'*.

The history of the institutions of the Church has at times been deficient in this quality, but the power of love is not to be denied and it will reshape all our futures.

Tom Nairn's damning phrase was shaped in jest, but there is a feeling in Scotland that the legacy of Calvinism had become an impediment and a hindrance rather than a help to a better future. The same is true in the public perceptions of the old Roman Catholic institutions of France, Spain and Ireland.

Hugh MacDiarmid once wrote that *"no nation ever remained strong whilst it neglected its land and no nation ever renewed its culture without restoring its cultivation. Scotland could be and should be one of the most prosperous and progressive countries in the world and the isles of the west and the north can be made to bloom like the rose"*.

Machynlleth is the pattern for that future, not the old outworn traditions of the past

July 11th 1995.